MODERNIZATION AND BUREAUCRATIC-AUTHORITARIANISM

Modernization

and

Bureaucratic-Authoritarianism

STUDIES IN SOUTH AMERICAN POLITICS

GUILLERMO A. O'DONNELL

Institute of International Studies
University of California, Berkeley

Standard Book Number 87725-209-2
Library of Congress Card Number 73-620029

I dedicate this book to Teresa,

which in so many, many ways

is as much hers as it is mine.

PREFACE

I wrote this work while doing graduate study in political science at Yale University. I returned to Argentina in May 1971, but because of other commitments I was able to make only minor modifications in the manuscript before submitting it for publication. Thus I have not incorporated in my analysis the important events of relevance that have occurred in 1972, or enriched it with the results of my examination of several valuable contributions by other authors which came to my attention too late. However, I feel it is not inappropriate for me to offer this text for the consideration of the reader as it stands. Its basic argument has not been invalidated by the events of the past year; rather, they seem to have been very much in line with the general tendencies perceived in the study.

The main concern from which this work originated is the evidence that (to put it mildly) the manifold changes that South American countries have been undergoing in recent decades do not seem to have increased the probability of the emergence and consolidation of more open political systems, or of collective action that might effectively diminish the conspicuous inequalities and injustices in these societies.

This observation is very much at odds with still widely prevailing conceptions about the interactions of the political, social, and economic dimensions. According to these conceptions, which are discussed in detail in the main text, the "advances" observable in some socio-economic indicators reflect change-processes that should be leading toward more effective political arrangements. On the contrary, it is in those South American countries where modernization has proceeded furthest in the last two decades that there have been the only successful attempts to implant a new type of authoritarian political system, which I have labelled "bureaucratic-authoritarianism."

Before this proposition and some of its more important implications can be evaluated by the reader, several preparatory steps are necessary. First, the sense in which the term "modernization" is being used must be discussed. This involves making explicit some important dissensions from dominant currents in political science and sociology--a discussion which I am afraid will be quite arid to many readers. The second requirement is a presentation of the analysis and data that support the view that bureaucratic-authoritarianism is a political phenomenon found only in situations of comparatively high modernization. A directly

related point is that there are crucial differences between
"bureaucratic" authoritarianism and other types (which I label
"populist" and "traditional") that in most of the literature are
represented as typical of the South American continent. Delinea-
tion of the specific characteristics of bureaucratic-authoritarianism is aided by placing it in a comparative perspective and
noting its similarities to systems in other, non-Latin American
situations of high modernization.

With the completion of the preliminary steps of defining
the concept of "modernization" and providing a typological char-
acterization of "bureaucratic-authoritarianism," the factors and
processes of high modernization that seem to be the most influential in attempts to inaugurate and consolidate bureaucratic-
authoritarian political systems can be explored. It is in relation to this dynamic, time-bound part of the historical process
that the most important analytical contribution is needed: the
explanation of the emergence of the new political forms and of
their effects upon the social context. However, several limitations of the study (among them the lack of adequate data) make
it impossible to provide such an analysis. The most that can be
achieved is to render plausible and open the way for future empirical work to test the hypothesis that--to put it in Weberian terms--
there is marked "elective affinity" between contemporary South
American situations of high modernization and bureaucratic-authoritarianism.

Thus, this work is only a preliminary exploration, a
point of departure for other investigations now in progress or
to be undertaken in the future. As I see it, it performs the
necessary task of clearing conceptual ground and proposing certain important correspondences between socio-economic and political dimensions. Without the completion of this preliminary step,
it would be impossible to work toward developing a strict explanation of these correspondences, to examine in detail their interactions through time, to make reliable predictions concerning the
evolution of the new political systems, and to refine distinctions
among the units (countries) that previous analysis at a high level
of aggregation has classified in the same typological "box."

Two additional remarks are in order here. First, insofar
as it was possible, for the static part of my analysis I have
preferred to use data from the late 1950's and early 1960's,
because those were the years that immediately preceded the attempts to inaugurate the bureaucratic-authoritarian political
systems on which this study largely concentrates. Second, the
empirical referent for this study is the set of South American
countries. Middle American countries have been excluded because,
except for geographical continuity and a hazily defined common
culture (both of poorly mapped political consequences), there do
not seem to be compelling reasons for including all Latin American

countries in the same universe of discourse. Rather, until more is known, it would seem that much is to be gained if, at a chosen level of analysis, the empirical referent is delimited to units whose relevant common contextual features can be unambiguously defined. For the purpose of this study, this delimitation is the set of South American countries.[1]

Acknowledgments

I was fortunate to spend three years (1968-1971) at Yale University's Department of Political Science, which in many ways provided the most helpful and congenial milieu possible for my work. Several scholars there offered me criticism and suggestions that have greatly improved this study. In particular, William Ascher, Natalio Botana, Ronald Brunner, Robert Dahl, John Fitch, Carlos Floria, Alfred Stepan, and Joseph Tulchin were very generous with their time and patience, criticizing in great detail earlier versions of the entire manuscript. I also had the privilege of being in very close contact with the work and the person of David Apter, who at all stages of this work provided advice, criticism, stimulation, and encouragement that I most gratefully acknowledge. Paul Gilchrist undertook, with talent equalled only by his patience, the colossal task of editing my Spanglish. The first period of my study in political science was supported by the Universidad Nacional de Buenos Aires and by Yale University. This monograph is an early result of research in progress generously funded by the Danforth Foundation. However, none of these persons or institutions should be blamed for the consequences of their support and criticism.

G. A. O.

Universidad del Salvador,
  Escuela de Ciencia Política

Centro de Investigaciones en Administración Pública,
  Instituto Torcuato di Tella

Buenos Aires, Argentina

---

[1]However, to be faithful to other authors' concepts, I will use the term "Latin America(n)" when referring to works that use that term.

CONTENTS

CONTENTS

LIST OF TABLES

LIST OF TABLES

LIST OF FIGURES

Chapter I

ASSUMPTIONS AND CLASSIFICATIONS

> We are so attuned to the idea of a close
> association among the different elements of
> "modernity" and "tradition" that whenever
> we find some evidence of industrialization
> we look for, and expect to find, those
> social and political changes that were
> associated with industrialization in many
> countries of the Western civilization.
>
> --Reinhard Bendix[1]

On Recent Studies

At least since Plato and Aristotle, social analysts have
maintained that the socio-economic structure of society has an
important influence on the type of political system it is likely
to have. There is much disagreement with respect to the nature
of this influence, the range of possible variation on the political side, and the degree of influence of other factors. Historical experience shows clearly that there is no necessary one-to-
one correspondence between socio-economic structure and type of
political system, but there is little doubt that knowledge about
the former allows us to make certain predictions concerning the
latter. Under given socio-economic conditions, some types of
political systems are very unlikely, while there is a strong
tendency for other types to emerge and/or consolidate themselves.
Particularly since Marx and Weber, this assumption has provided
a basic guideline for the study of the interrelations of politics
and other aspects of social life. However, as this book will
attempt to show, it offers only a point of entry to an enormously
complex subject-matter. Crucial questions concerning the definition and measurement of concepts, the hypothesized patterns of
interactions, and the historical-contextual validity of the
instruments of analysis must be answered before attempts can be
made to reach substantive conclusions.

In their search for empirical evidence, modern political
science and sociology, aided by the proliferation of aggregate

---

[1] Nation-Building and Citizenship (New York: Wiley, 1964).

1

data and by improvements in computing facilities, have continued the tradition of exploring the relationships between the socio-economic and the political dimensions. This has been a vast effort that has generated valuable new knowledge about many important aspects of these relationships. However, this effort has not been accompanied by a parallel reflection on the theoretical assumptions and consequences of the methods used by the various disciplines in dealing with this subject-matter. It will be seen that, at least for the conceptualization of the relationships between socio-economic structures and political systems in contemporary South America, such theoretical lag has led to some highly questionable results.

It seems quite clear that, at the level being referred to, the search for empirical evidence by modern "Occidental" political science and sociology has been permeated by the basic perception that most of the more affluent countries of the modern world are "political democracies,"[2] while among the poorer countries political democracies are very rare. There are important exceptions at all levels, but this seems to be the general pattern if one looks at the contemporary picture. But it is important to note that this pattern becomes apparent to the observer through the use of a more or less formal correlational study, which provides a static image of socio-economic levels and types of political systems at the present time. The correlation scores are quite high,[3] but they indicate very little about the problems with which this book will be mainly concerned. A correlation is like a snapshot. It tells us where the actors portrayed stand, but it does not give us any information about how they came to occupy their present positions or in which directions they are likely to move in the future. These latter involve, respectively, a genetic-explanatory and a predictive problem, which require very different techniques of study. Rather than a snapshot we need something closer to a "film" to answer questions raised by the genetic problem: How did the actors come to occupy their present positions? Are they repeating the same moves and following the same routes? How do previous moves of some of the actors influence the moves and routes of the rest? A film, by enabling us to detect the direction of movement of actors and recurrent patterns of interaction among them, would also help us with the predictive problem. Prediction is always a risky business, and

---

[2] A conceptually more accurate term is "polyarchy" (see Robert Dahl, A Preface to Democratic Theory [Chicago: University of Chicago Press, 1956], but here I prefer to follow the more established usage.

[3] Among many other studies on this correlation, see Bruce Russett, Trends in World Politics (New York: Macmillan, 1965).

if one wants to reduce the margin of error, one would be well-advised to choose seeing a film rather than merely a snapshot of its last scene.

Snapshots and correlations are useful, but with important limitations. They are of very little help for anything (such as explanation, retrospection, and prediction) that requires study along a time dimension. In fact, correlations can be very misleading if we attempt to extrapolate from them and try to say something about how things came about or where they are leading. This seems to be the case with many contemporary interpretations of the relationships between levels of economic development and types of political systems. Extrapolation from the experience of the presently richest countries on the basis of correlational (i.e., ahistorical) perspectives has been the foundation for sustaining the following expectations: (1) if other countries become as rich as the economically advanced nations, it is highly probable that they will become political democracies; (2) even though they may not achieve the highest levels of economic development, as the poorer countries become more affluent, the likelihood of their becoming political democracies will increase; (3) given two "underdeveloped" countries, the one that is relatively richer is more likely to be a political democracy.

These expectations can be said to constitute the basic "paradigm"[4] of comparative politics, as well as of social and political development literature, in spite of severe criticism and an impressive accumulation of case-study data that create serious doubts as to its validity.[5] This paradigm was given its

---

[4]The term "paradigm" is used here by analogy to the usage in Thomas Kuhn, The Structure of Scientific Revolutions (Chicago: University of Chicago Press, 1962).

[5]For these criticisms see esp. F. Cardoso and E. Faleto, Dependencia y desarrollo en América Latina (Siglo XXI, 1969); Samuel P. Huntington, "The Change to Change: Modernization, Development and Politics," Comparative Politics, 3 (1971); Joseph LaPalombara, "Political Science and the Engineering of National Development" in J. Powelson, ed., The Disciplines of National Development (forthcoming). From different viewpoints, most contemporary Latin American social science literature challenges this paradigm. For a pioneering critique by a U.S. scholar, focused on the Latin American context, see Alfred Stepan, "Political Development Theory: The Latin American Experience," Journal of International Affairs, Vol. XX, No. 2. As Huntington rightly argues, this paradigm pervades other areas in our disciplines, as shown by the "convergence hypothesis" of capitalist and socialist countries (see "Introduction" in S. Huntington and C. Moore, eds., Authoritarian Politics in Modern Society (New York: Basic Books, 1970).

first quantitative--and perhaps most influential--expression by Seymour Martin Lipset, and can be summarized in what might be called "the optimistic equation":

MORE SOCIO-ECONOMIC DEVELOPMENT =
MORE LIKELIHOOD OF POLITICAL DEMOCRACY[6]

Since Lipset's pioneering effort, numerous studies have elaborated the "left" side of the equation, adding factors such as literacy, communications, life expectancy, and many others that are seen as definitional components or as correlates of socio-economic development.[7] The intercorrelations of these variables are usually high, and their joint effect presumably increases the likelihood of political democracy (the "right" side of the equation). These studies derived from the basic paradigm are supposed to provide empirical support for the paradigm, as well as for the expectations that it embodies.

The basic paradigm and the aggregate-data studies that derive from it and appear to give it empirical validation deserve closer examination in several important respects. In the first place, they are old wine in new containers: they reformulate the Enlightenment's hope that social "progress" would generate "better" (from the point of view of the observer) forms of organization of political life. Political democracy is usually positively valued by the investigator. Many rich countries are political democracies, and vice versa; hence, as countries become more affluent, the likelihood of the emergence and/or consolidation of political democracy will increase in those countries.

Second, the only way these expectations can be justified is by assuming that the causal processes operating today are similar, at least in the most fundamental aspects, to those that led to the joint outcome "high socio-economic development--political democracy" in many of the richest countries. This assumption is crucial, since if it is not the case, it might be that countries whose economies are growing will not tend to become political democracies (and vice versa). Furthermore, it could be that because an "underdeveloped" country is more affluent than another, the poorer one is a political democracy while the richer one is not. These possibilities cannot be ruled out simply by

---

[6] Political Man (Garden City: Doubleday, 1960).

[7] A useful introduction to this literature is Raymond Hopkins, "Aggregate Data and the Study of Political Development," The Journal of Politics, Vol. XXXI, No. 1 (1969).

assuming the equivalence of causal processes: empirical evidence must be provided.[8]

Third, the basic paradigm is rendered immune to empirical falsification by treating the manifold observed incongruencies with the expectations derived from the paradigm (and its assumption of the equivalence of causal processes) as "deviations" or "regressions" due to "obstacles" (i.e., idiosyncratic factors that are regarded as superimposed on the more basic, equivalent processes). It is assumed that if the obstacles could be "removed," the more basic processes supposedly operating would produce their effects on political phenomena without "distortions." There is no doubt that if the basic paradigm were valid it would greatly simplify the conceptualization of an extremely complex subject-matter by establishing important commonalities across time and space. But if there is good reason to suspect that the paradigm seriously distorts the perception of relationships and tendencies in socio-economic and political interactions, there is no way to escape the need to be very specific about the historical contexts for which generalizations about these interactions are valid.[9]

---

[8]By "causal processes" of the units under study, I understand their initial conditions, the factors undergoing change through time, and the parameters that govern their relationships. The assumption of equivalence of these processes entails postulating that these aspects are fundamentally similar, or--where different --are irrelevant for determining the states of the units at the time they are compared. However, it can be formally demonstrated that if any of these three aspects are different, the behavior of the units compared will tend to be different, and these differences will tend to increase over time (see, on this point, the excellent discussion by R. Brunner and K. Liephelt, "Data Analysis, Process Analysis and System Change," paper presented to the 1970 annual meeting of the American Political Science Association). It should be obvious that such an assumption has a strong antihistoric and formalistic bias. It denies the causal significance of different historical contexts (or structures). It supposes that a factor such as level of social affluence, however defined and measured, exerts a similar influence over political phenomena irrespective of the constellation of factors with which it is interacting. However, if such constellations are different at different times and/or across different countries, there is no reason to expect that a similar level of social affluence will have similar effects on the political phenomena of these units.

[9]For a sharp criticism of the tendency toward broad generalizations, see J. LaPalombara, "Macrotheories and Microapplications in Comparative Politics: A Widening Gap," Comparative Politics, Vol. I, No. 1 (1968).

Fourth, and closely connected with the previous point, the empirical referent of theories and aggregate-data studies derived from the basic paradigm is usually the set of all or most contemporary polities. Since some positive correlation between socio-economic development and political democracy can be found, it may be concluded that this relationship holds for all the units (say, regions) included in that set. This would be fallacious.[10] A positive correlation at the level of the whole set does not preclude the possibility of a lack of association or even negative correlation at the level of a subset of the units studied.

Fifth, the basic paradigm and the optimistic equation that "translates" it for use in aggregate-data studies postulate a linear (or, more precisely, a positive monotonic) relationship between socio-economic development and the likelihood of political democracy--i.e., as development increases, the likelihood of democracy is also supposed to increase (by some unknown function). But, as previously noted, the data used refer to a set of countries at a single point in time, while the postulated relationship refers to changes over a period of time in each of the countries. Changes in socio-economic structure and the tendencies they presumably generate toward changes in the political dimension can only be studied with data from each unit and for the minimal time-period implied in the hypothesized relationships. The attempt to substitute "horizontal" data referring to many countries at only one point in time for this "longitudinal" data and still say something about causal, time-spanning processes within each unit is (as may be obvious) formally the same fallacy as the one discussed in the preceding paragraph.[11] Scholars using

---

[10]This has been labelled "the universalistic fallacy." For a good discussion with specific reference to Latin American studies, see Philippe C. Schmitter, "Nuevas estrategias para el análisis comparativo de la política en América Latina," Revista Latinoamericana de Sociología, Vol. 5, No. 3 (1969). In statistical terms, this fallacy is committed by ignoring part of the covariance components--for example, by assuming in a cross-tabulation that the within-cell scores are equal to the marginal frequencies (or show the same relationship as the latter). Both this fallacy and the one referred to in the text below have been shown to be formally equivalent to the better-known "ecological fallacy." On this point see the important article by Hayward Alker, "A Typology of Ecological Fallacies" in S. Rokkan and M. Doggan, eds., Quantitative Ecological Analysis in the Social Sciences (Cambridge, Mass.: The MIT Press, 1969).

[11]On this point see the excellent discussion by Brunner and Liephelt. See also Alker, and James Coleman, "The Mathematical Study of Change" in H. Blalock and A. Blalock, eds., Methodology in Social Research (New York: McGraw-Hill, 1968).

horizontal data can locate countries on a developmental continuum
(say, according to their per capita income as an indication of
their economic development) and then determine the type of political system that seems to correspond to each development score
or "stage." Up to this point they are within the logic of a
static correlational analysis, but any causal inferences drawn
on the basis of this exercise involve an unwarranted jump into
the logic of regression analysis. The only regression line that
can legitimately be used for studying tendencies, causal relationships, and changes over time within a unit is the one constructed
with data from that very unit. In sum: Constructing continuums,
performing regressions (explicit or implicit), and/or making
inferences about causation and change with horizontal data from
several countries at only one point in time may fit well with the
assumptions of the basic paradigm, but it inevitably involves the
fallacy that this enables us to say something about tendencies,
causation, and change in _one_ country--or in a _group_ of countries.

Sixth, in order to be useful the paradigm and its "optimistic equation" must be conceptually unambiguous, which creates
a number of problems. We will return to this subject later, but
it should be pointed out here that the "right side" of the equa-
tion--the political dimension--may be incorrectly defined. The
emergence of political democracy at some point in their history
has been, with some important exceptions, the general experience
of the presently more "developed" countries. There is little
doubt that socio-economic growth generates, or is highly correlated with, political pluralization.[12] But political pluralization and political democracy are not the same. Political pluralization refers to the numbers of, and interrelations among,
political units within a national context, whereas political
democracy is one possible institutional expression of a host of
factors--including political pluralization. As noted, political
democracy has been part of the historical experience of many of
the more developed countries, but nothing (except a tendency to
extrapolate from the known to the unknown) justifies a priori
expectations that such institutional expression will occur again
in the presently _less_ developed countries. Rather, political
pluralization might contribute to the emergence of types of
political systems that even with the most careless "conceptual
stretching" could not qualify as political democracies.[13] Thus,

---

[12]Later I will elaborate upon this assertion. For the moment,
let me define "political pluralization" as the emergence of more
political units interrelated in more complex ways.

[13]See G. Sartori, "Concept Misformation in Comparative Politics," _American Political Science Review_, Vol. LXIV, No. 4 (1970).
The frequent use in aggregate-data studies of wholly formalistic

it would seem advisable to provisionally revise the "equation" (which begins to lose its "optimistic" character) to reflect this possibility:

"MORE SOCIO-ECONOMIC DEVELOPMENT = MORE POLITICAL PLURALIZA-
TION $\neq$ MORE LIKELIHOOD OF POLITICAL DEMOCRACY"[14]

Another conceptual requirement is that the "left side" of the equation--the socio-economic dimension--be well-defined and that its indicators measure what they purport to measure. Other definitions and indicators than those now generally used could be found that better reflect the socio-economic dimension. If the new definitions and indicators alter the developmental rankings, the relationships observed under the previous conceptualization might be significantly changed. We will return to this point, but it is perhaps useful to note here that this would seem to be the case for contemporary South America: political authoritarian-ism--not political democracy--is the more likely concomitant of the highest levels of modernization.[15]

To this point we have discussed conceptual and methodolog-ical problems on a very abstract level. It is now possible to turn to studies specifically focused on Latin American countries and see how they apply, and with what consequences, the basic paradigm to this region.

Latin American Studies: Ranks and Classifications

The basic paradigm can be expressed either in its original form or by way of statements that are logically equivalent--for instance, statements of the form "Country X is 'deviant' (or 'paradoxical') because it is less democratic (or less 'politically developed') than it should be, considering its level of socio-economic development" or "Country X is more (less) democratic than it should be, considering its comparatively low (high) level of socio-economic development." Statements of this type can be

---

criteria (such as the holding of elections or the existence of a parliament, irrespective of their actual political import) for qualifying countries as "political democracies" seems to me an excellent example of the "conceptual stretching" that Sartori correctly criticizes.

[14]The symbol $\neq$ means "does not necessarily imply."

[15]The concept of "modernization" is defined and discussed below.

8

based on quantitative data and/or in qualitative judgments, and they may refer to a whole set of countries (e.g., Latin America), to a subset, or to just one country. But—to emphasize the point—in all cases they express the basic paradigm, and their import is the same: the likelihood of political democracy increases as the level of socio-economic development rises. Also, whether the data and conclusions are quantitative or qualitative, we remain within the logic of a simple model of regression analysis, with the expected values of the political dimension growing monotonically as a function of increases in the values of the "independent" variable(s) that define the socio-economic dimension.[16]

In all cases, the following operations must be explicitly or implicitly performed: (1) countries must be ordered, individually or by clusters, along a dimension of "socio-economic development"; (2) countries must be classified by their type of political system; (3) the relationships between the political and socio-economic dimensions must then be observed and, provided that the basic paradigm holds, statements such as those referred to above can be formulated. This is true not only of studies based on aggregate data,[17] but also of the more numerous studies based on qualitative observations and data,[18] as well as those focusing mainly on Argentina which conclude that the country is

_____

[16] Actually, the model implied by the studies to be cited is simpler, since the relationships between these dimensions are supposed to be linear. Concerning the statement that the logic of regression analysis also applies to qualitative-judgment studies of this type, see R. Fogel's discussion on "subliminal regressions" in "The Specification Problem in Economic History," The Journal of Economic History, Vol. XXVII, No. 3 (1967).

[17] See, among others, Robert Putnam, "Toward Explaining Military Interventions in Latin American Politics," World Politics, Vol. XX, No. 1 (1967); Robert Dix, "Oppositions in Latin America" in R. Dahl et al., eds., Regimes and Oppositions (forthcoming); Martin Needler, Political Development in Latin America (New York: Random House, 1968); and, for a wider-ranging example, A. Adelman and C. Taft Morris, Society, Politics and Economic Development (Baltimore: The Johns Hopkins Press, 1967).

[18] See, among many others, John Johnson, Political Change in Latin America (Stanford: Stanford University Press, 1958); Robert Alexander, Latin American Politics and Government (New York: Harper & Row, 1965); Edwin Lieuwen, Arms and Politics in Latin America (New York: Praeger, 1960); and M. Needler, Latin American Politics in Perspective (New York: Van Nostrand, 1967).

"paradoxical" in that its lack of political democracy and its recurrent political crises do not correspond to what "should be expected" according to its relatively high level of socio-economic development.[19] In what follows, special attention will be paid to studies based on quantitative data. They are only a small part of the numerous studies applying the basic paradigm and through its use reaching similar conclusions, but they have the advantage that their methodology permits close examination of their common approach and assumptions.

At this point it is important to recall that we are narrowing the scope of our discussion. We have been dealing with studies that focus on all (or at least a cross-regional sample of) contemporary countries. Now we will be concentrating on studies that focus on the Latin American region or some subset of countries of that region. This change in the empirical referent may appear to have some beneficial consequences vis-à-vis some of the problems noted in our analysis of the applications of the basic paradigm on a universal or cross-regional basis. In particular, focusing on a smaller sample may make it possible to gather and analyze more detailed data, which could be helpful in solving the problems of loose conceptualization. It could also facilitate the use of "longitudinal" data for each of the units analyzed. Furthermore, it may seem that the commonality of various contextual factors in a region (such as colonial origin, culture, and role in international power-relations) would result in a degree of intra-regional homogeneity that would enable scholars to avoid, for conclusions referring to that region, the problems posed by the "universalistic fallacy." Finding a substantial degree of positive association between "socio-economic development" and political democracy within the set of Latin American countries might then be construed as reasonable proof that, having controlled for the effects of the common contextual factors, the basic relationships and tendencies postulated by the basic paradigm hold true. Thus, with respect to the validity of the paradigm and of the fundamental causal processes that it postulates, intra-regional findings would seem to be of particular value, and therefore warrant close examination.

For the dimension of "socio-economic development," the studies we will be analyzing rank Latin American countries in terms of their per capita incomes (see Table 1). When more complex indices are generated by combining the gross national product (GNP) per capita with other per capita variables, the

---

[19] A. Whitaker, "The Argentine Paradox," The Annals of the American Academy of Political and Social Science, No. 334 (1961). A perusal of the social science literature on Argentina will show how frequent are assertions of this type.

Table 1

GROSS NATIONAL PRODUCT PER CAPITA AT MARKET PRICES
IN SOUTH AMERICAN COUNTRIES: 1966
(in U.S. dollars)

Country	Per Capita GNP
Venezuela	879
Argentina	818
Uruguay	613
Chile	576
Colombia	334
Brazil	333
Perú	271
Paraguay	220
Ecuador	219
Bolivia	178

Source: Statistical Abstract for Latin America--1968 (University of California, Los Angeles, 1969).

rank of Venezuela is lowered, reflecting the "Kuwait effect" of oil extraction on the Venezuelan GNP. The following clusters of countries[20] generally result: (1) at the "top"—Argentina, Chile, and Uruguay (and sometimes Venezuela); (2) in the "middle"--Peru, Colombia and Brazil;[21] (3) at the "bottom"--Bolivia, Ecuador, and Paraguay. These rankings are then plotted against the political dimension, conceptualized as "political democracy,"[22] "competitive politics" or "polyarchy,"[23] or (non)military intervention and "political development."[24] In all cases the measures of association postulated by the basic paradigm are similar or even better

[20]The Central American countries are excluded here.

[21]In some cases Brazil and Mexico are included as a subgroup within the middle level of socio-economic development. See, e.g., R. Vekemans and L. Segundo, "Essay of a Socio-Economic Typology of the Latin American Countries" in J. de Vries and J. Medina Echavarría, eds., Social Aspects of Economic Development in Latin America, Vol. I (Paris: Desclée, 1963), and G. Germani and K. Silvert, "Politics, Social Structure and Military Intervention in Latin America," Archives Européennes de Sociologie, No. 2 (1961).

[22]See, for example, Needler's plot of GNP against "stable democracy" in Needler, Political Development....

[23]Dix, "Oppositions...."

[24]Putnam, "Toward Explaining Military Interventions...."

than those obtained with universal or cross-regional samples. At
the higher levels of "development," Chile and Uruguay are the South
American political democracies, while Venezuela has elected three
consecutive constitutional Presidents and "survived" a change in
majority party. At the lowest level, the political systems are
definitely non-democratic. At the middle level, some problem
cases appear, but given firm a priori belief in the validity of
the basic paradigm, the mixed record of these countries can be
read as a reflection of "pulls" toward political democracy which
are still relatively weak because of their relatively low socio-
economic development. However, there is one blatant exception.
By any standard, Argentina's position in the political dimension
is significantly different from what would be expected on the
basis of the paradigm, considering its comparatively high level
of socio-economic development.

In spite of the Argentine discrepancy and the additional
assumptions required to resolve the ambiguities at the middle level,
the studies under consideration here have obtained measures of
association for the Latin American countries that have been interpreted as confirming the validity of the paradigm. The analysts
have been able to consider those cases "explained" that lie close
to the (explicit or implicit) regression line[25] and to construe
the other cases as "deviant." The only task remaining--in their
view--is that of examining the "deviant" cases to determine the
idiosyncratic (i.e., country-specific) factors that create obstacles
to the presumably universal tendencies implied by the paradigm.[26]

What are the implications of this procedure? To answer
this question a brief digression is necessary.

There are no "pure facts." Their very status qua facts,
as well as their interpretation and theoretical import, depends on
the frame of reference of the observer. For qualitative-data
studies this is intuitively (and quite trivially) obvious. But
it is also true for results derived from formal cr quantitative-
data studies. For example, the use of correlational or regression
techniques does not eliminate the classic requisites of clearly

---

[25]In less formal terms, the analysts have been able to consider
those cases "explained" whose political systems are appropriate
(in terms of the paradigm) to their level of socio-economic development.

[26]For an advocacy of this strategy, see, e.g., Dix and Putnam,
ibid. The same concept underlies country-studies that seek to
explain why a certain country is "exceptional" or "paradoxical."
This strategy is methodologically sound only if the conceptualization that generated the "explained" and "deviant" cases is valid.

defining concepts and adequately choosing indicators—otherwise the apparent "hardness" of their results is lost. The use of any statistical technique implies specifying in mathematical form a model of the reality to be studied. The adequacy of this model depends on the frame of reference and the basic expectations (or, as we have called it here, the "paradigm") that guide the inquiry. Thus, whether it is explicitly stated or not, the model specified for statistical manipulation presupposes crucial decisions concerning what questions are to be asked, how concepts are to be defined, which interrelationships are to be explored, and what indicators are to be chosen.

The same empirical referent analyzed from a different frame of reference and in terms of a different (quantitative or qualitative) model may generate very different results. Conceptualizations[27] at all levels and in all forms of analysis are tested by the results of empirical observation, but what these results are depends to a large extent on the conceptualization being tested. This circularity creates an ultimate uncertainty in even the most solid conceptualizations.

When, as is the case here, the evidence is at best weak, particular care and continued experimentation with alternative conceptualizations is advisable. It may turn out that "better" ones (in the sense that they fit observed phenomena more closely) exist, and that under them cases that were "normal" will become "deviant," and vice versa. If this is the case, insofar as previous studies and models for a particular subject-matter applied a dominant paradigm, the consequences for research may be serious. By postulating certain basic relationships, such a paradigm organizes the observer's perception of a highly complex subject-matter, generates the fundamental questions to be asked, and guides the formulation of specific hypotheses to be tested. For example, if a paradigm postulates that there is a tendency toward political democracy as socio-economic development proceeds, then this tendency is what analysts (and policy-makers) will expect from positive change in the socio-economic variables included in the definition of "development." The pattern of "normal" (or "explained") and "deviant" cases will make sense only if such expectations are valid. The conceptual structure of the subject-matter becomes greatly simplified. For example, if the tendencies postulated by the basic paradigm are operating in all the countries studied, then research questions can be focused primarily on determining what country-specific idiosyncracies can explain the "deviancy" of some of them. However, in contemporary South American countries

---

[27]"Conceptualization," as used here, is a very general concept which includes everything from loosely articulated frames of reference to very specific formal models.

some important tendencies might be operating which are very different from those implied by the basic paradigms.[28] The basic paradigm's organization of the perception of the subject-matter may be achieved at the price of postulating the wrong tendencies and, consequently, asking the wrong questions.

Suppose that instead of pulling South American countries toward political democracy, the causal processes triggered by their patterns of socio-economic growth are actually pulling them toward political authoritarianism? Would we then assume that political democracy will be the "natural" or the "normal" outcome? Would we then think, say, of Argentina in terms of her presumed "deviance" and try to find what factors distinguish her from most other South American countries? If it were the case that at higher socio-economic levels, political authoritarianism tends to become the norm, would we still assume that, as growth proceeds in less "advanced" South American political democracies, the outcome will be further democratization? These are not the types of questions that spring from belief in the validity of the basic paradigm, but they may be some of the more pertinent to ask about the contemporary South American reality. On these possibilities the accumulation of case-study evidence is impressive, but as observed above, it can always be interpreted as unable to falsify the paradigm. This highlights the importance of a dominant, basic paradigm. Contrary evidence can hardly be utilized insofar as the primary, pre-research perception of the subject-matter and its basic tendencies is not modified. The observer registers that evidence in his specific research (say, a country case-study), but when it becomes a matter of determining the theoretical import of those findings, it is the dominant paradigm, whatever the incongruencies on both levels of analysis, that is the source of the clues that guide that stage of analysis. It seems very difficult to analyze and appraise aspects of social life without some ideas or hypotheses about their fundamental tendencies and the directions in which the processes uncovered seem to be leading. This is the level, in many cases only implicit, at which the primary perception of the subject-matter performs a crucial intellectual function--particularly if such perception is articulated with the degree of specificity and scholarly consensus entailed by a dominant paradigm.[29] The resistance of that paradigm to empirical falsification strongly

---

[28] Or, for that matter, implied by the official ideology of the Alliance for Progress and of many South American public policies of the recent past.

[29] Attempts to formulate alternative conceptualizations are to be found in works cited in Chapter II that emphasize the problems of Latin American "dependence." However, this aspect must be conceptually clarified, empirically disaggregated, and incorporated into a broader theoretical perspective.

suggests that it must be attacked at a high level of conceptualization.[30] What follows in these pages can be interpreted as an attempt to make a preliminary contribution to that theoretical task.[31]

---

[30]This point can be seen more formally in relation to what is implied by aggregate-data studies that use statistical techniques for establishing and testing their findings. The results depend entirely on the requirement that the statistical model correctly specifies the relevant aspects of the segment of reality under study. If the model is misspecified, and if in addition it is not just-identified, its results are substantively meaningless. Econometricians have analyzed these requirements and insistently warned about the problems caused by models that do not meet them. For discussions of these important (albeit largely ignored in our disciplines) methodological problems, see W. Hood and T. Koopmans, eds., Studies in Econometric Method (New York: Wiley, 1953); F.M. Fisher, The Identification Problem in Econometrics (New York: McGraw-Hill, 1966); E. Malinvaud, Statistical Methods in Econometrics (New York, 1970); and P. Dhrymes, Econometrics: Statistical Foundations and Applications (New York: Harper & Row, 1970), among others. For a more elementary discussion, see R.J. and T.H. Wonnacott, Econometrics (New York: Wiley, 1970). If a wrong theory or sheer inadvertence leads to the specification of a wrong model (or to under- or over-identification of it), one can have no confidence that its apparently "hard" results are a fair approximation to the true values of the phenomena under study. If this is the case, meager (and almost always indeterminate) improvements can be attained by technical manipulation of the model in use. It is at the level of a revision of the model itself (and of the theory or conceptualization that it specifies) that these problems can be solved.

[31]Kingsley Davis has an excellent discussion of many of the issues raised here: "Unless the theory has analytic incisiveness and logical rigor, the results will be inconclusive no matter how 'good' the 'data' are. Since the original concepts governing the nature of the data to be obtained in different countries, as well as the method of gathering and presenting the information, are determined by the social theory brought to task, there is, in my estimation, no such thing as international 'raw data' existing apart from social science and yet ready to be utilized by it.... Things are comparable only with respect to certain criteria. If the criteria are scientifically insignificant, then the mere fact of comparability will be of little importance. It is possible to gather an infinite quantity of seemingly comparable information, but unless it is comparable with respect to analytically significant features of the material, it will be useless and, in some cases, misleading" ("Problems and Solutions in International Comparisons for Social Science Purposes," Population Reprint Series, Institute of International Studies, University of California, Berkeley).

Data and Averages

Most indicators used in the studies under discussion here are national averages (i.e., statistical means). This is current practice in sociology and political science, but for certain purposes it is difficult to justify. In one study based on aggregate data, Kalman Silvert proposes a classification of Latin American countries in terms of socio-economic development, but he includes a comment suggestive of the argument to be developed here:

> The most obvious difficulty with this [system of classification] as an indicator of development is the relatively low position of Brazil and Mexico. The figures are averages, of course, which means that the large peasant populations of these countries depress their rankings. If the statistics treated only of the non-Indian population in Mexico and of the south-eastern part of Brazil, the developed parts of both countries would take the [high] positions that they do, in fact, occupy" [italics added].33

National averages are means, obtained by dividing an aggregate indicator (say GNP) by the number of inhabitants. We know from descriptive statistics that means are measures of central tendency of a distribution, which by themselves do not tell us anything about two crucial factors: the form of the distribution of observations and the degree of their dispersion around the mean.34 These aspects can hardly be neglected, as can be seen from a hypothetical example of three distributions that have the same mean (see Figure 1).

Though their means are identical, a statement that the whole distributions are alike because their means are identical obviously would be fallacious. In political science and sociology, one is frequently interested in whole distributions, but aggregate data studies are almost always limited to working with, and reporting on, means. Several warnings have been issued, apparently without much effect, about the shortcomings of analysis and

---

33"Nationalism in Latin America," The Annals of the American Academy of Political and Social Science, No. 334 (1961).

34An outstanding discussion of the properties and limitations of different measures of central tendency can be found in J. Tukey, Exploratory Data Analysis (Reading, Mass.: Addison-Wesley, 1970). However, the basic point of my argument can be gleaned from any textbook on elementary statistics.

Figure 1

THREE HYPOTHETICAL DISTRIBUTIONS HAVING THE SAME MEAN

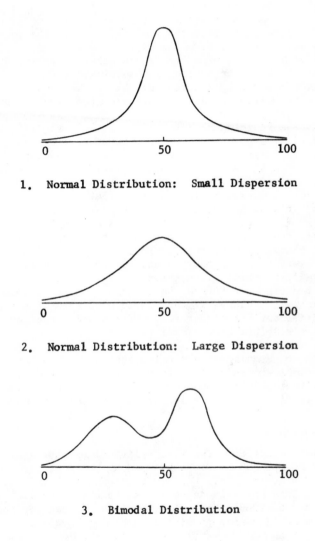

1. Normal Distribution: Small Dispersion

2. Normal Distribution: Large Dispersion

3. Bimodal Distribution

$Mean_1 = Mean_2 = Mean_3 = 50.$

inference based solely on means.[35] For cross-national comparative studies to be based solely on national means, it must be assumed either that the pattern of the distribution of observations and their degree of dispersion can be written off as irrelevant, or that both are known to be roughly similar. The hypothetical examples of Figure 1 show clearly that the first assumption would be very hard to justify. The second assumption needs further discussion. In the first place, it implies that the question "Mean of what?" (which in turn determines what unit of analysis is appropriate for the purposes of the particular inquiry) can be answered with the "obvious," almost always unexamined conclusion that the country at large is the universe of observations from which the mean is going to be computed. In the second place, the existence of a rough similarity in the form and in the degree of dispersion of the distribution is something that must be independently (and empirically!) determined before proceeding as if national means were adequate summaries of the data of interest.

In the "developed" countries the internal distributions of most variables are far more homogeneous than in most "less developed" countries, and these distributions and their degree of dispersion within the various countries are usually roughly similar. Under these conditions, taking whole nations as the units of analysis for assessing socio-economic effects on national political phenomena, as well as comparing the nations in terms of their mean values, may be justified. But for cross-national comparison of units where these features do not hold, the uncritical use of means must lead to erroneous results. Means are indicators, and indicators are useful only if they reveal the characteristics of the unit of analysis that, given the purposes of inquiry, are fundamental. Indicators refer to the processes and structure of the unit of analysis; hence, if they imply a texture of social reality that is different from the reality of the unit under analysis, they cannot help but be misleading.

In the quantitative studies that apply the basic paradigm to the Latin American region, parameters that would enable us to gauge the intra-national patterns of distribution of the variables used, as well as the dispersion of the observations made, are not

---

[35] See Bruce Russett, "The Yale Political Data Program: Experiences and Prospects" in S. Rokkan and R. Merritt, eds., Comparing Nations (New Haven: Yale University Press, 1966); R. Tufte, "Improving Data Analysis in Political Science," World Politics, Vol. 21, No. 4 (1969); and United Nations, "Report on International Definition and Measurement of Standards and Levels of Living" (E/CN3/3/179 and E/CN/5/299) and "International Definition and Measurement of Standards of Living: An Interim Guide," (E/CN3/270 Rev. 1, E/CN.5/353; Geneva, n.d.).

reported, and in most cases they are unknown.[36] Consequently,
countries are ordered along the socio-economic dimension solely
on the basis of the mean values of a number of variables.[37] From
this standpoint, statements are made about similarities or differences in levels of development among Latin American countries, thus
defining the independent variable "socio-economic development"--
that will be used to predict political phenomena. Here, again,
while the indicators are means, the empirical referents are whole
distributions. Hence the ordering of countries along the "development" dimension is likely to be erroneous if we are dealing with
variables differently distributed within those countries. At any
rate, it should be evident that inferences based on means are very
weak support for the strong conclusions entailed by the orderings
proposed by these studies.[38]

This point can be illustrated by another example, consisting of three countries at different levels of socio-economic
development (however measured), as shown in Figure 2.

Assume that Country A is fairly homogeneous, in that the
proportion of the population living in what may be called the
"peripheral area" is small. Since this implies comparatively
narrow dispersion around the means of numerous variables, a case
can be made that averaged national data give an acceptable "general picture"--at least for preliminary descriptive purposes at
the national level. Assume that Country B is a big country in
terms of population and territory. It is highly heterogeneous,
in that an important proportion of its population belongs to the
"periphery," where most socio-economic variables have extremely
low values. In this case, the distribution of most variables of
interest will tend to be bimodal and/or widely dispersed around

------

[36] Consider, for example, the most commonly used proxy for "economic development"--the gross national product--in countries
where minimally reliable data on income distribution are frequently
lacking.

[37] Or worse, on the basis of the grand mean or some weighted average of the means of assorted variables.

[38] To be fair, it should be added here that, besides the reasons
already suggested, the use of means for cross-national comparative
purposes is fostered by some convenient statistical properties of
means, as well as by the desire to enhance comparability by controlling for (i.e., annulling) the effects of the different size
of the units compared. But if, as I hope to show, in some cases
size itself is a factor of great importance, technical convenienc•
and substantive knowledge would seem to be sharply at odds.

the mean, whose usefulness is thus drastically decreased. Finally, assume that P is a small country, with heterogeneity similar to B; the same comments apply.

Note that, according to the very primitive intra-national disaggregations suggested in Figure 2, B's "modern center" is at least as large as A's. However, the big peripheral area of B will determine that, if national means are calculated, data from her modern center will be literally swamped with data from the periphery. Consequently, B's mean scores will be close to P's and significantly lower than A's. Pushing the example further, it might be that the "modern areas" (or "centers") of A and B are similar in many respects, while the same area of P differs markedly from both.

Are national means of variables appropriate for comparing these three countries? Since the general distribution--or, to put it in other terms, the "structure"--of A is very different from both B's and P's, the question cannot be lightly dismissed. Suppose now that analysts agree on the following points: (1) the population in the peripheral areas of all these nations participates only minimally in the production, consumption, and transmission of the cultural and material items broadly associated with modernity; (2) the "modern" areas contain an overwhelming proportion of those people that in some form "count" in the national political arena. If this is the case, even more serious doubts would be raised about the validity of using national means for purposes of comparison. If these are well-established empirical conditions, and if (as it is in the case of the studies analyzed) the goal of inquiry is to assess the effects of socio-economic phenomena on the type of political system and other features of national politics, would it not be a better strategy to think in terms of a "cross-modern areas" comparison? Would not such a comparison be likely to give a better indication of the constellation of factors that will explain most of the variance observed in the political dimension?

Let us say that countries A, B, and P are, respectively, Argentina (U$S 818 GNP per capita at market prices, 1966), Brazil (U$S 333), and Perú (U$S 271). On the basis of these per capita (i.e., mean) figures, the previously cited studies (quantitative and qualitative) place Brazil and Perú at roughly the same level of "socio-economic development," with Argentina well above both. But, as will be shown, the "modern" center of Brazil greatly exceeds all the values of the "modern" center of Perú, while it is very similar, in many important respects, to that of Argentina. Given the common goals of these studies and the present one, and given the aforementioned empirical conditions, which of these criteria is "more important"?[39] That is to say, which of these

_____

[39]Of course, there is no need to pose this question as a sharp

criteria give, in terms of data and conceptualization, a better insight into the processes that influence the state of the (political) dependent variables of interest? I suggest that the more important data are those that pinpoint the structural characteristics of each "modern" area.

At this point it should be obvious that questioning the unexamined use of national means leads to questioning the practice of always taking the whole nation as the "natural" unit of analysis for comparative purposes; the latter caveat is a logical step once the problem of the different effects of different types and degrees of intra-country heterogeneity becomes manifest.[40] It is possible now to start exploring what analytical yield can be obtained from the suggested alternative. Ideally, data should be disaggregated within each country along the lines in which the "modern areas-periphery" cleavage roughly lies, and the resulting "modern" subsets compared. Unhappily, current data analysis conventions are highly correlated with current practice in data collection and reporting. Sub-national South American data are scant and,

---

dilemma. As I will point out, the disaggregation I am proposing highlights the decisive political influence of the structural characteristics of each modern area, but it neglects the impact that the degree of national heterogeneity may have on those very characteristics. Given the severe data limitations within which my suggestion will have to be advanced, however, the alternative posed in the question seems realistic.

[40]It should be stressed that the selection of the units of analysis depends on the purposes of the inquiry. The units proposed here seem the most appropriate for a preliminary determination of the socio-economic factors that are most influential in shaping the characteristics of contemporary South American political systems (also the purpose of the studies we have analyzed). If the purpose were, say, more directly normative, the focus of attention would shift to the sectors of the population located in the peripheral areas. Or, if it were the more ambitious aim of explaining how the existing distribution of resources came about and is maintained, a focus on the whole national unit (including the effects on it of "external" factors) would be indispensable. (The purpose of these remarks is to rule out any interpretation that the analytical categories used here imply agreement with the theories of "structural dualism" originally proposed by J. Lambert in Os dois brasis [Companhia Editora Nacional, Brazil, 1957]. This conception and its numerous derivations have been aptly criticized elsewhere. See esp. Cardoso and Faleto, and R. Stavenhagen, "Seven Fallacies about Latin America" in J. Petras and M. Zeitlin, eds., Latin America: Reform or Revolution? [Greenwich, Conn.: Fawcett, 1968].)

when available, involve few dimensions with only limited comparability. This is a serious problem that will require the use of
an indirect approach, which will make possible only tentative
conclusions that will have to await more detailed data for careful
testing.

Intra-Country Heterogeneity

The distinction between "modern" and "peripheral" areas
is a very rough one. For the present purposes it will suffice
to define a "peripheral" area as one that has the following characteristics: (1) it is an agrarian region with an annual per
capita income of less than U$S 200; (2) its per capita productivity
is less than half the urban average of the country; (3) it has
minimal production and consumption of industrial goods; (4) it
has very low levels of organization (especially unionization) of
its wage and salary earners. In this first approximation, all
other areas are defined as "modern." It is important to note
that, according to this definition, the "modern" areas of each
country contain not only the "big"[41] urban centers, but also those
agrarian regions for which one of the specified conditions does
not hold--e.g., because of relatively high per capita income or
levels of unionization of its population. Thus, the distinction
proposed here does not always coincide with the conventional
"urban-rural" cleavage. (Further disaggregation may have been
useful, but the necessary data are lacking. There are good reasons to believe that much could be gained by discriminating among
the "big" urban centers in each South American country.)[42]

Several studies on income distribution in Latin America
have established patterns that are highly relevant for our purposes.
Argentina and Uruguay have been found "exceptional for the region"
due to "the almost total absence of a primitive [i.e., peripheral]
sector," while the patterns in other countries for which reasonably
detailed data are available are "in many ways, the reverse of the
Argentine situation."[43] (See Table 2.)

---

[41]This concept is defined below.

[42]A forceful plea for more research by political scientists on
the big Latin American urban centers (and an assessment of the
dismal state of the data available) can be found in R. Rabinovitz
"Data Resources for Cross-National Urban Research on Administration and Politics: A Proposal," Social Science Information, Vol.
IX, No. 3 (1970).

[43]UN-ECLA, Estudio económico de América Latina, "Estudios
especiales: Distribución del ingreso," (New York, 1970). See
also UN-ECLA, "Income Distribution in Latin America," Economic

Table 2

ESTIMATED STRUCTURAL DIFFERENCES AMONG SOUTH AMERICAN COUNTRIES:
C. 1965

Country	Percent Share of "Primitive Sector"		Percent of "Inframarginal Population" (per capita income less than U$S 100 per year) in Total Population
	In Total Employment	In Total GNP	
Argentina	7%	2%	10%
Venezuela	26	5	35
Chile	24	5	25/30
Brazil	42	10	35
Perú	56	14	N.A.
Ecuador	N.A.	N.A.	50
Uruguay	N.A.	N.A.	10

Sources: "Primitive Sector" data: Pinto, "Naturaleza . . . ;
"Inframarginal Population" data: D. Lambert.
"N.A." indicates data not available or not reported in
the source.

There is ample evidence that most of the population of the peripheral areas are deprived to the point that "they are excluded from consumption of manufactured goods, except for a minimum of clothing and other indispensable items."[44] And there is almost no industrial production in these regions. The extremely low measures of literacy, electricity, calory intake, and other factors are indicative of the bare subsistence level of most of those populations. It does not seem exaggerated to say that, except for the perhaps overemphasized effect of the transistor radio, the socio-economically marginal peripheral areas have had little or no exposure to the impact of modernity. More significant for this analysis, the level of ongoing nationally oriented political activity is very low in these areas. Even with respect to their "elites," their archetypical representative--the "absentee landowner"--is likely to be politically active in the big urban centers. These conditions are well-known to students of South American countries; they can be summarized in the sad fact that, except for short-lived "explosions," the preferences of an overwhelming proportion of the population of the peripheral regions do not count at all when decisions are made in the national arena. Only when the people migrate to the urban centers do they begin to have a slight chance to have some influence on national politics.

The degree of intra-country heterogeneity in South American countries reflected in Table 2 can be seen in a more indirect way by comparing the agrarian and urban regions of each country in terms of their income and productivity (Table 3). Again, the relative homogeneity (as compared with the other South American countries) of Argentina and Uruguay is evidenced, which is supported by the available, if scant, survey data. A 1966 national survey of Argentina shows that most regions have similar patterns of response in terms of political awareness, information, activism, allegiances, participation, and other political dimensions of interest here.[45]

Bulletin for Latin America, Vol. XII, No. 2 (1968); A. Pinto, "Naturaleza e implicaciones de la 'Heterogeneidad estructural' en América Latina," El Trimestre Económico, Vol. XXXI, No. 1 (1970); and D. Lambert, "Repartición de los ingresos y las desigualdades sociales en América Latina," Revista Mexicana de Sociología, Vol. XXXI, No. 2 (1969).

[44]UN-ECLA, The Process of Industrial Development in Latin America (New York, 1966), p. 252.

[45]This survey is reported in J. Kirkpatrick, Leader and Vanguard in Mass Society: A Study of Peronism in Argentina (Cambridge: The MIT Press, 1971). I am grateful to the author for her authorization to transcribe below some of her survey data from a prepublication manuscript.

Table 3

COMPARISON OF PRODUCTIVITY AND INCOME IN
AGRARIAN AND NON-AGRARIAN AREAS IN SOUTH AMERICAN COUNTRIES:
C. 1965

Country	Per Capita Productivity (Non-agrarian index = 100)		Average Income (Agrarian index = 100)	
	Agrarian Areas	Non-agrarian Areas	Agrarian Areas	Non-agrarian Areas
Argentina	111	100	100	115
Brazil	49	100	100	273
Chile	41	100	N.A.	
Colombia	60	100	N.A.	
Perú	25	100	N.A.	
Uruguay	120	100	N.A.	
Venezuela	23	100	100	250
Ecuador	45	100	N.A.	
Other[a]	27	100	N.A.	

[a]"Other" category in source includes not only Bolivia and Paraguay, but also Panamá and the Dominican Republic.

Source: UN-ECLA, Estudio Económico....

The contrary seems to be true for the other South American countries.[46]

Our preliminary conclusions concerning intra-heterogeneity can be summarized as follows:

Proposition 1: The degree of intra-country heterogeneity is relatively low in Argentina and Uruguay, is greater in Chile, and is very high in Brazil, Colombia, Ecuador, Perú, and Venezuela. Bolivia and Paraguay are homogeneous, but in an inverse sense--i.e., a "modern" sector has only barely emerged.

Proposition 2: Given the differences indicated in Proposition 1, for the purpose of assessing national political correlates of socio-economic characteristics, a "cross-center" strategy of comparison may be preferable to the current practice of utilizing national means.

Definitions and Indicators

Until now we have utilized the terms "modern" (or "center") and "periphery" with some misgivings because of their unwanted connotations. At this stage it is possible to sharpen our concepts by using an important analytical contribution: David Apter's theory of "modernization" as a primarily derivative process, consisting of the spread into "modernizing" societies of roles and institutions originating in and around industry in the more industrialized societies.[47] This definition has important advantages for our analysis:

(1) It provides straightforward guidelines for operationalization;

---

[46]See, for Brazil, J. Lane, "Isolation and Public Opinion in Northeast Brazil," Public Opinion Quarterly, Spring 1969.

[47]See David Apter: The Politics of Modernization (Chicago: University of Chicago Press, 1965), Conceptual Approaches to the Study of Modernization (Englewood Cliffs: Prentice-Hall, 1969), and Choice and the Politics of Allocation (New Haven: Yale University Press, 1971). For similar, albeit less elaborated, conceptions specifically focused on the Latin American context, see UN-ECLA, El cambio social y la política de desarrollo social en América Latina (New York, 1969) and R. Adams, The Second Sowing (San Francisco: Chandler, 1967). The pioneering contributions of Harold Lasswell should also be mentioned here; see esp. World Politics and Personal Insecurity (New York: McGraw-Hill, 1935).

(2) It opens theoretical access to data gathered, mostly by economists, on the productive structure of South American countries--especially on their industrial sectors.[48] The "transplantation" of roles and institutions that characterizes modernization results from (and in turn exerts an important influence upon) a fundamental aspect of the productive structure of society: that which pertains to industrial production and its manifold, urban-based, directly related complementary activities--marketing, publicity, communications, transportation, and the financing of industrial activities. The comparative differences, and the changes over time, in the productive structures of societies--and, in particular, of their urban-based industrial structures--are classic bases for the study of socio-economic effects upon political phenomena, and will be used extensively here;

(3) It has no implication of correspondence between "modernization" and the connotations associated with the term "development." Thus it avoids the vexing problems of definition and measurement of "development," whether by way of indices (some of whose problems have already been mentioned) or by some standard of performance--say, sustained growth or increasing equalitarianism--in which all South American countries are conspicuously failing;

(4) By emphasizing the effects that are produced in each modernizing context by the "transplantation" of roles and institutions from highly industrialized societies, it directs attention toward the study of the particular constellations that result in the former. The dynamic elements in each situation result from the interaction of the effects of these transplantations with other factors that are expressions of more autonomous internal sources. This concept of modernization indicates the need to specify the particular constellations that characterize each unit of analysis as a fundamental requisite for the interpretation, explanation, and prediction of behavior--with maximum certainty and determinacy--of the elements that constitute each unit;[49]

---

[48]The term "industrial sector" will be used to refer to industry and its directly related activities, "industry" to the production of industrial goods, and "productive structure of the national centers" to the activities of production and marketing of goods and services in those areas.

[49]For further elaboration of this point of view in the "structural" (or "contextual") tradition, see Chapter III below. The point may seem fairly obvious, but its neglect leads to the fallacy of expecting similar behavior from nominally similar actors,

(5) It provides that proper importance is given to the effects
of "external" linkages and supra-national power relations in
shaping each national situation.[50]

---

irrespective of the particular contexts in which they may be operating. For example, "the emergence of a middle class" should not
lead us to expect that actors included in this category will behave as they did in Western Europe. Even if the similarity were
more than nominal (which in this case it is not) the fact that the
actors are inserted in different contexts prevent us from expecting
that they will behave in the same way. Such behavior depends on
interactions with the other factors that define the specific context. (For a good critique of "the emergence of the middle sectors" literature, see J. Graciarena, Poder y clases sociales en
el desarrollo de América Latina [Paidós, 1967].) But, as E.
Hobsbawm points out, the same erroneous expectation has pervaded
the analysis of other sectors (urban workers, peasants) that have
received more attention from the left ("Latin America as U.S.
Empire Cracks," The New York Review of Books, March 25, 1971).
In all cases, such expectations lead to mistaken predictions and
unfortunate public policies, as well as breed the phenomenon of
"fracasomanía" that A. Hirschman has commented on in his Journeys
Toward Progress (The Twentieth Century Fund, 1963).

[50]Latin American social scientists have paid more attention than
any others to this crucial consideration. See esp. Cardoso and
Faleto; T. dos Santos, "La Crise de la théorie de développement
et les relations de dépendence en Amérique Latine," L'Homme et la
Société, 12 (1969) and "The Structure of Dependence," The American
Economic Review, LX, 2 (1970); T. dos Santos et al., La crisis
del desarrollismo y la nueva dependencia (Moncloa Campodónico
Editores, 1969); H. Jaguaribe et al., La dependencia político-
economica en América Latina (Siglo XXI, 1970); A. Quijano, "Dependencia, cambio social y desenvolvimiento social" in F. Cardoso
and F. Weffort, eds., América Latina: Ensayos de interpretación
sociológico-política (Editorial Universitaria, Chile, 1970); C.
Furtado, Dialéctica del desarrollo (FCE, 1965) and Subdesarrollo
y estancamiento en América Latina (Eudeba, 1966); M. Alonso Aguilar, Teoría y política del desarrollo latinoamericano (UNAM, 1967);
J. Nun, "Marginalidad y participación social: Un plateo intro-
ductivo," Instituto Torcuato di Tella, 1969 [mimeo]; G. Cárdenas,
Las luchas nacionales contra la dependencia (Editorial Galerna,
1969); O. Sunkel, "Política nacional de desarrollo y dependencia
externa," Estudios Internacionales, I, 1 (1968) and "La universidad latinoamericana ante el avance científico y técnico: Algunas
reflexiones," Estudios Internacionales, III, 4 (1970); and O.
Ianni, Imperialismo y cultura de la violencia en América Latina
(Siglo XXI, 1970). But see also Apter, Choice...; D. Chalmers,
"Developing on the Periphery: External Factors in Latin American
Politics" in J. Rosenau, ed., Linkage Politics: Essays on the
Convergence of National and International Systems (New York, 1969);
and I. Horowitz, Three Worlds of Development (New York, 1967).

(6) Finally, as may be obvious, it departs from the basic paradigm in that it denies the usual ".toward democracy" teleology and helps in the exploration of the likelihood and consequences of different types of political systems at different levels of modernization.

With Apter's concept it is possible to make a further specification of the "modern-periphery" dichotomy. A peripheral area is one where, besides the conditions already stated, a very limited degree of modernization is observable: the penetration of institutions and roles associated with industry and modern technology is minimal. Conversely, the penetration of institutions and roles associated with industry and modern technology becomes a fundamental criterion for the study of each modern area: it is the main guide for drawing the "modernization profile" of the modern areas to be cross-nationally compared. As an indicator of the structural characteristics of each modern area, this "profile" is, I believe, the best tool available for the comparative study of contemporary South American political concomitants of the socio-economic situation of each country.

The "modern-peripheral" distinction proposed is, of course, only a first step. As will be seen, even at this level serious data problems exist. But for the purposes of this analysis, such dichotomization serves well to reflect the lack of political impact on national decisions of certain sectors of the population. The assumption here is that most of the variance at the national political level can be explained by focusing on each South American "modern area" and, within it, particularly on "political demands" formulated by "(activated) political actors" and "incumbents of technocratic roles." These concepts, which will play an important part in this analysis, are defined as follows:

Political Demands (or more briefly, demands) are preferences about governmental policies held by political actors who are able to place those preferences on a continuing basis within the field of attention (whether for compliance, denial, or repression) of national policy-makers.

Political Activation refers to the capacity of sectors of the population living in modern areas to transform their political preferences into political demands. For political activation to exist, two conditions must be met. First, the sector must have a permanent organizational basis that is not entirely subordinated to the domination of other sectors. Second, the sector must be within a network of communications that enables it to be easily contacted by, and quickly responsive to, its leadership. Otherwise, the sector has not yet developed sufficient political capabilities to transform its preferences into demands.[51] Political

---

[51]Instead of the clumsy word "activation," a better term for

activation has both <u>scope</u> and <u>intensity</u>. <u>Scope</u> refers to the number and proportion of individuals that are politically acti- vated within an area, <u>intensity</u> to the frequency and degree of organizational support of political demands.[52]

<u>Political Actors</u> are social sectors (classes, groups, and organizations) whose political activation enables their leadership to participate on a continuing basis in the national political process. When a significant proportion of the individuals in a sector participate directly in the formulation of demands (say, by striking, demonstrating, or plotting a military coup), they constitute a "(politically) activated sector."

<u>Technocratic Roles</u> are positions in a social structure which require application of modern technology as an important part of their daily routine.[53] To perform these roles, each

---

this concept would have been (political) "mobilization"; but I was afraid that the latter would be confused with "mobilization" as used in the influential writings of Karl Deutsch and Gino Germani. (See Deutsch, "Social Mobilization and Political Devel- opment," <u>The American Political Science Review</u>, 55 [1961], and Germani, <u>Política y sociedad en una epoca de transición</u> [Paidos, 1962].) In my usage, the concept does not entail any assumptions of transitions from the breakdown of "traditional" society (and insofar as this latter situation may exist, it seems unlikely that it would involve sectors of the population that would be "politically activated" in the sense intended here). The relation of my concept to Samuel Huntington's "political mobilization" (see <u>Political Order in Changing Societies</u> [New Haven: Yale University Press, 1968]) is closer, but I place greater emphasis on the organization and communication variables as requisites for the continued, nationally oriented, attention-getting political activity that transforms poorly or sporadically articulated pref- erences into "political demands." Sectors lacking those requisites might be able occasionally to have their preferences expressed at the national political level, but they will be unable to keep them before the attention of national policy-makers.

[52]The interconnections of this concept with others used in this analysis will be spelled out below when the focus is on dynamic processes. As will be seen in Chapter II, political activation is conceived to be dependent on the productive-industrial structure and on the degree of social differentiation of each modern area, as well as on the political expression of the latter--political pluralization.

[53]It is important to note that this category is constituted by individuals <u>applying</u> modern technology, and not by those concerned mainly with the expansion of scientific-technological knowledge.

incumbent must have prolonged schooling geared to provide the
necessary technical expertise. In addition, he must keep abreast
of developments (during and after schooling) in the more industrialized societies, where most of these roles originated and
where the qualifying expertise is being expanded. The scope of
technocratic roles refers to how many social sectors and activities
they have penetrated in each area; their density refers to the
degree they have penetrated each social sector or activity. Technocratic roles are an elite phenomenon. The incumbents are a
subset of the "politically activated population" and of "political
elites."[54]

Some examples will further clarify these concepts. Within
the modern area an important proportion of "wage earners" (e.g.,
industrial workers) and "salary earners" (e.g., primary school
teachers) is likely to be politically activated. Their leaders,
in that case, will be part of the political elite of the country:
the activation of their constituency enables them to make political
demands (i.e., to express political preferences on a more than
sporadic basis and by means that capture the attention of national
policy-makers). But most of these leaders will not belong to the
elite subset formed by the incumbents of technocratic roles: their
activities do not usually require extensive education and routine
application of modern technology. Technocratic roles tend to
develop around the managing of such activities as non-artisan
industry, planning, government, the military, and communications
and control. The degree of penetration of these roles into such
areas of activity is of fundamental importance. The broader the
"scope" of their penetration, the more social activities in which
this subset has expertise; and the greater the "density" of penetration, the more incumbents of these roles are to be found. At
some point, the scope and density of penetration profoundly change
the supporting institutions. "Modern" or "professional" military
officers are able to dominate military institutions, to redefine
their goals and strategies, and to reshape the curricula of military academies. Old patrones are replaced by individuals with
formal training in administration. Business creates organizations
and promotes public relations activities geared to increase contacts among managers schooled in "modern administration" and with
other incumbents of technocratic roles. Ministers of Economy are
no longer lawyers, but are professionally trained economists, and

_____

[54]The term "elite" is used here in the very general sense of
referring to those individuals that have a reasonable chance of
capturing the attention of national policy-makers whenever they
feel that an issue at hand deserves it. Thus individuals may be
part of the political "elite" even though their demands are sys-
tematically rejected or repressed.

their staffs are correspondingly changed. New publications, as well as new consumption and prestige "markets," appear.[55]

As will be seen below, the degree of political activation and of penetration of technocratic roles (as well as of "social differentiation" and "political pluralization"--to be analyzed in the next chapter) are closely related to the productive structure of each South American modern area, in particular to the type of industrialization in those regions. All vary together: the more industrialization, the more social differentiation, the more polit- ical pluralization and activation, and the more penetration of technocratic roles. This concept will underlie statements of the form "Country X is more modernized than Country Y." Such state- ments are elliptical expressions of the notion that these several dimensions are jointly higher in Country X than in Country Y.

In terms of the available data, the distinction between "modern" and "peripheral" areas serves for a first approximation to determining the political actors in each country. Given the severe limitations stemming from the lack of sub-national South American data, the problem is to find indicators clearly related to political activation. For example, data on hospital beds or radio receivers are of little value because there is not enough evidence that they are closely related to organizational support and continued demand-formulation. Another difficulty stems from the fact that national data are frequently not disaggregated. It must be well-established that the indicators refer to variables that are overwhelmingly concentrated in the modern areas--say, industry (output, employment, use of complex technology), advanced educational facilities, innovative activities, skilled labor and professional management, modern types of communication and trans- port, labor unionization. Insofar as the condition of overwhelming concentration in the modern areas applies, it is possible to work with total, non-averaged, national data as a first approximation to the dimensions of interest within each national modern area. Examination of country studies suggests that, for these variables, 20 percent could be safely "discounted" from national totals to approximate the values for each modern area.[56] However, in the tables that follow, to avoid giving a misleading impression of accuracy, total national figures are reported. Furthermore, since

---

[55] In the next chapter, I will deal with these phenomena in more detail, and will explore their political consequences.

[56] In Figure 2 it can be seen that, depending on the degree of heterogeneity of each country, the "space" covered by each modern area varies. But given the properties of the indicators chosen, all are overwhelmingly concentrated in all South American modern areas, irrespective of the "space" that these areas occupy within the whole national territory.

Figure 2

FIGURATIVE REPRESENTATION OF DIFFERENT DEGREES OF
INTRA-NATIONAL HETEROGENEITY

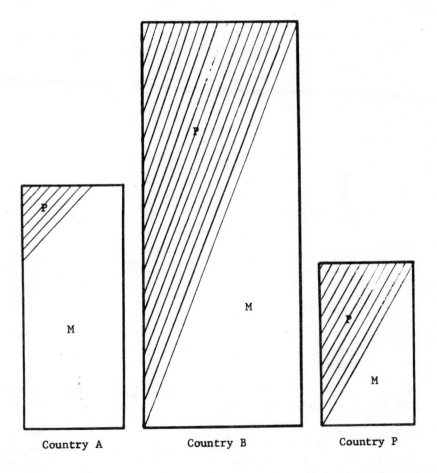

Country A   Country B   Country P

 Peripheral areas

Modern areas

the interpretation of these data may be based upon different orders of magnitude in different countries, exact statistical comparisons have not been attempted. However, these differences in national data are consistent and large enough to support conclusions about very different levels of modernization in contemporary South American countries. This will be the starting point for the exploration of political correlates to be undertaken in Chapter II.

Approximations to Actual Values

Size

The size of each South American domestic market is shown in Table 4. Although cases like Sweden and Israel demonstrate that it is not a universal proposition, it is unquestionably true that among South American countries the larger their domestic market the further they have advanced in industrialization.[57]

Table 4

GROSS NATIONAL PRODUCT AT MARKET PRICES: 1966
(U$S millions)

Argentina	18,733
Brazil	27,711
Chile	5,150
Colombia	6,209
Perú	3,256
Uruguay	1,686
Venezuela	7,938
Bolivia	668
Ecuador	1,169
Paraguay	460

Source: University of California, Los Angeles, Statistical Abstract of Latin America-1969.

---

[57]On the ambiguous intra-national relationships between market size and economic development, see E.A. Robinson, ed., The Economic Consequences of the Size of Nations (London: St. Martin's Press, 1960). However, the relationship for the Latin American area between market size and degree of industrialization is very strong. The coefficient of determination (R^2) between log size and log industrial output for Latin America is .906 (UN-ECLA, The Process of Industrial Development..., Statistical Annex [mimeo]).

A UN-ECLA study observes:

> The countries with the largest domestic markets are gen-
> erally those that have gone further with import substitu-
> tion and where industrialization has reached the most
> advanced stage . . . . The countries where the external
> sector is still relatively important, and where there
> would seem to be a broad field open for [import] substi-
> tuting activities, are in fact those in which the size
> of the domestic market imposes the most severe restric-
> tions, even at the earliest stages of [industrial]
> development through which they are now passing.[58]

This study classifies Latin American countries in terms of their
industrial development, as follows: the most advanced--Argentina,
Brazil, and México; intermediate--Colombia, Chile, Perú, Uruguay,
and Venezuela; the least advanced--Bolivia, Ecuador, and Paraguay,
as well as all the Middle American countries (with the exception
of Cuba, for which data were not available).[59]

Another aspect of size is population. If the strategy is
to "discount" the politically "inactive" population in the peripheral areas, a useful procedure would be to examine the data on
urban units. There is general agreement that in contemporary South
America the big cities are more and more the main arena of national
politics.[60] Here again a somewhat heretical concept will be

---

[58] Ibid., p. 54.

[59] It is significant that this is close to the way these countrie
have stratified themselves, in terms of relative economic development, in the Latin American Free Trade Association (LAFTA). This
perception of relative development by national policy-makers (whi
determines very important differences in the preferences to be
granted within LAFTA) is similar to the classification proposed
in this work, but is very different from the developmental rankings
generated by the nationally averaged data strategy I have criticized.

[60] Useful surveys on this question are F. Rabinovitz, "Data Resources," and "Urban Development and Political Development in Latin
America" in R. Daland, ed., Comparative Urban Research: The Administration and Politics of Cities (Beverly Hills: Sage Publications,
1969), and I. Horowitz, "Politics, Urbanization and Social Development in Latin America," Urban Affairs Quarterly, 2, March 1967.
However, the systematic study of the big South American centers,
to say nothing of their political correlates, has barely begun.
Important recent contributions in this direction can be found in
J. Hardoy and C. Tobar, eds., La urbanización en América Latina
(Editorial del Instituto, 1969), and F. Rabinovitz and F. Trueblood,
eds., Latin American Urban Research, I (Sage Publications, 1970).

advanced. Urbanists are far from agreement about "when a city is a city," but it has become standard practice for sociologists and political scientists to use some figure such as 2,000 or 20,000 inhabitants as an arbitrary cutoff point. This--it seems to me-- is all too often a way of avoiding difficult conceptual problems. In particular, if one wants to assess the effects of urban areas on national politics, it is by no means clear that the use of something like 2,000 or 20,000 as a cutoff is sensible. It entails giving equal political weight to any citizen living in a unit above the 2,000 (or 20,000) cutoff point, and lumps together small towns and large urban centers. This practice may be useful for many purposes, but for tracing urban influences on national politics it seems necessary to use different definitional criteria. The classification "urban" should be applied where the internal com- plexity, non-artisan industry, inward and outward communications, and existence of national government institutions and services create a locus of political activation significantly impinging upon the national political arena.[61] On wholly impressionistic grounds I believe that the lower limit for "urban" in contemporary South America should be placed around 300,000 inhabitants. Table 5 provides the resultant data.

These data raise some important questions. In particular, are there related patterns in terms of industrialization, roles, political activation, communications, innovation? In the following pages we will attempt to provide answers to some of these and other closely related queries.

---

[61]Reflecting on this definition problem, Gino Germani says: "The problem of their [the indicators of urbanization] validity remains open, however--that is to say of their relevance or repre- sentativeness for the phenomena studied. It is a theoretical problem, since the task is one of defining the concept of urbani- zation and, then, of examining to what extent, among the many possible indicators of that concept, some of them--for example, density and size--will be more useful for its study. A sociologi- cal definition of the concept ought to be based on those traits specifically associated with the particular social structure that characterizes urban society" (Sociología de la modernización [Paidos, 1969], p. 147; translated from Spanish by this author). For a good discussion of this problem by a demographer, see Eduardo Arriaga, "A New Approach to the Measurements of Urbanization," Economic Development and Cultural Change, XVIII, No. 2 (1970). Arriaga criticizes current definitions and measurements of urban- ization on grounds similar to those advanced here and, with more sophisticated handling of more detailed data, arrives at measures of concentration of urban population in urban units that parallel the pattern indicated in Table 5.

Table 5

"URBAN" AREAS IN SOUTH AMERICAN COUNTRIES: C. 1960

Country	Number of Cities of More than 300,000 Inhabitants	Population of Major City (000's)
Argentina	9	6,000 (Buenos Aires)
Brazil	10	3,250 (Sao Paulo) 3,000 (Rio de Janeiro)
Chile	1	1,900 (Santiago)
Colombia	4	1,100 (Bogotá)
Perú	1	1,900 (Lima)
Uruguay	1	1,150 (Montevideo)
Venezuela	2	1,250 (Caracas)
Bolivia	1	450 (La Paz)
Ecuador	2	450 (Guayaquil)
Paraguay	1	300 (Asunción)

Source: UN-ECLA, Statistical Bulletin for Latin America, IV, No. 2 (1964).

Industrialization

Z. Slawinski distinguishes five "stages" of industrial development, of which the fifth, not yet reached by any Latin American country, is represented by the more advanced economies. The fourth stage, which--according to Slawinski--Argentina, Brazil, and México have "started," involves

more complex forms of processing, and the production of complex equipment. Some notable features are: the production of special steels, the creation of petrochemical industries; the production of synthetic chemicals; high precision electrometalical industry on the one hand, and heavy equipment industry on the other; and, in general, the production of high caliber machines and equipment of complex design manufactured or assembled by complex processes. The high technological level required by this stage entails the extensive use of skilled manpower.[62]

The third stage is characterized by

basic industries producing simple equipment . . . the emergence and development of the steel industry, supplemented by the processing of simple metallic products; by the large-scale development of the cement industry; by petroleum refining and the development of basic chemical industry; and by the production of simple chemical products.[63]

The first and second stages, where at some point Bolivia, Ecuador, and Paraguay are located, are indicated by the prevalence of cottage and artisan industry and traditional consumer industries, respectively.

This ordering is well supported by the available data. For example, an UN-ECLA study divides the South American countries into three groups and each national industrial sector into "dynamic" and "slow-growth" industries, with the results indicated in Table 6.

Two points are in order here. First, the dichotomization between "dynamic" and "slow-growth" industries understates the between-group differences; if the data were disaggregated to the level of more technologically complex and more capital-intensive industries, these differences would be even more pronounced. Second, if a distinction between "artisan industries" (those employing less than five workers) and "factory industries" is utilized, artisan employment as a proportion of total industrial employment is 40.7 percent in Group I, 48.6 percent in Group II, and 82 percent in Group III.[64]

Another important indicator of the different types of industrialization--the import coefficient--is much lower in countries of Group I than in the remaining countries (see Table 7).[65]

_____

[62]"Structural Changes in Employment in the Context of Latin America's Development," _Economic Bulletin for Latin America_, X, No. 2 (1965), p. 166.

[63]Ibid., p. 167.

[64]Computed from UN-ECLA, _The Process of Industrial Development..._, p. 75.

[65]Ibid.

ASSUMPTIONS AND CLASSIFICATIONS

Table 6

GROSS VALUE OF OUTPUT IN U$S (x 1,000) AND PERCENTAGES OF
TOTAL VALUE BY "DYNAMIC" AND "SLOW-GROWTH" INDUSTRIES
IN SOUTH AMERICAN COUNTRIES: 1960[a]

	Gross Value of Output		
	Dynamic	Slow-Growth	Grand Total
Group I[b]	17,750	18,284	36,034
Group II	3,862	6,260	10,122
Group III	289	1,386	1,675

	Percentage Composition		
	Dynamic	Slow-Growth	Grand Total
Group I	49.3	50.7	100.0
Group II	38.2	61.8	100.0
Group III	17.3	82.7	100.0

[a]"Dynamic" industries are paper and paper products, rubber products, chemicals, petroleum, non-metallic minerals, metallurgy and
metal transformation; "slow-growth" industries are foods, bever-
ages, tobacco, textiles, footwear, clothing, wood products, furni-
ture, and printing and allied industries.

[b]Group I: Argentina, Brazil, and México; Group II: Chile,
Colombia, Perú, Uruguay, and Venezuela; Group III: Ecuador and
Middle American countries. Cuba, Bolivia, and Paraguay are
excluded by lack of comparable data. (The two latter could be
classified in Group III, but their inclusion would only minimally
change the figures above.)

Source: UN-ECLA, The Process of Industrial Development..., p. 87.

Table 7

IMPORT COEFFICIENTS OF SOUTH AMERICAN COUNTRIES: 1963

Country	Import Coefficient
Argentina	5.5%
Brazil	4.4%
México	7.0%
Chile	12.8%
Colombia	8.2%
Perú	13.8%
Uruguay	10.0% (1961)
Venezuela	19.4%
Bolivia	16.9%
Ecuador	11.6%
Paraguay	7.7%

Source: UN-ECLA, The Process of Industrial Development...,
Statistical Annex [mimeo].

Another way to look at the same phenomena is to consider data on vertical industrial integration. Table 8 shows that in the industrially more advanced South American countries the share of consumption goods declines and the share of intermediate and capital goods production correspondingly increases. This pattern suggests that, as a movement is made toward more advanced industrialization, important consequences may follow in terms of the increasing adoption of more and more complex technologies, as well as of a larger role for skilled labor and management. (This point will be explored below.)

Table 8

ESTIMATES OF THE COMPOSITION OF INDUSTRIAL OUTPUT OF
SOUTH AMERICAN COUNTRIES ACCORDING TO DESTINATION, 1960:
ABSOLUTE AND PERCENTAGE DATA

	Intermediate Goods	Consumption Goods	Capital Formation	Other
Absolute Figures (U$S 000's)				
Group I[a]	12,903	18,272	2,868	
Group II	2,696	6,004	239	
Group III	375	1,106	20	
Percentages				
Group I	35.8	50.7	8.0	5.5
Group II	26.6	59.3	2.4	11.7
Group III	22.4	66.0	1.2	10.4

[a]For breakdown of groups, see Table 6.

Source: UN-ECLA, The Process of Industrial Development..., p. 88.

For the moment, the data already considered enable us to formulate the following proposition:

Proposition 3: In contemporary South American countries, the larger the size of the domestic market and the greater the concentration of population in urban units, the more advanced their industrial establishments.

Roles and Stratification

Pursuing the strategy of asking "How many?" instead of "What average?" it can be shown that the differences summarized in Proposition 3 are related to differences in role and stratification patterns. Countries of Group I have a significantly larger number of both unionized and industrial workers, heavily concentrated in the big urban areas, as shown in Table 9.

Table 9

NUMBER OF INDUSTRIAL WORKERS AND UNION MEMBERS
IN SOUTH AMERICAN COUNTRIES: C. 1960

Country	Union Members (000's)	Industrial Workers (000's)
Argentina	2,576	1,855
Brazil	2,500	2,055
Chile	493	428
Colombia	330	655 (1964)
Perú	550	410 (1961)
Uruguay	197	211 (1963)
Venezuela	1,500	287 (1961)
Bolivia	200	109 (1950)
Ecuador	85	210 (1962)
Paraguay	20	34

Sources: Union members: Needler, Political..., p. 96; industrial
workers: International Labour Organization, International Labour
Statistics (Geneva 1967), with the exception of Paraguay, obtained
from Pan-American Union, América en cifras (Washington D.C., 1967).

In political terms, sheer numbers are important here.
More unionized workers located at the centers of national politics
greatly increase the likelihood of their gaining the degree of
organizational strength, and being placed within a network of
modern communications, that make possible effective demand formulation. This does not necessarily mean more revolutionary mili-
tancy,[66] nor a balanced power position vis-à-vis more established

---

[66] See Stepan, "Political Development ...," and W. Cornelius, "The
Political Sociology of Cityward Migration in Latin America" in
Rabinovitz and Trueblood. It is important to note, however, that

sectors, but it does mean that an important proportion of the population located in the modern areas, until then politically "inert" and lacking in organizational resources, can become politically activated.[67]

South American countries are no exception to the general rule that capital- (and technology-) intensive industries are well above the national industrial averages in the proportion of highly trained managers, technicians, and engineers, as well as skilled workers, that they employ.[68] This is also true for "big" industries in general. These categories of industry--capital-intensive and "big"--partially overlap, and the countries of Group I have more of both types than do the other two groups of countries (and Group II has more than Group III). Structural differences in industrial establishments are related to other important differences--i.e., at various occupational levels, roles requiring more specialized skills emerge in higher numbers and in higher proportion within each modern area.

Educational institutions are the main suppliers of the skill inputs required at different levels of industrialization. Hence, it can be assumed that educational data will reflect such differences, as is illustrated by Table 10.

Probing further, we can determine approximately how many books are being read in each country and, particularly, how many translations are being read (an indication of the outwardly directed attention that is a hypothetical consequence of moderni-zation as the concept is defined here). In addition, on the assumption that technical books bear a more direct relationship to non-primitive productive processes and their associated roles

---

the evidence discussed by these authors refers to slum-dwellers, a category with limited overlap with industrial and/or unionized workers. In Chapter II, I will analyze the impact on the more established Argentine and Brazilian sectors, especially in the period that preceded their 1966 and 1964 coups, of this massive presence in the big urban centers.

[67]This point will be discussed from a broader and more dynamic perspective in Chapter II.

[68]See Slawinski; Consejo Nacional de Desarrollo (Argentina), Educación y desarrollo económico en la Argentina (2 vols.; 1969); Instituto Torcuato di Tella, Los recursos humanos de nivel técnico y universitario en la Argentina (1964); OECD, Education, Human Resources and Development in Argentina (1967); A. Petreli Gastaldi, A economia brasileira e os problemas do desenvolvimento (Edicao Saraiva, 1968).

Table 10

EDUCATION ENROLLMENT (000's) IN SOUTH AMERICAN COUNTRIES: C. 1968

Country	Technical Schools (Secondary Level)	Total University Enrollment	Total Engineering	Total Natural Sciences	Total University Degrees Granted
Argentina (1965)	425	243	16.6	31.2	15.9
Brazil (1964)	380	155	6.9	22.1	20.1
Chile (1964)	125	43	N.A.	2.0	3.4
Colombia (1965)	96	37	3.1	7.7	3.2
Perú (1962)	64	46	4.1	4.1	4.0
Uruguay (1965)	26	16	N.A.	0.5	0.7
Venezuela (1963)	93	46	1.6	5.7	2.9
Bolivia (1965)	8	13	1.2	1.5	N.A.
Ecuador (1965)	40	15	1.7	2.3	0.6
Paraguay (1959)	3	3.7	0.5	N.A.	0.2

Source: Compiled from UNESCO, Yearbook of Educational Statistics, 1968 (Paris, 1969).

than to primitive processes and roles, it is interesting to know approximately how many of these books are being read in each South American country. The data in Table 11 show a pattern that is clearly consistent with the already observed cross-modern area differences.

Proposition 4: In contemporary South America, the more advanced the industrial establishments, the more industrial and unionized workers there are.

Hypothesis 1: The more unionized and industrial workers there are, given their concentration in big urban centers, the greater the likelihood of their political activation.

Proposition 5: The more advanced the industrial establishments, the more roles with specialized skills directly related to productive processes are required, and the more secondary socialization patterns are geared to provide them.

Table 11

NUMBER OF BOOKS AND TRANSLATIONS PUBLISHED ANNUALLY
IN SOUTH AMERICAN COUNTRIES: C. 1965

Country	Books Published	Translations Published	Translations of Technical Books
Argentina	3,620 (1966)	488	212
Brazil	4,975 (1964)	629	226
Chile	1,478 (1966)	170	52
Colombia	709 (1965)	N.A.	N.A.
Perú	985 (1966)	21	12
Uruguay	266 (1966)	26	16
Venezuela	N.A.	16	8
Bolivia	N.A.	N.A.	N.A.
Ecuador	N.A.	N.A.	N.A.
Paraguay	N.A.	N.A.	N.A.

Source: UNESCO (see Table 10 above), Table 9.

Innovation

Educational data have been interpreted here as indicative of structural differences across modern areas. It might be argued that some interpretations of Latin American culture suggest that education is remote from and bears little relationship to structural differences in industrial productive processes. Such an argument would be difficult to sustain in face of the data in the preceding tables in this text, but it merits further examination. If there is one point of general agreement in the literature on the different aspects of "development," it is that more complex societies tend to have higher rates of innovation.[69] Hence, a critical test of the appropriateness of the different rankings of South American countries would be to look at data about the innovations generated in each of them. If the differences among these countries are better accounted for by the studies I have criticized at the beginning of this chapter, this ought to be reflected in the pattern of data on innovation. If, on the contrary, they are better accounted for by the classification I am proposing, the pattern of data on innovation should correspond to the latter. If neither type of classification is appropriate, these data could suggest a different alternative or show a pattern of innovations in each country not significantly different from what sheer chance would have produced.

For this to be a truly critical test, there had to be a high degree of assurance that the indicated innovations were "authentic" on a universal basis. Therefore, I used the register of inventions--by South American country--in the U.S. Patent Office rather than the inventions register in each individual country. The pattern of the data obtained, shown in Table 12, is strikingly similar to the ordering of South American countries proposed here.

Communications

Continuing with the "How many?" strategy, it is useful to examine data on those communications media that require from the user something more than passive exposure--e.g., telephones and newspapers (see Table 13). These data provide a preliminary answer to the question of how many people are more than passively involved in a network of modern communications. (Data on television sets and radio receivers are excluded from Table 13, although their pattern coincides with the other media patterns.)

---

[69] For statements on this topic see Apter, Politics of Modernization, and Lasswell, "The Policy Sciences of Development," World Politics, XVII, No. 2 (1965).

Table 12

TOTAL NUMBERS OF INVENTIONS REGISTERED IN THE U.S. PATENT OFFICE
BY COUNTRY OF REGISTRANT, SOUTH AMERICAN COUNTRIES:
1951-1961

Argentina	425
Brazil	123
Chile	37
Colombia	35
Perú	28
Uruguay	46
Venezuela	89
Bolivia	N.A.[a]
Ecuador	N.A.
Paraguay	N.A.

[a]Source fails to indicate if countries for which data are not reported is due to lack of registrations, or because numbers were considered too small to be worth reporting.

Source: Journal of the Patent Office Society, XLVI, No. 2
(February 1964), pp. 168-169.

Transportation is a requisite of the social, psychological, and geographical mobility broadly associated with modernity. The importance of transportation stems not only from the number of users, but perhaps even more from (1) the numbers of workers engaged in vehicle-fabrication--a technologically complex, production-line, "worker-unionizing" activity; (2) the wide network of auxiliary industries--repair shops and gas stations, as well as the advertising that the automobile industry generates, exposing a wide range of people to one of the more "glamorous" aspects of modernization. Table 14 includes only data relating to automobiles. Railway data have been excluded because it seems questionable whether they relate very directly to modernization.

On the basis of the data in Tables 12-14, the following propositions can be derived:

Table 13

NUMBER OF INSTALLED TELEPHONES (1967)
AND DAILY NEWSPAPER CIRCULATION (1960)
IN SOUTH AMERICAN COUNTRIES

Country	Telephones Installed: 1967 (000's)	Total Daily Newspaper Circulation: 1960 (000's)
Argentina	1,553	3,186
Brazil	1,472	3,837
Chile	289	998
Colombia	734	787
Perú	152	350 (1952)
Uruguay	195	540 (1962)
Venezuela	327	646
Bolivia	29	92
Ecuador	45	226
Paraguay	16	N.A.

Source: UNESCO (see Table 10 above), Table 9.

Proposition 6: In contemporary South America, the more advanced the industrial establishments, the higher the rate of scientific-technological innovation generated.

Proposition 7: Data on innovation can be used as an independent and critical test of the adequacy of orderings reflecting structural (socio-economic) differences.

Proposition 8: The more advanced the industrial establishment, the larger the number of individuals directly connected by modern communications and transportation networks.

Table 14

TRANSPORTATION DATA (AUTOMOBILES) FOR SOUTH AMERICAN COUNTRIES:
C. 1965

Country	Yearly Gas Consumption (millions of liters)	Total Automobiles Registered (000's)	Yearly Automobile Production (000's)	Yearly Tire Production (000's)
Argentina	4,455	1,653 (621)[a]	137 (42)	2,936
Brazil	6,839	2,396 (1,050)	135 (89)	5,241
Chile	1,233	215 (107)	N.A.	555
Colombia	2,219	251 (115)	1.8 (0.9)	N.A.
Perú	1,492	285 (107)	None	N.A.
Uruguay	390	198 (80)	None	None
Venezuela	3,182	550 (165)	44 (12)	N.A.
Bolivia	191	23 (N.A.)	None	None
Ecuador	358	41 (N.A.)	None	None
Paraguay	62	11 (N.A.)	None	None

[a]Figures in parentheses refer to commercial vehicles.

Source: Pan American Union, América en cifras, 1967.

Preliminary Recapitulation

We have shown that differences in size (of the domestic market and of urban units) are closely related to important differences in the productive structure of modern areas and, more specifically, in the type of industrialization of contemporary South American countries.[70] These, in turn, involve important

[70]At this stage of the discussion it may be easier to understand

differences in social structure--including, among other phenomena mentioned above, a larger organizational base for more urban workers and more roles that require specific technical skills. Along all the dimensions summarized in the preceding tables, the differences among the three groups into which I have classified the South American countries are large and consistent enough to support the assertion that there are significant differences in the degree of modernization of their national "centers."[71] The "political side" of this assertion will be elaborated in the next chapter, but for the moment it suffices to observe that a pattern has emerged that is strikingly different from the one generated by the preponderance of recent studies. The "new" breakdown is as follows:

---

why using national averages, among the other consequences analyzed, misleads by concealing the effects of the size variable on the data. The effects of size on the structural characteristics of social units have frequently been shown to be of major importance, but the study of this factor is scattered across disciplinary boundaries and still awaits systematic investigation. See esp. H. Simon, "The Architecture of Complexity," General Systems Yearbook, 10 (1965); M. Haire, "Biological Models and Empirical Histories of the Growth of Organizations" in M. Haire, ed., Modern Organization Theory (New York: Wiley, 1959); Kenneth Boulding, "Toward a General Theory of Growth," Canadian Journal of Economic and Political Science, 19 (1953); D'Arcy Thompson, On Growth and Form (Cambridge: University Press, 1966); K. Deutsch and M. Kochen, "Toward a Rational Theory of Decentralization," American Political Science Review, 63 (1969); S.R. Klatzky, "Relationship of Organizational Size to Complexity and Coordination," Administrative Science Quarterly, XV, No. 4; R. Dahl, After the Revolution (New Haven: Yale University Press, 1970), as well as research in progress by R. Dahl and R. Tufte on size and democracy. I am grateful to R. Brunner for introducing me to this fascinating literature.

[71] The general strategy followed here coincides with the multiple-dimension, multiple-indicator approach pioneered by K. Deutsch in "Toward an Inventory of Basic Trends and Patterns in Comparative and International Politics," The American Political Science Review, 54 (1960). Insofar as various indicators which have a plausible relationship to the concepts guiding the inquiry show distinctly consistent patterns, one can feel confident that the general theory that summarizes the findings corresponds to the empirical reality to which it refers.

Group	Country	Degree of Modernization in "Centers"	Type of Political System
I	Argentina Brazil	High	Non-democratic
II	Chile Colombia Perú Uruguay Venezuela	Intermediate	Democratic (except Perú)
III	Bolivia Ecuador Paraguay	Low	Non-democratic

Better data would allow the introduction of more refined distinctions on the "socio-economic side," but close examination of the highly aggregated data used here and of country-specific information suggests that Perú and Ecuador might be better seen as boundary cases, the former at the lower bound of Group II and the latter at the higher bound of Group III.

This preliminary classification leads to the following proposition:

Proposition 9: In contemporary South America, the higher and lower levels of modernization are associated with non-democratic political systems, while political democracies are found at the intermediate levels of modernization.

The end-result of this chapter is another "snapshot"--a static pairing of analytical categories along a socio-economic dimension, and a preliminary step towards a typology of the political dimension.[72] In the next chapter the approach shifts to a

---

[72]In addition to the other difficulties already discussed in this chapter, the use of analyses based on conclusions drawn from data at only one point in time produces unreliable results. Studies that use data from the periods in which Argentina had elections and political parties (i.e., was a "democracy" according

dynamic perspective that will enable us to explore some of the
processes that have led to the observed political outcomes. The
change of focus will also make possible a much more refined categorization of the political dimension that will supersede the
very rough one included here.

---

to the highly formalistic criteria used in most of these studies)
do not find the country a "deviant case." But during the same
periods, Brazil and Perú also had elections and parties (i.e.,
they also were "democracies"), and they tended to become "deviant":
more "democratic" than would have been predicted by their level
of "socio-economic development." Such movements toward and away
from the (tacit or explicit) regression line may not greatly
affect the overall measures of association obtained in a sample
of Latin American countries, but it is difficult to see how this
erratic composition of "normal" and "deviant" cases is consistent
with the basic paradigm of those studies. See e.g., J. Coleman,
"Conclusion: The Political Systems of Developing Areas" in G.
Almond and J. Coleman, eds., The Politics of Developing Areas
(Princeton: Princeton University Press, 1960), and C. Wolf, "The
Political Effects of Economic Programs: Some Indications from
Latin America," Economic Development and Cultural Change, XIV,
No. 1 (1965).

Chapter II

TOWARD AN ALTERNATIVE CONCEPTUALIZATION
OF SOUTH AMERICAN POLITICS

The relationships between the political and socio-economic
dimensions are a time-bound interplay, and only a longitudinal
perspective can reveal their interactions. The static, "horizontal" approach used in the first chapter must be abandoned, and a
shift made toward providing a genetic explanation of certain fundamental characteristics of contemporary South American political
systems. For this purpose, the accumulation of work in the field
(particularly country-studies) provides a rich background of information, but unfortunately there are many problems involved in
the utilization of these data for comparative purposes. Thus,
being careful about the status of the conclusions to be drawn, I
will use the term "proposition" for those statements that are
reasonably well-supported by available data, while reserving the
term "hypothesis" for those that, even though they appear plausible
in the light of the information at hand, must await more stringent
testing.

In this chapter I will make use of a distinction that will
later serve to improve the preliminary political classifications
proposed in Chapter I. This distinction, relating to contemporar
South American political systems, is whether or not governmental
action is geared to exclude the already activated urban popular
sector (working class and segments of the lower middle class) fro
the national political arena. Such exclusion means consistent
governmental refusal to meet the political demands made by the
leaders of this sector. It also means denying to this sector and
its leaders access to positions of political power from where they
can have direct influence on national policy decisions. This
political exclusion can be achieved by direct coercion and/or by
closing the electoral channels of political access. (It is important to note that the concept of "exclusion," as I am proposing
to use it, assumes previous "presence" in the national political
arena: an excluded sector is a politically activated sector.
Politically "inert" sectors are not part of the set of political
actors [see the definitions in the preceding chapter]; they remain outside the national political arena.) The exclusion of
political actors involves an intentional decision to reduce the
number of persons who have a significant voice in determining what
goes on at the national political level. Of course, attempts at
exclusion have varying degrees of success. At one extreme, the
political deactivation of an excluded sector may be achieved: it

becomes politically inert through destruction of its resources (especially its organizational bases) and can no longer make genuine political demands. At the other extreme, the attempted exclusion of a sector may not achieve its political deactivation, in which case it will retain the capacity to continue pressing its political demands, and the set of political actors will tend to reconstitute into the number that existed before the exclusion was attempted. A system that attempts the exclusion of the already activated urban popular sector will be called an "excluding political system."[1]

---

[1]Definitions of this type are intended as analytical tools for cutting through complex empirical phenomena. As so frequently happens, the use of the concept raises problems that cannot be solved without introducing distinctions. In particular, I have chosen to include within the category of "excluding political systems" those cases where, besides the other conditions specified in the text, the electoral arena no longer exists, whether by outright suppression or because only government-sponsored parties can participate in it. A situation which is not included within the "excluding" category is when, as will be seen in Chapter IV, the electoral arena remains, but under the constraint that it cannot serve as a means for gaining important governmental positions for leaders and political parties representing the popular sector. In this case, even though the possibilities for political influence of the popular sector are severely limited, as long as it is politically activated and represents an important proportion of the total vote, there is a high probability that political candidates from other sectors will attempt to gain its votes through campaign promises. Even though these promises are rarely kept, they are a means by which some indirect--and not insignificant--political influence can be exerted by the popular sector through the electoral process. (In Chapter IV I argue that this is why the closing of the electoral arena is often a fundamental goal of most of the other sectors in situations of highly modernized South American systems.) Other authors have made similar observations on this point: see, e.g., Furtado, Subdesarrollo..., pp. 110-117. In the case of the suppression of the electoral arena, the popular sector's voting strength obviously does not count any more. Suppression does not affect other sectors of less voting strength but better informal channels of political access; rather, it enhances their relative effectiveness. It dispossesses the popular sector of a major political asset, but this sector is left--as long as governmental coercion is not too severe--with other means of demand formulation outside the electoral arena: direct action, strikes, demonstrations.

The analytical connection between the requirement of previous political activation of the popular sector and the suppression of the electoral arena for producing an "excluding political

The **opposite**--an "incorporating political system"--is defined as a political system that purposely seeks to activate the popular sector and to allow it some voice in national politics--or that, without deliberate efforts at either exclusion or incorporation, adapts itself to the existing levels of political activation and the given set of political actors. The "incorporating" categorization allows for a good deal of variation, but it is sufficient for the purposes of our analysis, which will focus on the exclusion systems and the processes that have led to them.

In the sense defined, the only two contemporary South American systems that are "excluding" are Argentina and Brazil. These are the countries that, as Chapter I has shown, have advanced furthest in modernization. Here we shall study the processes that in both countries led, first, to incorporation and, later, to exclusion. We shall then briefly examine other contemporary South American political systems. Finally, a sketch of the "political game" in highly modernized contemporary South American political systems will be proposed, and a new classification of political systems with respect to modernization to supersede the preliminary one proposed in Chapter I.

Argentina and Brazil: From Incorporation to Exclusion[2]

The Period of Populism and Horizontal Industrialization. Until the 1930's, in both Argentina and Brazil, the economically

---

system" is underscored by the contemporary Peruvian case. Given the low level of the popular sector's political activation in Perú, the suppression of the electoral arena is not aimed at the exclusion of the largely inert popular sector. In the categories I am proposing, the Peruvian case is an "incorporating political system," in that it does not intend to deny the popular sector's preferences and is even attempting its political activation. Of course, the suppression of elections makes a difference within this category also, as is illustrated by the tight vertical controls within which political activation is being fostered by the Peruvian system.

[2]This and the following section are brief summaries only. In many respects my analysis is similar to that in Cardoso and Faleto, but certainly is no substitute for this excellent study. My main general sources have been: O. Ianni, O colapso do populismo no Brasil (Editorial Civilizacao Brasileira, 1968); L. Martins, Industrializacao, burguesia nacional e desenvolvimento (Editora Saga, 1968); Philippe C. Schmitter, Interest Conflict and Political Change in Brazil (Stanford: Stanford University

more dynamic and politically more powerful sectors were in the nationally owned agrarian areas producing exportable goods, and in the largely foreign-owned network of financial and export intermediaries. In both countries the world crisis of the 1930's greatly accelerated the emergence of domestic industry and an urban working class. The increased urbanization and industrial-ization changed the distribution of political power and provided the basis for a broad "populist" coalition.[3] It was formed by relatively new sectors.[4] What the coalition was against was quite obvious: the old oligarchies, the highly visible foreign-owned firms mediating between the international and the domestic market, and the policies of free trade with which the old rulers

---

Press, 1971); Alfred Stepan, The Military in Politics: Changing Patterns in Brazil (Princeton: Princeton University Press, 1971); Thomas Skidmore, Politics in Brazil, 1930-1964 (New York: Oxford University Press, 1967); H. Jaguaribe, Desarrollo político y desarrollo económico (Eudeba, 1964); J.B. Lopes, Sociedade in-dustrial no Brasil (Difusao Européia do Livro, 1964); Germani, Sociología . . .; J.L. de Imaz, Los que mandan (Eudeba, 1964); M. Kaplan, La formación del estado nacional en América Latina (Editorial Universitaria, 1969); UN-ECLA, El cambio . . .; UN-ECLA, El desarrollo social de América Latina en la post-guerra (Solar-Hachette, 1963); J.F. Marsal, Cambio social en América Latina (Solar-Hachette, 1967); Graciarena, "Estructura . . ."; Furtado, Subdesarrollo . . ., Dialéctica . . ., and Teoría . . .; C. Mendes, Nacionalismo e desenvolvimento (Instituto Brasileiro de Estudos Afro-Asiaticos, 1963); and Torcuato di Tella, Hacia una política latinoamericana (Arca, 1969).

Too late for utilization in this book, a new and important contribution by F.H. Cardoso came to my attention--Ideologías de la burguesía industrial en sociedades dependientes [Argentina y Brasil] (Siglo XXI, 1971). Cardoso's analysis further develops a line of reasoning used in Cardoso and Faleto, with which this chapter to a large extent agrees (see esp. Cardoso, pp. 94-130).

[3] The best study of this populism is Torcuato di Tella, "Populism and Reform in Latin America" in C. Véliz, ed., Obstacles to Change in Latin America (New York: Oxford University Press, 1965). See also F. Weffort, Estado y masas en el Brasil (ILPES, 1967), and "Le Populisme," Les Temps Modernes, 257 (October 1967); Ianni, O colapso . . ., and Martins, Industrializacao . . . .

[4] "Relatively" new because some members of the old oligarchy shifted part of their activities toward domestic market-oriented industrial production. In this sense they participated in, and benefitted from, the new economic policies, but a substantial proportion of them, including their associations, maintained their former activities and openly opposed the new policies.

had traditionally been associated. In terms of what it was <u>for</u>, the new coalition agreed on two basic points: (1) industrialization and (2) the expansion of the domestic market.[5] Though it originated in the drastic drop in export earnings due to the world crisis, the growth of industry soon took on a dynamic of its own. For its advocates, industrialization was the way to insulate the country from international crises, as well as the means for eliminating the economic and political dependence that was beginning to be widely resented. These hopes, added to the close ties between foreign-owned firms and the traditional rulers, made industrialization (combined with nationalism) the "ideological glue" of the new coalition.

Argentina and Brazil established import and exchange restrictions for the purpose of saving international currency; this left a wide range of unsatisfied consumer demand, which offered a ready-made market for the expansion of domestic industry. The populist leaders (Perón in Argentina and Vargas in Brazil) made the need to save international currency an argument for a policy of domestic expansion and nationalism, and the high tariff protection that they established preserved the national market for domestic producers after the more severe years of international trade had passed.

As noted, the populist coalition was built around this dynamic core of rapidly expanding domestic industry. The broadening of the functions of the state, entailed by the abandonment of free trade and laissez-faire policies, provided employment for many middle class <u>empleados</u> and <u>técnicos</u>; the nationalism <u>cum</u> industrialization argument had direct appeal for the military; the expansion of industry and government, together with the growth of the economy, benefitted urban workers, created more jobs, fostered migration to the urban-industrial centers, extended the market economy, raised consumption levels, and increased unionization; in the agrarian sector, the producers of non-exportable goods benefitted greatly from the expansion of the domestic market.

The great "but . . ." was that the "enemy"--the export-oriented sector--was the provider of international currency. The populist response was to reduce this sector's real income and redistribute it for the benefit of domestic industrial expansion and consumption. But even though the export sector had lost its traditional hegemony, and the government had succeeded in extracting a significant portion of its income, the exporters' situation as sole international currency earners allowed them to

---

[5]For a valuable study of this coalition, see Cardoso and Faleto, pp. 102-122.

retain a degree of political influence disproportionate to their decreasing share of the Argentine and Brazilian GNP. The nationalistic populist policies never went much further than recurring deprecation of the "oligarchy" and expropriation of the more visible symbols of foreign presence. Under cover of these largely symbolic actions, Vargas' and Perón's governments developed a complex pattern of accommodations and ambiguous relations with the export sector, which in its role as foreign currency earner was crucially important for the carrying out of populist domestic-expansion policies.

An aspect of the drive toward industrialization which would have enduring consequences was that since the 1930's the expansion of industry was "horizontal" or "extensive"--i.e., aimed at satisfying the demand for finished consumer goods (mostly light and nondurable). It is a moot question whether, given the technological, financial, and managerial resources available, it would have been possible to proceed otherwise, but this horizontal expansion of industry meant that few inroads were made into the production of intermediate and capital goods. The results were fractionalization into many consumer-goods producers and very high costs. Another consequence was a heavy dependence on imports of intermediate and capital goods, as well as of technology, without which the industrial establishment could not continue operating.[6]

The entry of vast segments of the popular sector as consumers in the urban economies was fostered by (and a requisite of) the expansion of domestic industry. Their entrance into an expanding governmental and labor market was, of course, part of the same phenomenon. As long as the export sector could provide the necessary international currency and the industrial domestic firms could continue to expand horizontally, no incompatibility seemed to exist among the interests of the members of the populist coalitions. Vargas and Perón encouraged workers' unionization, in part because it provided allegiance for them and in part because it facilitated governmental control over the newly incorporated segments of the popular sector. Both leaders used their control of governmental resources for gaining power over

---

[6] These characteristics have received a lot of attention from students of the economy of Latin American countries. A good recent summary is UN-ECLA, "Industrial Development in Latin America," Economic Bulletin for Latin America, XIV, No. 2 (1969). See also Furtado, Teoría . . ., and Raul Prebisch, "Change and Development: Latin America's Great Task" (ILPES and IDB, 1970; mimeo). The articles by O. Sunkel cited above, as well as Cardoso and Faleto, offer valuable guidelines for exploring the socio-political consequences of this pattern of industrialization.

existing labor unions and for creating new ones. This policy
deprived the popular sector of the opportunity to develop more
autonomous organizations and ideologies, and it gave Perón and
Vargas increased capacity for manipulating labor. But it also
had the effect of giving urban workers an organizational basis
that, with all its weaknesses considered, was incomparably
stronger than anything they had before. Unions would by and
large support Perón and Vargas and, during their governments,
union leaders would be dependent on their approval for keeping
their positions. But even in this subordinate position, the
urban popular sector was given its first chances to have some
effective weight in national politics, and its leaders were able
to participate in bargaining within the populist coalition. When
the populist period lost its dynamism and the populist governments
had been ousted, in both Argentina and Brazil there remained an
urban popular sector with a high degree of organization, political
allegiances hostile to the established sectors, and ideological
tendencies amenable to more radical formulations than anything
proposed by Perón or Vargas during their years in power.

Another aspect of populist policy deserves emphasis here.
The period of horizontal economic growth began with a domestic
industrial sector having few links with foreign-owned firms, most
of which (as noted above) were up to then devoted to export-
oriented activities. The expansion benefitted all industry. It
seemed merely a matter of maintaining high tariff protection and
of obtaining more resources from the state, and industry would
be able to meet existing consumer demand and the broadening of
demand by the entry of new segments of the popular sector into
the market. Public policies reflected the cohesiveness of industrialists' interests and were, in this sense, quite simple
and straightforward. The displaced rulers could complain, of
course, but to the members of the populist coalition, indiscrimi-
nate industrial expansion and tariff protection seemed the obvious
policies.

Perhaps above all, the periods of the politically incorporating and economically expanding Argentine and Brazilian
populist systems were times of quite generalized exultation.
The broad "developmentalist alliance" had found the way for "take-
off into sustained growth," the old rulers had been replaced and
the ties of external dependence severed, all participants in the
populist coalition were receiving payoffs roughly proportionate
to their expectations, and no source of fundamental conflict among
them was apparent.

But this situation contained elements that would lead in
a short time to its collapse. In the following section we will
trace the main features of the crisis of populist policies and the
creation of new alignments that would later preside over the "excluding" phase of the Argentine and Brazilian political systems.

The End of Argentine and Brazilian Expansion. What happened in the Argentine and Brazilian economies came to be known as the "exhaustion" of the "easy" stages of industrialization-- i.e., the end of the period of extensive, horizontal industrial growth based on substitution for imports of finished consumer goods.[7] Import substitution proved to be an import-intensive activity.[8] During the horizontal industrialization period international prices for exports were erratic, contributing to a declining economic situation further aggravated by the poor productivity of the export sectors, which were "paying the bill" of populist policies. Combined with the increasing need for imports of intermediate and capital goods to support the existing domestic industry, these factors led to severe foreign exchange shortages.[9] As Table 15 shows, increases in import substitution by Argentina and Brazil did not alleviate the problem at all.[10]

---

[7]There is a large bibliography on this subject-matter. See esp. UN-ECLA, El desarrollo económico de América Latina en la postguerra (New York, 1963); M.C. Tavares, "The Growth and Decline of Import Substitution in Brazil," Economic Bulletin for Latin America, IX, No. 1 (1964); UN-ECLA, The Process of Industrial Development . . . and El cambio . . .; Furtado, Subdesarrollo . . . and Teoría . . .; S. Macario, "Protectionism and Industrialization in Latin America," Economic Bulletin for Latin America, IX, No. 1 (1964); W. Baer, Industrialization and Economic Development in Brazil (Homewood: R. Irwin, 1965); N. Leff, "Import Constraints and Development: Causes of the Recent Decline of Brazilian Economic Growth," Review of Economics and Statistics, November 1967; D. Felix, "The Dilemma of Import Substitution in Argentina" in G. Papanek, ed., Development Policy: Theory and Practice (Cambridge: Harvard University Press, 1968). A. Hirschman, "The Political Economy of Import-Substituting Industrialization in Latin America," The Quarterly Journal of Economics (February 1969); and C. Díaz Alejandro, Essays on the Economic History of the Argentine Republic (New Haven: Yale University Press, 1970), have criticized some of the more rigid interpretations of the concept of "exhaustion."

[8]The expression is from C. Díaz Alejandro, "On the Import Intensiveness of Import Substitution," Kyklos, 3 (1965).

[9]See, among others, UN-ECLA, External Financing of Latin America (New York, 1965); CNRS, Les Problèmes des capitales en Amérique Latine (Paris, 1965); and Prebisch.

[10]Moreover, even though in more recent years Argentina and Brazil (especially the latter) siginificantly increased domestic production of capital goods, the demand for imports of heavy and high technology equipment kept rising. See, for Brazil, Nathaniel

Table 15

COMPENSATORY INTERNATIONAL FINANCING PLUS DECREASE IN NET
MONETARY RESERVES USED BY SOUTH AMERICAN COUNTRIES TO
COVER INTERNATIONAL BALANCE OF PAYMENTS DEFICITS:
1946-1961

(in U$S millions)

Argentina	1,129.0
Brazil	1,471.6
Chile	232.7
Colombia	339.0
Perú	-49.1
Uruguay	207.1
Venezuela	-161.4
Bolivia	37.6
Ecuador	17.7
Paraguay	4.4

Source: Computed from UN-ECLA, The External Financing of Latin
America (New York, 1965).

The foreign exchange shortage has been at the core of
many of the countries' economic problems.[11] It became a question
of importing either raw and intermediate materials (thus maintaining existing levels of industrial activity, but hindering
growth) or capital goods (thus favoring growth, but creating
serious socio-political crises as a consequence of drastic short-
term drops in output). More important, it became evident that
the existing domestic industrial structure could not effect "intensive" industrialization--i.e., the vertical integration of
domestic industry for the production of a wide range of raw,
intermediate, and capital goods. The period of "horizontal"
industrialization left a schedule of supply which included a
disproportionate (in amount and variety) share of consumption
and luxury items, as well as myriad small producers co-existing

Leff, The Brazilian Capita' Goods Industry, 1929-1964 (Cambridge:
Harvard University Press, 1968), and, for Argentina, Alejandro,
Essays . . ., and data in Chapter III below.

[11] I examine these problems in greater detail in Chapter III
below, focusing on the Argentine case.

with a few big firms, all under the umbrella of minimum competition and maximum state protection. This composition of the industrial sector has contributed to costs that are well above international standards, has multiplied inefficient allocations, and has exerted an increasingly negative effect on income distribution.[12] When (circa 1960) the economies of Argentina and Brazil had evidently exhausted the possibilities of "easy" horizontal industrial growth, the problems that this generated made clear to many sectors that important and quite painful policy innovations were required--though they were far from agreeing on what those policies should be.

The type of industrial undertaking needed for vertical integration (both for the development of "basic" and capital goods industries, as well as for the huge infrastructure investments required) is very different from the small shop that frequently was sufficient for entrance into industry during the horizontal expansion stage. The size of the new investments, their period of maturation, and their technological requirements in most cases greatly exceed the capabilities of Argentine and Brazilian firms, and greatly strain available public resources.[13] The populist hopes concerning the reduction of foreign dependence have become an unwitting irony. The assimilation of masses into urban life has consolidated consumption expectations modeled after the highly developed economies, "vertical" industrial projects have depended more and more on capital, and technology transfers from abroad[14] and the increasing penetration of technocratic roles has consolidated linkages of dependence with the "originating" societies from which such roles have been "transplanted" (see pp. 81ff. below). Even more important, foreign firms have been encouraged to "jump over" the tariff barriers. The larger the domestic market, the greater the incentives for the "Argentine" General Motors and the "Brazilian" ITT to enter directly into these markets. Table 16 shows how, circa 1960, the pattern of U.S. direct investments varied with the size of each domestic market (and consequently with the differences in degree of modernization of each South American country).

---

[12] For good overviews of this pattern and some of its socioeconomic consequences, see UN-ECLA, Estudio económico . . .; O. Sunkel, "Politica . . ." and "La universidad . . . ."

[13] Cardoso and Faleto, esp. pp. 143ff., elaborate on the crucial differences that, vis-à-vis the less industrialized South American countries, are generated for the more industrialized [and more modernized--Author] ones by this situation.

[14] See esp. Sunkel, "Politica . . ." and "La universidad . . . ."

Table 16

U.S. PRIVATE INVESTMENT IN SOUTH AMERICAN COUNTRIES,
DIRECT AND DIRECT INDUSTRIAL: C. 1960

(U$S millions)

	Total, Direct Private Investment (1)	Subtotal, Direct Private Industrial Investment (2)	(2) ÷ (1) = Percent
Argentina	828	454	55%
Brazil	1,128	663	59
Chile	768	27	4
Colombia	465	120	26
Perú	448	60	14
Uruguay	51	20	39
Venezuela	2,807	202	7
Bolivia, Ecuador, and Paraguay	635	29	5

Source: U.S. Department of Commerce, Survey of Current Business, August 1964.

In the more modernized South American countries, foreign-owned industrial firms producing for the domestic market are no longer the isolated, highly visible, export-oriented firms characteristic of lower levels of modernization. These firms have created a wide network of satellite, nationally owned production and marketing firms, and pay higher than average wages in the great urban areas.[15] The towering, isolated symbols of foreign

---

[15]This situation contrasts with the still largely prevailing pattern in other South American countries, where the largest proportion of foreign investment is concentrated in export-oriented firms (mainly mining-extractive enclaves, plantations of highly specialized exportable agrarian products, and financial-commercial intermediaries with foreign trade). The links that most of those firms establish with the domestic market and with domestic entrepreneurs are far less numerous than in those cases where marketing and consumption also take place within the same domestic market. Furthermore, even though enclaves and plantations tend to pay higher wages than the national averages, in most cases they are located at great distances from the large urban centers of these countries. See Furtado, Teoría . . ., and Cardoso and Faleto, pp. 48ff.

presence in former periods have now spread into the largest South American markets, establishing multiple connections with domestic entrepreneurs and with workers who depend on these foreign-owned firms for maintaining their relatively privileged positions.[16] In Argentina and Brazil this new situation reflects profound socio-economic transformations which (as I will argue in more detail below) have had a profound impact on their political problems and have changed their constellations of political actors and policy concerns.

The foreign exchange shortage, combined with consumption demands from all sectors which became more and more difficult to satisfy, have been at the heart of the inflation that has plagued these nations. The countries that have suffered the most infla-tion are those which began their drive toward industrialization earliest (Argentina, Chile, and Uruguay) and those that, because of their larger domestic markets, have advanced furthest in their industrialization (Argentina and Brazil),[17] as can be seen in Table 17.[18]

With Argentina and Brazil, Chile and Uruguay share a history of "stabilization plans" based on the diagnosis that the

---

[16]Furthermore, of those industrial firms that have retained (at least nominal) national ownership, those that are of larger size and those that work in more dynamic or more technologically com-plex activities are the ones that, by far, have the closest links with foreign firms--in terms of royalties, minority shares, and financing. (See the highly illustrative data and analysis of the Brazilian case by V. Faría, "Dependencia e ideología empresa-rial," Revista Latinoamericana de Ciencia Política, No. 1 [April 1971].) These findings are particularly significant if we remem-ber from Chapter I that the more highly modernized South American countries are those which have both more "big" and more "techno-logically complex and capital-intensive" industrial firms.

[17]Because of the market-size factor Chile and Uruguay were stalled at a lower level of industrialization. On this point see data in Chapter I above, and UN-ECLA, The Process of Industrial Development . . . and its Statistical Annex [mimeo].

[18]In accordance with the aims enunciated in the Preface to this book, inflation data have been chosen that closely pre-ceded the 1964 and 1966 Brazilian and Argentine attempts to inaugurate "excluding" political systems, on the assumption that these data reflect situations that immediately influenced these events. But, as is the case with much of the other data, more recent rates of inflation in South America maintain the pattern indicated in Table 21 (in spite of a recent reduction of Brazil's rate of inflation).

Table 17

YEARLY AVERAGE RATES OF INFLATION: 1960-1965

(Percentages)

Argentina	23.2%
Brazil	60.0
Chile	27.0
Colombia	12.4
Perú	9.4
Uruguay	29.7
Venezuela	0.0
Ecuador	3.8
Bolivia	5.1
Paraguay	5.3

Source: UN-ECLA, Estudio económico de América Latina, 1969 (New York, 1970).

containment of excess demand, a restrained monetary policy, and the elimination of "marginal" (i.e., inefficient) producers are prerequisites for stopping inflation and that, in turn, stopping inflation is a prerequisite for further growth. These policies have been the subjects of heated debate.[19] Whatever their merits, they were rendered politically impracticable by the enormous social tensions they created. Inflation and growth followed a wild pattern, alternating between the recessionary effects of the "stabilization plans" and the return to more relaxed policies.[20]

_____

[19]For surveys of this voluminous "structuralists vs. monetarists" debate, see W. Baer and I. Kerstentzky, eds., Inflation and Growth in Latin America (Homewood: R. Irwin, 1965), and W. Baer, "The Inflation Controversy in Latin America," Latin American Research Review, 2 (1967).

[20]Commenting on the Brazilian experience, Samuel Morley writes: "A natural desire to stop inflation rapidly generates programs which are partially abandoned after their politically disastrous first effects on output and employment. If they are reapplied later, the economy alternates between periods of real stagnation and inflationary growth. Such a policy is as bad as no inflation program at all. It weakens the private sector, makes advance planning and investment more difficult, and extends the period

Among other important effects, it did not take long for many Argentine and Brazilian sectors to reach the conclusion that stabilization programs (as well as other economic policies to be discussed below) required, as a political pre-condition, postponement of popular consumption and power participation demands.

As a consequence of these policies, inflation was on the average very high in Argentina and Brazil, but with substantial yearly fluctuations. The alternation of recessionary and inflationary public policies created a volatile situation to which many public and private decision-makers found it difficult to adjust.[21] Another important indication of the exhaustion of horizontal industrial expansion is given by data on aggregate economic growth, almost nil in Argentina and declining sharply in Brazil during the years immediately preceding the 1964 military coup.[22]

---

of recessionary adjustment without controlling the inflation" ("Inflation and Stagnation in Brazil," Economic Development and Cultural Change, XIX, No. 2 [1971]). For similar conclusions concerning the Argentine case, see G. Maynard and W. van Rijckeghem, "Stabilization Policy in an Inflationary Economy: An Analysis of the Argentine Case" in Papanek, ed., as well as the analysis and sources cited in Chapter III below.

[21] A UN-ECLA study, "Industrial Development . . .," advances the interesting suggestion that these difficulties are greater the more industrially advanced the country is. According to this study, the greater technological requirements for further vertical integration, as well as the greater size of investments and their longer terms of maturation, require a more stabilized context over which public and private decisions can span. In contrast, industrial establishments in which less capital- and technology-intensive firms and projects still predominate are better able to adjust to sudden contextual variations. This suggests the hypothesis (to be explored further below) that the perceived need of achieving a high degree of stabilization and predictability in the social context will increase with the degree of modernization achieved in each country. I emphasize that this seems to be a perceived need, because the UN-ECLA study presents it as an objective need imposed by a situation of more advanced industrialization.

[22] For Argentina, see Chapter III below. For Brazil, see Baer, Industrialization . . . and "Inflation and Economic Efficiency: Brazil," Economic Development and Cultural Change, 11 (1963), and Skidmore.

Trends in employment also should be mentioned.[23] The adoption of technology from settings where the combination of factors of production is very different has meant that the more modern and more dynamic industries usually have small labor-absorption capacity.[24] Resulting trends in employment have led to the well-known phenomenon of disproportionate size of the services sector. But here again structural differences in the modern areas make a difference: Argentina's and Brazil's industrial employment as a percentage of the non-rural employment peaked around twenty years ago. For most other South American countries, such employment peaked later, or the growth rate flattened, but never at the levels reached by Argentina and Brazil (see Table 18), supporting the assertions in Chapter I concerning the important structural differences observable in the modern sectors of South American countries.

The crucial point here is that horizontal industrial growth advanced much further in Argentina and Brazil than in the other South American countries. But this growth was severely limited and of short duration. When it was over it left a heritage that included the breakdown of the populist coalition, new policy issues, a profoundly modified social structure, and many shattered illusions.[25] In a fundamental sense, after reaching in this way the high point of modernization of their "centers," Argentina and Brazil have had to deal with "problematic spaces"[26] that have crucial aspects that are significantly different from those of their pre-expansion period and from the present problematic spaces of other, less modernized South American countries.

---

[23] For data and analysis, see Slawinski, and F. Cardoso and L. Reyna, "Industrialization, Occupational Structure, and Social Stratification in Latin America" in C. Blasier, ed., Constructive Change in Latin America (Pittsburgh: University of Pittsburgh Press, 1968).

[24] This aspect has been receiving considerable attention; for a good analysis see Furtado, Dialéctica . . . .

[25] On the breakdown of the populist coalition (or, as some authors prefer to label it, the "developmentalist alliance"), see-- among others--Cardoso and Faleto; Ianni, O colapso . . .; Torcuato di Tella, El sistema político argentino y la clase obrera (Eudeba, 1964).

[26] I will use this term to combine two partially overlapping concepts: "salient social problems" (social problems that are high on the agenda of concerns of political actors) and "developmental bottlenecks" (problems that from the point of view of the observer seriously hamper the probabilities of future socio-economic growth).

Table 18

PERCENTAGES OF TOTAL NON-RURAL EMPLOYMENT IN INDUSTRIAL (FACTORY)
EMPLOYMENT IN SOUTH AMERICAN COUNTRIES: 1945-1960[a]

	1945	1950	1955	1960
Argentina	20.6%	18.5%	16.9%	15.3%
Brazil	16.9	17.3	15.8	15.0
Chile	12.7	13.1	13.3	12.4
Colombia	9.1	9.8	9.1	9.6
Perú	8.5	11.0	11.9	13.0
Uruguay	N.A.	N.A.	N.A.	N.A.
Venezuela	9.2	8.1	9.7	10.8
Other (includes Middle American countries)	11.6	10.7	11.1	11.4

[a]Underlined figures are the maximum percentages for each country
during the 15-year period.

Source: UN-ECLA, The Process of Industrialization in Latin America (New York, 1966), Statistical Index [mimeo].

This is a point that will be stressed and elaborated in the rest
of this chapter--i.e., different levels of modernization, in all
the dimensions that this concept entails, generate different
constellations of issues that define each country's problematic
space. In turn, the set of political actors and their political
responses (actors' goals and coalitions, public policies, and
political system types) are molded by these different constellations and by the different structures in which these constellations have emerged. These are, I believe, useful analytical
tools for the comparative exploration of socio-economic and political interactions in contemporary South America.

In Argentina and Brazil, the homogeneity of interests
that once existed within the industrial sector has evidently dis-
appeared. More and more "experts" since the late 1950's agree
that, if growth is to begin again, the market must be cleared of
"marginal" producers by eliminating all restrictions on those
firms that are technologically more advanced, more capital-
intensive, and financially more powerful. Of course, this issue
cuts deep across the industrial sector. In addition to its obvious economic importance, it becomes a major political problem

because most of the more advanced firms are foreign (mostly U.S.)
owned.[27] In addition to being domestically owned, the more marginal industrial firms tend to employ more labor-intensive production techniques, which means that their elimination would
aggravate the unemployment crisis. Thus, what would seem to be
"economically rational" (leaving aside for the moment the less
than optimal effects of oligopolic concentration) raises prospects
of more dependence and more unemployment. As C. Díaz Alejandro
puts it, the issue may be no less than the viability of national
capitalism without national capitalists.[28] Nationalism and preservation of the social peace can be used as effective arguments
by those domestic industrialists whose elimination is threatened
by expert advice, by "stabilization" plans, and by the interests
of the more powerful producers. As will be seen below, this issue
also has profound significance for the military and the técnicos
placed in strategic points for national economic planning and
decision-making.

The end of horizontal industrial growth had other closely
related effects. No longer were there isolated, highly visible
"enemies" or the hope of devising policies that would provide
satisfactory payoffs for all the participants in the old populist
coalition. What remained for some time was the pattern or erratic
policies that resulted in more inflation and less growth. In
that situation, the nature of salient social problems in Argentina
and Brazil profoundly changed: new issues were discussed by a
different set of political actors, both of which reflected the
changes in social structure and the new cleavages that the high
modernization of their "centers" had brought about in these countries. There is little doubt that in all South American countries
further growth requires, among other things, quite drastic changes
in their economic structures. But in Argentina and Brazil of the
1960's and today, conflict and debate no longer center on solutions to be achieved by expropriating extractive or export-oriented, foreign-owned firms. Before their horizontal industrial
growth these were central issues, as they are now central issues
in the contemporary scene of most other, less modernized South
American countries.[29]

---

[27]The data in Table 16 are relevant here. It is in Argentina
and Brazil that there is more (and in greater proportion) domestic-
market oriented U.S. direct industrial investment.

[28]Essays . . ., p. 272.

[29]This crucial change in the nature of issues to be faced at
higher levels of Latin American modernization is also noted, with
less emphasis, in Cardoso and Faleto.

The bigger size of their domestic markets allowed Argentina and Brazil to advance further than the other South American countries in the modernization of their "centers," particularly in the broad base of production entailed by industry and its manifold directly related activities (marketing, publicity, communications, transport, financing), as well as in the penetration of roles required for the performance of these activities and the "external" linkages channeled through these roles. Changes within the same country, as well as cross-national differences in levels of modernization, involved crucial differences in the structure and in the control of many increasingly influential productive processes. These in turn led to changes in the social structure of the "centers," as well as in the pattern of coalitions and in the goals of political actors—which began to cluster around the new issues and the new cleavages that expressed the changed problematic space. All these changes created new problems with respect to the modified bases of power of political actors, the policy options they perceived as available to them, and the types of institutional political arrangements they were likely to opt for.[30]

Political Actors in Argentina and Brazil after Populism.

Given the strained economic situation that resulted from the "exhaustion" of horizontal industrial growth, the consumption and power demands of the popular sector seemed to other sectors to be very difficult to satisfy. But now those demands were formulated from the more solid and broader organizational bases achieved during populism, and were addressed to civilian governments very vulnerable to civilian strife. Furthermore, the populist period generated a large urban electorate to whom political leaders could appeal—mostly with promises of distributionist, populist-type economic policies. Before the 1964 (Brazil) and 1966 (Argentina) military coups, all political actors operated more and more on the basis of pressure and threats. The main assets of the popular sector were its electoral weight and its capacity to strike, demonstrate, and disrupt. As a consequence, the scope and intensity of its political activation grew markedly in both countries in the years that preceded the coups.[31] The active

---

[30] In spite of its serious data limitations, the comparative strategy I am proposing makes possible an approximation to these crucial changes and differences, which are likely to remain concealed by the use of a static approach and nationally averaged data.

[31] For Argentine and Brazilian data on the popular sector's increasing political activation (indicated by number of strikes and strikers), see Samuel Baily, Labor, Nationalism and Politics in Argentina (New Brunswick: Rutgers University Press, 1967);

presence of the popular sector in the great urban centers was
perceived as profoundly threatening by most other social sectors.
After economic expansion had ended, the workers' demands were
assessed by their former coalition partners as leading to a reshaping of society far more radical than anything they were
willing to accept.[32] In spite of "complications" that originated
the new inter-industry cleavage, most propertied Argentine and
Brazilian sectors agreed that the popular sector's demands were
excessive (both in terms of consumption and of power participation), and that capital accumulation would be impossible if those
demands were not tightly controlled.

We have been careful not to equate high modernization
with any implication of socio-economic "development." The concept
of modernization has been used for studying changes taking place
within a national context of manifold social rigidities, a highly
skewed distribution of resources, and external dependence. Within
such a context, the possibilities of economic expansion were quite

---

R. Rotondaro, Realidad y cambio en el sindicalismo argentino
(Pleamar, 1971); and Schmitter, Interest Conflict . . . . For
interpretations that agree that the growing rate of popular activation was a major factor in the 1964 and 1966 coups, see, among
others, Cardoso and Faleto; F. Weffort, Estado . . . and "Le
Populisme"; N. Aguiar Walker, "Movilización de la clase obrera
en el Brasil," Revista Latinoamericana de Sociología, I, No. 3
(1965); Ianni, O colapso . . .; L. Martins, "Aspectos políticos
de la revolución brasileña," Revista Latinoamericana de Sociología,
III, No. 3 (1967); J.B. Lopes, "Etude de quelques changements
fondamentaux dans la politique et la société brésilienne," Sociologie du Travail, No. 3 (1965); and José Nun, "The Middle Class
Military Coup" in C. Véliz, ed., The Politics of Conformity in
Latin America (New York: Oxford University Press, 1967).

[32]For data and analysis concerning the fears of entrepreneurs
and their organizations raised in Argentina and Brazil by the
increasing rates of activation of the popular sectors, see F.
Cardoso, Empresario industrial e desenvolvimento econômico
(Difusao Europeia do Livro, 1964); J.M. Freels, El sector industrial en la política nacional (Eudeba, 1970), and "Industrialists and Politics in Argentina: An Opinion Survey of Trade Association Leaders," Journal of Inter-American Studies and World
Affairs, XII, No. 3 (1970); and the Argentine and Brazilian
studies of UN-ECLA in El empresario industrial en América Latina,
as well as the sources cited in the preceding footnote. See
also the vivid testimonials about pre-coup Argentina by two
economists--Alejandro, Essays . . ., and Everett Hagen, The
Economics of Development (Homewood: R. Irwin, 1968), pp. 339-
340.

limited, as the populist experience so clearly showed. But high modernization generated increasing rates of popular political activation. This led most of the propertied sectors to perceive popular political demands as serious threats to the survival of the existing social arrangements--particularly the class structure, the power distribution, and the international alignments of the countries. The resulting polarization made the strong class component of the situation even more visible, facilitating the collaboration of most of the propertied sectors in accepting a political "solution" that supposedly would eliminate such threats by the political exclusion of the popular sector. For reasons that will be discussed below (the inter-industry cleavage being one of them), the collaboration did not extend much further than this, and the major role in the determination of the content of the new policies was played by a very small segment of the propertied sectors. This segment was constituted of the individuals that, because of the level of modernization in Argentina and Brazil, controlled the more complex organizations and the more advanced technologies, and had the closest links abroad. But the limited collaboration sufficed for ensuring the united support of the propertied sectors for the coups, and for the initial decisions taken by the new "excluding" political systems of Argentina and Brazil. (We will return to this point below.)

The Cuban revolution frightened many sectors, and seemed to confirm their assessment of the implications of popular political activation. The specter of a socialist revolution was raised, and was greatly enhanced by the manifold activities that U.S. policy-makers undertook to prevent and repress "subversion" in the South American continent. The impact of the Cuban revolution and of increasing social unrest were at the core of an expanded definition of the role of the military. The United States undertook to provide training in anti-subversive warfare, French and U.S. "anti-subversive" and "civic action" doctrines were taught, and the military's capabilities for political leadership were stressed as parts of the evolution of the military. "National security" was redefined to include the achievement of "socio-economic development" and the suppression of "internal enemies"--the "agents of extremist subversion."[33] Social crises, government inefficiency, and social unrest were perceived to

---

[33]For general surveys on the evolution of the military, see Liisa North, _Civil-Military Relations in Argentina, Chile, and Perú_ (Berkeley: University of California, Institute of International Studies, 1966); W. Barber and N. Ronning, _Internal Security and Military Power_ (Columbus: Ohio State University Press, 1966); Stepan, _The Military . . .;_ L. Einaudi and A. Stepan, "Latin American Institutional Development: Changing Military Perspectives in Perú and Brazil" (Santa Monica: Rand Corporation, 1971); and P.V. Beltrán, ed., _El papel político y social de las fuerzas_

constitute the "internal subversion" whose elimination had fallen within the range of specific military duties.

The income situation of the large salaried middle class deteriorated steadily in both Argentina and Brazil during the years that preceded the 1964 and 1966 coups. This sector showed unequivocal signs of disaffection with the situation, in which deprivation, political disorder, and a formally democratic system appeared linked. Reacting in a characteristic way, they responded to a "law and order" appeal.[34] (One critical subset of the middle class--the técnicos occupying governmental positions--found that the "politicians" could offer them only precarious tenure in public office and were usually unwilling, and always unable, to follow their advice. But the técnicos belong in the technocratic roles category, and will be considered below under that rubric.) Most agrarian exporters reasserted their dislike for mass politics and their conviction that they could not achieve much permanent gain under elected governments subject to the pressure of the urban popular sector.

The result of these developments was the political isolation of the popular sector.[35] Lacking their previous populist allies and direct political access, and suffering from unfavorable income redistribution, they required increasing political activation to obtain decreasing returns on their demands. In the other sectors, growing fears of subversion coupled with shrinking payoffs had the effect of further eroding the weak support they had given to the pre-coup Argentine and Brazilian political systems.

The deteriorating performance of government was reflected in net decreases in the resources available to the governments

---

armadas en América Latina (Monte Avila Editores, 1970). For a sense of this issue as seen by Argentine military officers, see the sources cited in the final section of Chapter III below. For Brazil, see Gen. Couto e Silva, Geopolítica do Brasil (Livraria Jose Olimpo Editora, 1967) and the comments by O.S. Ferreira in "La geopolítica y el ejército brasileño" in Beltrán, ed. See also the quarterly Argentine journal Estrategia and Revista Brasileira de Estudos Politicos, special issue on "Seguranca Nacional" (1967).

[34]See esp. Furtado, Dialectica . . . and Subdesarrollo . . .; Weffort, Estado . . .; Martins, Industrializacao . . .; and Ianni, O colapso . . . . See also the sources cited in the three preceding footnotes and data included in Chapter III below.

[35]Besides the sources cited in this subsection, see di Tella, El sistema . . ., and D. Cantón, "Revolución argentina de 1966 y proyecto nacional," Revista Latinoamericana de Sociología, V, No. 3 (1969).

during the periods that preceded the 1964 and 1966 coups. Lower tax revenues and smaller shares of governmental income in the GNP, decreased real salaries of civil servants, overstaffing at the lower ranks and an exodus at the higher levels, recurrent cabinet crises--all indicated marked decay in governmental problem-solving capabilities in both countries.[36]

Various currents in political development literature have emphasized the importance of some correspondence between the performance of the political system and political demands.[37] As the Argentine and the Brazilian populisms show, periods of socioeconomic expansion tend to increase the activation of more political actors. But the many developmental bottlenecks lead to situations in which, while overall social performance is improving slowly, further political demands are being formulated, supported by further political activation. The "gap" between performance and demands generates political action to reduce it. What action will be taken by which political actors? This seems to depend on the patterns of social differentiation resulting from changes in the socio-economic structure.

The data from Chapter I and the processes described in this chapter can now be brought together. It has been suggested that the size of South American domestic markets and the productive structure of their modern areas--particularly their type of industrialization--are the major factors in determining the pattern of social differentiation of each modern area. (These are the more general aspects of the concept of modernization being used here.) Furthermore, the increased differentiation of the social structure means greater social complexity--i.e., more social units (sectors, classes, institutions, and roles) interrelated in more complex ways. Political pluralization is the political expression of social differentiation: it means greater complexity of political interaction--i.e., more political actors inter-

---

[36]For Argentina, see esp. Chapter III below. For Brazil, see esp. Instituto Brasileiro de Estatistica, Series estatisticas retrospectivas (IBGE, 1970).

[37]See, among others, Huntington, Political Order . . .; LaPalombara, "Political Science . . .," and "Penetration: A Crisis of Governmental Capability" in L. Binder et al., Crises and Sequences in Political Development, forthcoming; Lasswell, "The Policy Sciences . . ."; and K. Deutsch, The Nerves of Government (New York: Free Press, 1963). See also the useful survey by A. Diamant, "The Nature of Political Development" in J. Montgomery and W. Siffin, eds., Approaches to Development: Politics, Administration, and Change (New York: McGraw-Hill, 1966).

related in more complex ways.[38] In all these dimensions the overarching concept of modernization has guided the analysis and the
choice of indicators. More important, in all these dimensions the
available information suggests that there are significant differences among the three groups of South American countries. These
differences, and the different problematic spaces they entail,
are seen here as major determinants of the different patterns of
political phenomena (in particular, of the different types of
political systems) that distinguish the countries in each group
from those in the other groups.

Social differentiation proceeds in a "contrapuntal interplay"[39] with problems of social integration. "Social integration" is almost impossible to define and measure with precision.
It is a concept used frequently in social theories that postulate
equilibrium assumptions that are not shared here. But in spite
of its limitations, it points to an aspect of social reality that
cannot be ignored. The emergence of new social units (classes,
sectors, institutions, roles) often conflicts with patterns consolidated during previous stages of society--in particular when,
instead of emerging from more or less spontaneous processes of
conflict and adjustment of internal forces, highly influential
social units (in particular, institutions and roles) result from
"transplantations" from more advanced and more industrialized
societies.[40] Modernization entails social differentiation, and

---

[38]As E. Kenworthy puts it: "[Social differentiation entails]
the assumption that there is a plurality of groups relevant to
the political process. In developmental terms, this alerts one
to the emergence of new actors in the political scene, and often
of new power resources as well (organized labor and the general
strike are examples of each). This, after all, is the political
meaning of differentiation. Unfortunately, the development literature often has viewed differentiation as mass politicization,
as if only one group were emerging in the political arena . . . .
Differentiation not only gives rise to a plurality of groups but
to a variety of political resources" ("Coalitions in the Political
Development of Latin America" in S. Groennings et al., eds., The
Study of Coalition Behavior [New York: Holt, Rinehart and
Winston, 1970]).

[39]The expression is from Neil Smelser, The Sociology of Economic
Life (Englewood Cliffs: Prentice-Hall, 1960), p. 110.

[40]Perhaps the best examples of the emergence of new social units
from internal processes are to be found in Western Europe and the
United States. On the other hand, "transplantations" have been
the general rule in the "late modernizers," including, of course,
South American countries. Such differences in the patterns and

the latter generates competing interests, conflicting normative
claims, and divergent behavioral expectations. Insofar as some
"fit" is not achieved among these aspects and across social units,
social integration lags behind social differentiation. The incorporation of newly differentiated social units exponentially
increases the possible permutations and combinations among them,
at the same time that structural sources of conflict increase and
the commonalities of behavioral expectations decline. A frequent
result is a low level of social cohesion and generalized uncertainty. Political actors begin to focus more and more on short-
term gains, the boundaries of socially and politically permissible
behavior are blurred, and the capacities of political systems to
incorporate sectoral goals into broader perspectives are diminished.[41]

In Argentina and Brazil, the "differentiation-integration
gap" contributed to the previously mentioned "demands-performance
gap." Both were consequences of the high levels of modernization
reached in the national "centers," and led to a political situation that Samuel Huntington has aptly described as "mass praetorianism."[42] The "political game" became, on the one hand, broader,

---

sequences of modernization, as well as in the degree of its "fit"
with preexisting patterns, are further evidence against the assumption of equivalence of causal processes discussed in Chapter
I.

[41]For excellent discussions of these aspects, see cited works
by D. Apter, esp. Choice . . . .

[42]Political Order . . . . According to Huntington, "praetorianism" emerges when the levels of political participation and
mobilization markedly exceed the level of political institutionalization in a society (p. 80). "Mass praetorianism" exists when
the institutionalization lag occurs in highly modern and mobilized
societies, where large-scale social movements and complex organizations play a decisive role (pp. 88ff.). Huntington discusses
the main aspects and consequences of "[mass] praetorianism" in
several passages; see, e.g., p. 196: "In all societies specialized social groups engage in politics. What makes such groups
seem more 'politicized' in a praetorian society is the absence
of effective political institutions capable of mediating, refining,
and moderating group political action. In a praetorian system
social forces confront each other nakedly: no political institutions, no corps of professional political leaders are recognized
or accepted as the legitimate intermediaries to moderate group
conflict. Equally important, no agreement exists among the groups
as to the legitimate and authoritative methods for resolving conflicts . . . . In a praetorian society, however, not only are

in that more demands, brought forth by more political actors, were focused on governmental decisions. On the other hand, the "game" became more unconstrained, in that formally prescribed political behavior was less and less important vis-à-vis naked power strategies, both among political actors and against the governments. Political institutions in both countries (parties, parliament), which had never been particularly strong, were even further weakened, and the executive became the primary focus of a glut of political demands. In this situation, the pre-coup Argentine and Brazilian governments were victimized by, and collaborated in, praetorianism. Some authors have depicted the situation as a "stalemate," with high levels of unrestrained conflict, sharp differences in demands, and weakness of governments preventing the implementation of any policy.[43] This governmental incapacity aggravated the social situation, breeding more praetorianism. Inside the government, with few possibilities for effective decision-making, concern for survival in office became paramount. This led to the adoption of sequences of policies designed to placate the more threatening political actors, with little concern for general problem-solving.[44]

These processes threatened the survival of the existing political system. Salient social problems remained unsolved, competition was increasingly zero-sum, gains were precarious, and praetorianism undermined the problem-solving capabilities of existing institutions. The threshold for a definitive crisis in the political system was reached when most of the political actors focused on changing the rules of the "political game" altogether, instead of trying to obtain gains within the existing rules. Coalitions were formed with the preeminent goal of ending the "stalemate" by implanting a new political system that would allow effective decision-making in line with the preferences of the coalition members. As Huntington's analysis suggests, after a praetorian period the tendency is to define the situation as one

---

the actors varied, but so also are the methods used to decide upon office and policy. Each group employs means which reflect its peculiar nature and capabilities. The wealthy bribe; students riot; workers strike; and the military coup.

[43]For the initial statement of this concept, see di Tella, El sistema . . . . Other authors have explored its implications; see, for example, Kenworthy, "Coalitions . . .," and Irving L. Horowitz, "La norma de ilegitimidad: Hacia una teoría general del desarrollo político latinoamericano," Revista Mexicana de Sociología, XXX, No. 2 (1968).

[44]This aspect is discussed in greater detail in Chapters III and IV below.

requiring the placement of severe constraints on the political activities of those who are outside the winning coalition. The tendency, thus, was toward a highly authoritarian political system, but the specific characteristics of such authoritarianism, as well as the major goals of the winning coalition, were deeply influenced by the degree of [high] modernization and the type of [mass] praetorianism.

It may be useful here to briefly recapitulate what has been said to this point in this chapter . . . . The end of populism in Argentina and Brazil meant the dissolution of the broad coalition that had supported it, and was tied closely to the exhaustion of the possibilities of "easy" horizontal industrial growth. Manifold unsolved problems (inflation, erratic economic growth, social mis-allocations, persistent rigidities in social structure, modified but in many ways increased foreign dependence) indicated to many political actors the need for a major reshaping of the social structure: a populist system could not produce the needed changes. It was obvious to observers from all points of the ideological spectrum that the financial and technological requirements, as well as the social changes imposed by economic growth, had drastically altered conditions in Argentina and Brazil. The effects of modernization were visible in increased social differentiation, which expressed itself in political pluralization, in the emergence of deep inter-industry cleavages, in further penetration (in scope and in density) of technocratic roles, and in increased political activation of the popular sector. A period of mass praetorianism resulted in both countries, which worsened the social conditions and led to a broad consensus that the existing political system had reached its "ceiling."[45]

By way of summary, the following propositions can be stated:

Proposition 10: The "problematic spaces" of South American countries at the highest levels of modernization are significantly different from those that existed prior to their horizontal industrial expansion and from those existing at lower levels of modernization in other South American countries. New salient social problems and new developmental bottlenecks are generated by a higher level of industrialization, by further social differentiation, by greater penetration of technocratic roles, by new sets of political

---

[45] The concept is from Apter, Choice . . . .

actors and new political coalitions, by increasing rates of
political activation, by new policy issues, and by new patterns of dependence.

Proposition 11: Situations of high modernization are likely
to create serious demands-performance and differentiation-
integration "gaps." These add to the agenda of salient
social problems and intensify political demands, leading to
mass praetorianism. "Gaps" and praetorianism are effects
(and in turn causes) of diminished problem-solving capabilities of the existing political system.

Proposition 12: On the one hand, the deterioration of the
social context results in declining payoffs for most sectors.
On the other hand, the mass praetorianism which often ac-
companies a high level of modernization leads to a high
degree of political activation of the urban popular sector.
Given these conditions, the contraction of the political
system by the exclusion of the popular sector is likely to
become a basic point of agreement among most of the other
social sectors.

The point of agreement referred to in Proposition 12
was for many sectors in Argentina and Brazil a vague and preliminary one. As subsequent events showed, the content of the
public policies to be adopted after the exclusion of the popular
sector became a crucial issue. This point is closely related
to a phenomenon to which we now turn--i.e., the penetration of
technocratic roles at high modernization.

Technocratic Roles. Until now we have worked at two
levels of analysis. At both levels, important changes have taken
place as modernization has proceeded in Argentina and Brazil.
The first has been the level of the agenda of salient social
problems and developmental bottlenecks; the second, the level
of social structure, the productive-industrial base, and the
differentiation, emergence, and political activation of new
social sectors and political actors. Structural analysis can
be carried on at a lower level of generality, focusing on roles--
smaller units at the intersection of social structure and the
behavioral tendencies of their incumbents. The concept of modernization being used here requires the analysis of roles (particularly of what I have called "technocratic roles") as a
crucial component of the overall modernizing situation. In the
framework I am proposing, the political variables can readily be
seen as interacting with social factors at these three levels
of analysis.[46]

---

[46]At an even lower level of generality, the hypotheses to be
formulated here need testing by interview and content analysis

Advances in modernization are evidenced by further social differentiation at one level of analysis, and by further penetration of technocratic roles at a lower level. As the data in Chapter I suggest, the complexity of social structure produced by high modernization (and its key component, industrialization) creates public and private management needs in which technology plays an ever-increasing part. This seems to be true irrespective of the type of political system. Larger organizations engaged in more complex production, the effects of industrialization upon communications, marketing, publicity, and information-processing services, as well as the need for coordination of more diversified social units and activities--all require increasing "inputs" of persons who have gone through prolonged training in techniques of production, planning, and control. As modernization proceeds, more technocratic roles are to be found in more and more social activities. These roles are always a small proportion of the total role-incumbent population, but both their scope and density of penetration increase markedly with modernization.[47]

Are there stages at which the incumbents of technocratic roles feel capable of dealing with broad social problems in "their own ways?" What are their prevailing biases for perceiving, assessing, and acting upon social problems? These are among the questions to be explored in this section.[48]

---

research. This cannot be done here, but the task being undertaken in this book is not deprived of its value--structural analysis at several levels is a requisite for the interpretation and determination of findings at the "micro" level. See on this point, which departs from current reductionist approaches, the recent methodological discussions of E. Verón, Conducta estructura y comunicación (Jorge Alvarez Editorial, 1969); Apter, Change . . .; A. Przeworski and H. Teune, The Logic of Comparative Social Inquiry (New York: Wiley, 1969); R. Holt and M. Richardson, "Competing Paradigms in Comparative Politics" in R. Holt and J. Turner, eds., The Methodology of Comparative Research (New York: Free Press, 1970); Sidney Verba, "The Uses of Survey Research in the Study of Comparative Politics: Issues and Strategies" in S. Rokkan et al., Comparative Survey Analysis (The Hague: Mouton, 1969); P. Bourdieu et al., Le Métier de sociologue (The Hague: Mouton and Bordas, 1969); as well as the constant advocacy for "contextual analysis" to be found in Harold Lasswell's work.

[47] See definitions in Chapter I.

[48] As I stated at the beginning of this chapter, answers to these questions will be phrased as hypotheses that require further testing, since the evidence on which they rest is sketchy. Several authors writing about contemporary South American politics

A lot of attention has been paid to the "revolution of rising expectations" at the mass level, but very little scholarly effort has been devoted to a closely related and perhaps more important phenomenon: the transplantation of expectations produced by incumbency in technocratic roles in modernizing societies.[49] Executives attending business schools molded after prestigious U.S. models, military officers studying abroad and in military academies that adopt curricula and approaches proposed by foreign advisory missions, and técnicos getting their degrees abroad--all learn role-specific techniques, but above all they learn role-models. How role-incumbents in the "originating" societies perform, what support they have and what rewards they can expect, what the criteria for achievement are--all are transmitted together with the more specific technical expertise of each profession.

This is a crucial point. What is transmitted from the "originating" societies is a complex constellation, of which the technical expertise is only one element. In addition to the latter (rather, encompassing it), the individual learns a role-model; and his conception of his role, which derives from that learning, must interact with a social context that in a modernizing situation differs greatly from that of the society in which his role (and his conception of his role) originated. Given the unavoidable effects of a different social context, a key question

---

have referred to this elite subset of incumbents of technocratic roles. See A. Costa Pinto, Nacionalismo y militarismo (Siglo XXI, 1969); M. Kaplan, "Aspectos políticos de la planificatión en América Latina," Aportes, XX (April 1971); R. de las Casas, "L'Etat autoritaire: Essai sur les formes actuelles de domination impérialiste," L'Homme et la Société, 18 (1970); C. Mendes, "Sistema político e modelos de poder no Brasil," Dados, 2 (1966), "O governo castello branco: Paradigma e prognose," Dados, 3 (1967), and "Elite de poder: Democracia e desenvolvimento," Dados, 5 (1969); F. Cardoso, Cuestiones de sociología del desarrollo (Editorial Universitaria, 1968), pp. 106ff. See also the discussion on the emergence of a "technobureaucracy" in Cardoso and Faleto, p. 156. But to my knowledge, the elite subset delimited by the concept of "technocratic roles," and its political import in contemporary South America, has not yet received the systematic study that it deserves.

[49]On role expectations see T.R. Sarbin and V.L. Allen, "Role Theory" in G. Lindzey and E. Aronson, eds., The Handbook of Social Psychology, Vol. I (Reading, Mass.: Addison-Wesley, 1968). Writing about "fascination effects" of more developed countries over Latin American elites, Torcuato di Tella points to the type of problems examined here (see "Populism . . .," p. 48).

is what dimensions of the role-model will be adjusted (and in what directions) in the modernizing situation.

Even the specific technical expertise is more dependent on the social context than is usually recognized. Techniques are "adequate" only in certain contexts. If, as frequently happens, the role-incumbent's social context differs substantially from the one presupposed by the techniques he learned, his specific technical knowledge may be of little use. As would be expected from what has been said here, the most casual acquaintance with incumbents of technocratic roles in modernizing contexts reveals severe frustration stemming from a "failure" of the context to meet their expectations. This situation can threaten the achievement of the rewards they are "normally due" according to their role-models.

Their frustration can easily be channeled into a drive to reshape the social context in forms that, it is hoped, will be more congenial to the learned expertise and the reward aspirations of these individuals--a course which can easily be rationalized. Their consciousness of their expertise convinces incumbents of technocratic roles that, by molding the social context to serve their own aspirations, they would at the same time improve the social situation. At this point the interaction of roles with the other structural levels is crucial: I hypothesize that the extent to which frustration by incumbents of technocratic roles may be channeled into political action aimed at reshaping the social context is a multiplicative function of the degree of penetration (density and scope) of these roles in a modernizing situation.

High modernization (including one of its components, the high industrialization of modern national centers) involves the emergence of more technocratic roles in more social sectors and activities. Artisan industries are replaced by complex, highly bureaucratized organizations; technically trained military officers replace the old barracks generals; modern marketing, information, publicity, and communication services spread; more potential "planners" and civil servants yearn for governments that would follow their advice and grant them effective decision-making power.[50] On the basis of the data in Chapter I, it can quite confidently be asserted that, at the level of productive-industrial processes and their closely related activities, high levels of South American modernization entail a high degree of penetration of technocratic roles in the modern centers. The

[50]Besides the sources cited in the preceding footnote, see J.L. de Imaz, "El 'técnico' y algunos sistemas políticos latinoamericanos," unpublished paper (1970).

point to be stressed here is that the possibilities of linkages among incumbents of these roles across the sectors in which they are operating increase as a multiple function of the overall penetration of these roles. Before the 1964 and 1966 coups in Brazil and Argentina, business and military academies became common meeting places for incumbents at the "top" of large business organizations and the military.[51] Several equivalents of _Time_ and _Fortune_ magazines appeared, providing further intercommunication among these role incumbents and lending them social prestige vis-à-vis other social sectors. Numerous publicists diffused the outlook of what came to be called the "modern" or "technocratic right."[52]

---

[51]On the linkages established in pre-coup Brazil through the Escola Superior de Guerra and the big-business IPES, see Stepan, _The Military . . .,_ and Skidmore. For the pre-coup Argentine period, see Chapter III below and the works cited there. It is noteworthy that the evolution of military institutions (including the degree of penetration of technocratic roles) seems to be more independent of the social context (and more directly dependent on U.S. policy) than other sectors are. Thus, in the 1960's the Peruvian military achieved a degree of technical training and penetration of technocratic roles not inferior to the Brazilian and the Argentine military. See, on this aspect and on the political impact of CAEM (the Peruvian higher military training institution), Einaudi and Stepan, North, and Einaudi, "The Peruvian Military: A Summary Political Analysis" (Rand Corporation, 1969). But, as I will argue below, the lower level of modernization of the Peruvian social context (which meant less penetration of technocratic roles in other social sectors) determined that the political intervention of the Peruvian military took place under a different coalition and for very different goals than in Brazil and Argentina.

[52]These statements (and those that follow in this subsection) are phrased in the general terms that correspond to the type of information (mostly impressionistic and to a large extent derived from my own "participant-observer" experience) from which they stem. It is only by research explicitly geared to test them that it would be possible to answer many questions that my formulation raises but cannot answer. For example, it would be necessary to know what percentage of those with technical expertise in a highly modernized context are predisposed in the directions suggested and, especially, to actively supporting an attempt to implant an "excluding" political system. (It is my impression that these percentages are significantly higher among incumbents at the top of business organizations and the military than among governmental técnicos, but that the scores are high in all cases.) Second, to what extent does a "halo effect" operate, by which persons

The effects of the penetration of technocratic roles are multiplicative: greater scope and density leads to the emergence of a wide network of institutions and channels of communication across the social sectors in which the roles most deeply penetrate--the military, large and technologically complex business organizations, and governmental areas of economic decision-making and planning.[53] At lower levels of modernization the lesser penetration of technocratic roles hinders the formation of these important linkages, even though individual incumbents have the same training as those operating in more modernized contexts.

Linkages promote mutual recognition. Whatever the social sector in which they operate, the incumbents of technocratic roles share many important characteristics. Their role-models, and through them their basic expectations about the "proper" state of the social context, originate in the same societies. Their training stresses a "technical" problem-solving approach. Emotional issues are nonsense; the ambiguities of bargaining and politics are hindrances to "rational" solutions; and conflict is by definition "dysfunctional." Their underlying "maps" of social reality are similar. That which is "efficient" is good, and efficient outcomes are those that can be straightforwardly measured; the rest is noise that a "rational" decision-maker should strive

---

lacking their backgrounds are attracted by the social prestige and the image of efficiency of incumbents of technocratic roles, and on that basis are willing to support the latters' political stands? (This is where the _Time_ and _Fortune_ equivalents, as well as more elementary training institutions, seem to make an important contribution.) Third, to what extent is that "halo effect" indicated by the adoption of terms of the technocratic jargon (most of them in English) that are barely understood by most users? (This is a topic of which the Argentine humorist "Landrú" has made much use.) Fourth, what are the interrelations between the interests of the sectors that technocratic roles have most densely penetrated, on the one hand, and the predispositions that are hypothesized here to stem from their incumbency, on the other hand? (I will return to this important point below.)

[53] It is perhaps worth recalling here that, according to the definition given in Chapter I, the concept of "technocratic roles" applies to those individuals who, as an important part of their daily business, _apply_ modern technology. This requires fairly prolonged training and continuing attention to developments in the field of technical expertise, but should not be confused with what might be called "scientific roles," which are primarily concerned with expanding knowledge in particular fields--not with the application of what is more or less received wisdom in a specialty.

to eliminate from his decision premises. The texture of social
reality is radically (in some cases, one is tempted to say "bru-
tally") simplified. Such simplification may not be denied, but
is seen as an indispensable requisite for being able to manipulate
reality in the direction of "efficiency." The resistance of so
many problems to solution through efficiency considerations alone
tends to be interpreted as an indication of how much "progress"
in formal rationality remains to be achieved. (This may be an
oversimplified depiction of a mentality rarely found in its pure
state, but it seems to me that it corresponds quite closely to
the position taken by many technocratic role-incumbents in their
appraisal of the pre-coup Argentine and Brazilian social contexts.
It corresponds even more closely to the conceptions that inspired
the socio-economic policies that immediately followed the 1964
and 1966 coups.)

There are also important similarities in the career patterns of most incumbents of technocratic roles. They become members of bureaucratic elites who arrive at positions of social
eminence after successful organizational careers.[54] Combined perhaps with more "central"[55] predispositions, it might be that such
career patterns would reinforce desires for an orderly world in
which levels of authority are clearly defined and where policy
is decided by those who have presumably gained special expertise.

Mutual recognition is promoted by the development of a
common "language." The old scorn of unlearned military, ignorant
businessmen, and humanistic intellectuals for one another has
undergone substantial modifications. Many individuals in each of
these categories have gained a common technocratic background and
have discovered that they share a common technical language (or
"jargon"). This facilitates communication across specialties,

---

[54]An interesting subject for speculation is the degree to which
the findings of modern organization theorists can be utilized
for illuminating the political behavior of technocratic role-
incumbents (see esp. J. March and H. Simon, Organizations [New
York: Wiley, 1958]; J. Cyert and J. March, A Behavioral Theory
of the Firm [Englewood Cliffs: Prentice-Hall, 1963]; J. Thompson,
Organizations in Action [New York: McGraw-Hill, 1967]; and M.
Crozier, Le Phénomène bureaucratique [Paris: Editions du Seuil,
1963]). For a preliminary speculative effort, see G. O'Donnell,
"High Modernization and Military Coups: Theory, Comparisons, and
the Argentine Case" in D. Apter, ed., Embourgeoisement and Radi-
calization in Latin America (forthcoming); Spanish version in
Desarrollo Económico, October-December 1972.

[55]Milton Rokeach, The Open and the Closed Mind (New York: Basic
Books, 1960).

but makes communication more difficult with other social sectors lacking this common background. Increasingly, common coding and decoding of information across technocratic roles fosters their cohesion, but by the same token further isolates them from other social sectors and their norms, preferences, and demands.[56]

Mutual recognition and a common "language" promote a heightened assessment of their combined capabilities by incumbents of technocratic roles. The more they penetrate social sectors, the more likely they are to believe that their combined expertise can ensure effective problem-solving throughout a broad range of social problems. In less modernized contexts, the necessarily more isolated incumbents of technocratic roles may withdraw from political involvement, or since a coalition centered around these roles would be too weak to be effective, may search for alliances with other groups for channeling their political action. But in situations of high modernization that have resulted in mass praetorianism, a coup coalition[57] is likely to be formed with the

---

[56] In my opinion this is a central problem for consideration in a fully developed theory of modernization. The strong positivist bias still prevailing in sociology and political science has isolated these disciplines from recent philosophical and linguistic work on the meaning of signs and symbols in the texture of social life. On the other hand, philosophers and linguists until now have shown little interest in tracing the social-structural correlates of their findings. Major exceptions to these regrettable disciplinary disconnections are Lévi-Strauss's social anthropology and the work of David Apter, Clifford Geertz, and Harold Lasswell. Significant recent contributions are Verón, and D. Bennet, "Ideology as Language: A Strategy for Research," unpublished paper, Yale University (1970). The emergence of new labels for old phenomena (e.g., "social unrest" becoming "subversion"), the emergence of a technocratic "dialect" (i.e., "the particular linguistic competence of a particular grouping of people"--D. Bennet), with its indication of changed maps of social reality, its indication of (and effects upon) changed social structure, the linkages that it promotes and those that it eliminates, and above all the complex patterns of interrelation among these dimensions are an area of investigation that the study of modernization cannot ignore. Speculation about this problem, in some respects similar to my own, can be found in M. Landau, "Linkage, Coding and Intermediacy: A Strategy for Institution Building," Journal of Comparative Administration, II, No. 4 (1971).

[57] As used here, the term "coup coalition" refers to the military officers and civilian personnel who directly participate in creating the political conditions conducive to a military coup, as well as organizing, setting the main goals, and executing it.

predominant participation of incumbents of technocratic roles. These individuals have already achieved dense penetration (and consequently a high degree of control) of crucial social sectors. Because of this, they are far more likely than in less modernized contexts to be highly confident of their capabilities for governing effectively. The basic goal of these role-incumbents will be a quite drastic reshaping of the social context, aimed at the creation of conditions that will permit much more extensive application of their expertise, and the expansion of influence of the social sectors they have most densely penetrated.[58]

Operating in a different social context, technocratic role-incumbents in situations of high modernization are likely to act in contrast to their usually politically liberal role-models, and to constitute the core of the coalition that will attempt the establishment of an authoritarian, "excluding" political system. The usual verbal allegiance to political democracy is apparently the weakest component in their role-models. It is easily abandoned to promote an authoritarian political system that will (it is believed) facilitate more effective performance by the role-incumbents.[59]

The following hypotheses can now be formulated:

Hypothesis 2: The transmission of technical expertise from advanced to modernizing societies is only one aspect of a more complex phenomenon--i.e., the transmission of role-models,

---

[58]There is little doubt that one consequence of the modernization processes in Argentina and Brazil has been a significant increase in the political and economic weight of the social sectors (the armed forces, large modern firms, and the national government) that technocratic roles have most densely penetrated. This is an important link between the social structure and the role levels. It is tempting to interpret this link by postulating that factors at the role level merely "express" the objective interests of social sectors (particularly classes) and organizations. This is a fairly common basis for interpretation, especially in some varieties of Marxism, but it is my impression that the causal processes are far more complicated, with both sets of factors (at the role level and the social-structural level) making independent and important contributions.

[59]Of course, this shift produces profound psychological dissonance. Dissonance is evidenced in the repeated Argentine and Brazilian assurances since their coups that the resulting political systems were the only ways to achieve "authentic democracy" in the future. In Chapter III, I suggest that this method for reducing dissonance is far from new.

which include career and social expectations derived from the originating societies.

Hypothesis 3: Role-performance (including the application of learned expertise), which is highly dependent on the state of the social context, cannot be carried out in the same way as in the originating societies. The consequent frustration of incumbents of technocratic roles is very likely to be channeled into political action.

Proposition 13: High modernization entails a substantial increase in the density and scope of penetration of technocratic roles in the modern centers of each national unit.[60]

Hypothesis 4: The greater scope and density of penetration of technocratic roles multiplicatively facilitates communications and inter-institutional linkages among the incumbents of these roles.

Hypothesis 5: The greater the penetration and number of linkages, the more favorable the assessment of their combined social problem-solving capabilities by the incumbents of technocratic roles and the greater their degree of control of crucial social sectors and activities.

Hypothesis 6: If high modernization results in mass praetorianism, the assessment by technocratic role-incumbents of their combined capabilities is likely to generate a coup coalition that has these incumbents at its core. This coalition will aim at reshaping the social context in ways envisioned as more favorable for the application of technocratic expertise and for the expansion of the influence of the social sectors that the role-incumbents have most densely penetrated--i.e., an "excluding," authoritarian system.[61]

There is ample evidence of the numerous linkages established among incumbents of technocratic roles during the periods of Argentine and Brazilian praetorianism, as well as of their crucial influence in the 1964 and 1966 coups.[62] Their coup coalitions could count on the acquiescence of many sectors for the first "round" of decisions, which included the exclusion of the popular sector, the postponement of popular demands, and the

---

[60] See Chapter I above.

[61] In the next section the characteristics of the political system that results from this process will be analyzed.

[62] See esp. footnotes 2, 31, 33, 48, 49, and 51 of this chapter.

closing of the electoral channels of political participation.
Once in power, the coalitions made a second "round" of decisions,
and the policy implications of the coups were spelled out. Then,
many of the original supporters of (or acquiescers to) the coups
discovered that the choice of a new political system over continued mass praetorianism was not a very happy one. The first round
of decisions is related to the inauguration of the post-1964 and
-1966 Argentine and Brazilian political systems, while the second
round is related to their performance and subsequent evolution.
Strictly speaking, it is the first phase only that falls within
the scope of this book; it will be the subject-matter of the
section immediately following. But in this section I will yield
to the temptation to speculate briefly about the second phase.

Bureaucratic-Authoritarian Political Systems in Contemporary South America

The exclusion of an activated popular sector can sometimes
be achieved with psychological or economic payoffs; otherwise,
the exclusion requires the application of strong and systematic
coercive measures. This has been the experience of the authoritarian political systems emerging in highly modernized contexts
which have attempted to exclude, and eventually to deactivate,
the popular sector.

Robert Dahl has proposed a heuristically useful model of
the emergence of "polyarchy" ("political democracy," as used here)
as a function of decreasing costs of tolerance and increasing
costs of suppression ("exclusion," as used here).[63] As social
differentiation proceeds, more and more autonomous groups appear,
and it becomes harder for the government to suppress them--or for
them to suppress each other. At this stage a political system
which accepts the legitimacy of diverging interests and actors,
and regulates them peacefully, is likely to emerge. Dahl's model
ends at this point, but for the sake of my argument I have extended it further--see Figure 3.

In the right hand third of the model depicted in Figure
3, social differentiation has increased with further modernization, and with its increase the costs of suppression (i.e., exclusion) have risen steadily. But social integration has lagged,
and praetorianism has resulted, such that the costs of toleration
have risen even more rapidly. In this situation, it is likely
that suppression will be attempted again, but now at a much higher
cost than at any previous stage.

---

[63] Polyarchy, Participation and Opposition (New Haven: Yale
University Press, 1971), pp. 15-16.

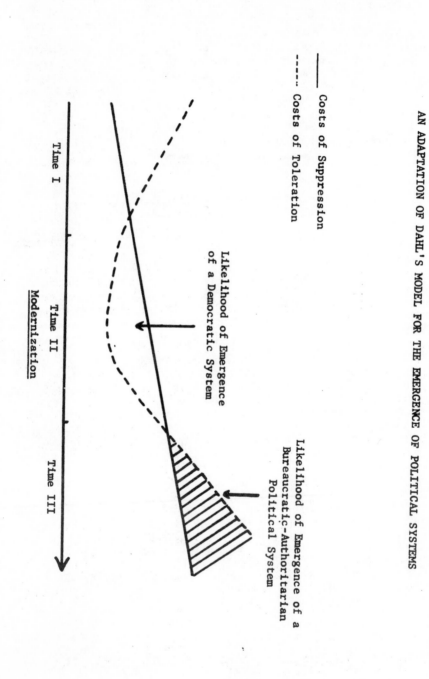

Figure 3

AN ADAPTATION OF DAHL'S MODEL FOR THE EMERGENCE OF POLITICAL SYSTEMS

Proposition 14: Political pluralization is the political expression of social differentiation. The levels of political
activation (especially of the popular sector) are likely to
increase with differentiation and pluralization. Given such
political activation in a highly modernized context, mass
praetorianism is likely to result. In that situation, the
exclusion, and eventually the political deactivation, of the
popular sector will be attempted through the use of a high
degree of coercion (as well as the inauguration of an authoritarian political system to apply it).[64]

With reference to the "demands-performance gap" discussed
earlier (see pp. 70ff.), in principle governmental action could
be taken to meet any unfulfilled demands. But since on the basis
of even the most optimistic assessment, only slow improvements in
performance could be expected, immediate political action would
be taken to block demands that are perceived as excessive, given
the state of the social context. First, political parties and
elections would be eliminated, and with them the political personnel who were particularly sensitive to the demands of the popular
sector. Second, the "domestication" of the labor unions, the most
important organizational channel for the formulation of popular
demands, would be attempted by cooptation of the leaders and by
coercion. Third, an attempt would be made to bureaucratically
"encapsulate" most social sectors, in order to maximize control
over them. This would be accomplished by ensuring that the sectors were politically represented by organizations whose legal
existence was dependent upon government authorization. Bargaining
and interest representation would be limited to leaders at the top
of these organizations, and spontaneous modes of demand-formulation, as well as dissent, would have no legitimate place under
the new political conditions.

The proponents of these policies assume that the exclusion of the popular sector and its demands would make possible a

---

[64]It is of some interest to compare this proposition with the
"optimistic equation" discussed in Chapter I above. In the situation analyzed here, socio-economic changes have resulted in increased political pluralization (i.e., more political actors
interrelated in more ways), but the tendency is not toward political democracy, the general acceptance of the existing set of
political actors, and the peaceful adjustment of conflicts.
Rather it is toward the implantation of an authoritarian system,
the rejection of the existing set of political authors, and the
exercise of a high degree of coercion. Is it possible to consider this pattern an accidental or transitory "deviation"? In
the pages that follow I will bring to light elements to strengthen
the belief that the answer to this question must be negative.

reconversion of the socio-economic structure that would stimulate
economic growth by a general increase in efficiency and by allowing political hegemony and capital accumulation in the more "dynamic" sectors. Political democracy and wider distribution of
wealth and power would <u>then</u> be possible.[65] Of course, the main
beneficiaries of the earlier accumulation of political power and
socio-economic resources would be the sectors most densely penetrated by the coup coalition of incumbents of technocratic roles--
the more "efficient" producers (i.e., larger, more modern firms,
the armed forces, and, to a lesser extent, the government). As
will be seen below, some of these aims were not achieved, but
along with the high degree of coercion required if the authoritarian efforts were to succeed, they played an important part in
determining the characteristics of the post-1964 Brazilian and
the post-1966 Argentine political systems.

These political systems have a theoretical import extending beyond the specific Brazilian and Argentine cases. In his
broad-ranging study in historical sociology, Barrington Moore
finds, in addition to bourgeois and communist revolutions, a third
historical path toward industrialization.[66] This path involves a
coalition of the public bureaucracy and the propertied sectors
(including a subordinate industrial bourgeoisie) against the
peasantry and an emerging urban proletariat. It is a conservative
reaction to "the strains of advancing industrialization," to "a
weak push toward parliamentary democracy," and to the entry of
the "masses" into the political scene. This "third path" is not
unlike what has occurred in Argentina and Brazil.

Moore deals with countries that have come to play an
important role in international affairs, but in a recent paper
Andrew Janos studies weaker, more dependent countries that bear
illuminating similarities to the South American cases analyzed

---

[65]This might be considered an extremely naïve (or cynical?)
version of the "optimistic equation."

[66]<u>Social Origins of Dictatorship and Democracy</u> (Boston: Beacon
Press, 1966). For another important study that suggests many
points similar to Moore's and to the considerations proposed here,
see Alexander Gerschenkron, <u>Economic Backwardness in Historical
Perspective</u> (Cambridge: Harvard University Press, 1962). See
also A. Organski, <u>The Stages of Political Development</u> (New York:
Knopf, 1965). The first detailed analysis of a historical situation marked by defensive political reactions of the propertied
sectors was by Marx; see <u>El 18 Brumario de Luis Bonaparte</u> (Bar-
celona: Ediciones Ariel, 1968), which is still a source of
valuable insights.

here.[67] Janos deals with the Eastern European countries of the 1930's, many of which became what he calls "bureaucratic regimes." Like contemporary Argentina and Brazil, these countries had advanced well beyond stereotypical "traditional" societies, they had relatively large modern centers, there was high political activation of the urban popular sector, developmental bottlenecks had appeared, social-structural rigidities had persisted longer than in the earlier modernizing countries, and social integration had lagged far behind social differentiation. Eastern European "bureaucratic regimes" were based on a coalition of military, high-level civil servants, big businessmen, and sectors of the traditional landowning strata, with the initial support of a large dependent urban middle class. This coalition attempted to consolidate traditional forms of domination in the rural areas and to deactivate the urban popular sector. In this way the "bureaucratic regimes" tried to accelerate industrialization and to minimize the chances of social revolution.

Janos points out that these regimes were distinguished from those of Italy and Germany during the same period in that they lacked the mobilizational force and ideological appeal of the latter. He attributes this difference to the fact that the elites of the "bureaucratic regimes" (as is true in the Argentine and Brazilian cases under study here) belonged to already well-established sectors of their societies.

There is little doubt that the present political system of Spain can be categorized as a "bureaucratic regime," even though the events that preceded its inauguration differed in several important respects from events in the Eastern European countries.[68] The present-day system of Greece is strikingly similar to such a regime in all the aspects discussed here.[69] The Brazilian and Argentine political systems inaugurated in 1964 and 1966, respectively, also belong in this category. All these political systems are authoritarian systems emerging from conditions of high modernization. It is impossible to say, without systematic comparative research, but it is a disquieting possibility that such authoritarianisms might be a more likely outcome than political

---

[67]"The One-Party State and Social Mobilization: East Europe between the Wars" in S. Huntington and C. Moore, eds., Authoritarian Politics in Modern Societies: The Dynamics of Established One-Party Systems (New York: Basic Books, 1970).

[68]See esp. Juan Linz, "An Authoritarian Regime: Spain" in S. Rokkan, ed., Mass Politics (New York: Free Press, 1970).

[69]See Keith Legg, Politics in Modern Greece (Stanford: Stanford University Press, 1969).

democracy as other countries achieve or approach high modernization.

Two authors--David Apter and Juan Linz--have made important contributions to the study of this type of political system. Though Apter's analysis is at a relatively high level of abstraction while Linz's analysis is derived mainly from his examination of the specific case of Spain, a comparison of Apter's "bureaucratic system"[70] and Linz's "authoritarian regime."[71] reveals that they are referring to the same empirical phenomenon. Apter's bureaucratic system emphasizes control and vertical authority arrangements, operating by means of predominantly instrumental norms (i.e., without consummatory, mobilizational ideologies). Linz's authoritarian regime is characterized by limited pluralism and low ideological content, as well as by attempts at political deactivation and the development of relative autonomy of government vis-à-vis social groups. Linz points out that these regimes come to power "after periods of considerable organized political strife, lack of consensus under democratic governments and aborted revolutions."[72]

If these systems obviously are not political democracies, they also have characteristics that clearly distinguish them from totalitarianism. They lack solid legitimation and a comprehensive ideology; they do little to indoctrinate the population; they prefer political apathy and accept "limited pluralism."[73] The basic paradigm discussed in Chapter I, as well as the dichotomy "democracy-totalitarianism," assumes that authoritarianisms are only transitions toward more definitive or more stable types of political systems; this has made it difficult to recognize the theoretical import of specific authoritarianisms. As Linz says:

> We prefer for purposes of analysis to reject the idea of a continuum from democracy to totalitarianism, and to stress the distinctive nature of authoritarian regimes. Unless we examine the distinctive nature of authoritarian regimes, the conditions under which they emerge, the conception of power held by those who shape them, regimes which are not clearly democratic or totalitarian will be treated merely as deviations from those ideal types and will not be studied systematically and comparatively.[74]

---

[70]Apter, Politics . . ., Conceptual . . ., and Choice . . . .

[71]Linz, "An Authoritarian . . . ."

[72]Ibid.; emphasis added.

[73]Ibid.   [74]Ibid.

I will call the political system that was implanted in
Brazil in 1964 and in Argentina in 1966 "bureaucratic-authoritarian." This awkward term is in part used to indicate its
derivation from Apter's and Linz's contributions,[75] but also
because it facilitates the use of the term "authoritarian" as
a genus that includes other types of non-democratic South American political systems associated with lower levels of modernization.[76] The term "bureaucratic" suggests the crucial features
that are specific to authoritarian systems of high modernization:
the growth of organizational strength of many social sectors, the
governmental attempts at control by "encapsulation," the career
patterns and power-bases of most incumbents of technocratic roles,
and the pivotal role played by large (public and private) bureau-
cracies.[77]

---

[75]In his study of Brazilian politics, Philippe Schmitter (Interest Conflict . . .) adopts Linz's "authoritarian" type for
characterizing the present political system.

[76]The other South American authoritarianisms, which will be
briefly discussed below, will be categorized as "populist" and
"traditional."

[77]The decision to exclude the Middle American countries from
the focus of this study has meant excluding México, a country
that with respect to all the indicators used in Chapter I clearly
belongs in the same group of high modernization as Argentina and
Brazil (with a degree of intra-country heterogeneity similar to
the latter). In my view the Mexican case highlights the importance of a phenomenon not present in Argentina and Brazil: the
entrance into high modernization with a high degree of legitimacy
of the political system and generalized allegiance of the population at large (for survey data on this point see G. Almond and
S. Verba, The Civic Culture [Princeton: Princeton University
Press, 1963], and the excellent discussion by Robert Scott,
"Mexico: The Established Revolution" in L. Pye and S. Verba,
eds., Political Culture and Political Development [Princeton:
Princeton University Press, 1965]).
Such legitimacy and allegiance--stemming from a revolutionary
process that had not occurred in Argentina and Brazil--allowed a
high level of institutionalization of the Partido Revolucionario
Institucional (PRI), through which it has been possible to achieve
a high degree of "encapsulation" of the Mexican popular sector.
(The degree to which such encapsulation has been achieved with
other social sectors is disputed among specialists, but it seems
clear that it holds for the popular sector; see R. Scott, Mexican
Government in Transition [Urbana: University of Illinois Press,
1959], and the survey of the state of this question in M. Croan,
"Is Mexico the Future of East Europe?: Institutional Adaptability

The Workings of the Argentine and Brazilian Bureaucratic-Authoritarian Systems

For a first approximation to this subject-matter, it may be useful to focus for a moment on the situation faced by the Brazilian and Argentine systems in the approximately two-year period immediately following the 1964 and 1966 coups--especially on the socio-economic policies most closely associated with Minister Campos of Brazil and Minister Krieger Vasena of Argentina.

Ideological legitimation by corporatist ideologies (which would have facilitated attempts at "encapsulating" social sectors) may have been feasible in the 1930's, but it is no longer possible today. Developmental bottlenecks and policies that favored capital accumulation in the more "dynamic" or "efficient" sectors produced declines in real wages and salaries in both

---

and Political Change in Comparative Perspective" in S. Huntington and C. Moore, eds.)

These same factors have contributed in the Mexican case to the stability of governments and tenure in public office, which is to be contrasted with the extreme instability of the high modernization periods in Argentina and Brazil, and which can be interpreted as greatly facilitating more effective public decision-making and a longer-range horizon of decisions for public policy. In terms of my analysis, the Mexican revolutionary heritage made possible the entry into high modernization with a low level of popular political activation and demands, most of them channeled through established and largely "encapsulating" political institutions. By the same token, the demands-performance and differentiation-integration "gaps" have been far less pronounced than in Argentina and Brazil, and have not led to mass praetorianism.

But it should be noted that the consequence of these factors has not been markedly different in terms of political system type and public policies. Rather, the legitimacy of the political, system and the low level of popular political activation in México has made it possible for the policies of authoritarianism at high modernization to be pursued at relatively (in comparison to Argentina and Brazil) low cost and high efficiency. Several comments should be made to clarify this statement.

First, only by "conceptual stretching" can the Mexican system be classified as a political democracy. In spite of the broad allegiance that makes electoral defeat unlikely, there are abundant indications that there is no chance for genuine political opposition.

Second, it is clear that "encapsulation" has advanced much further in the Mexican case than under the Argentine and Brazilian bureaucratic-authoritarian systems. An important consequence has

countries, as well as in the shares of wages and salaries in their GNP's.[78] Under such conditions, there were few psychological or economic payoffs with which to "ease" the exclusion and the attempted political deactivation of the popular sector. Hence coercion[79] became widespread--particularly after intellectuals and university students added their determined opposition to the socio-economic policies of the new governments and their efforts to exclude and deactivate the popular sector.

The limited psychological and economic payoffs were reflected in popular unrest, terrorism, and manifold indications of growing general disaffection. Even among those sectors that had originally supported the coups, many urban empleados discovered that they were not faring any better than before. But even more important for the dynamic of these systems was the inter-industry cleavage that emerged around considerations of efficiency versus nationalism and maintenance of levels of employment. This cleavage had important repercussions within the military, which by and large favored "efficiency" but not without "nationalistic" deviations (much more marked in Argentina than in Brazil). As noted before, the roots of this conflict between efficiency and nationalism lie in the great difficulties faced by domestically

---

been the almost complete "domestication" of Mexican labor unions-- an important requisite for the "success" of authoritarian policies and for achieving (maintaining, in the Mexican case) a low level of political activation of the popular sector.

Third, in terms of allocation of resources, México is not more equalitarian than Brazil and certainly much less so than Argentina. Furthermore, the trend since the 1950's has been (as in the other Latin American situations of high modernization) toward income redistribution against the interests of the popular sector and in favor of the more "dynamic" entrepreneurial sectors (see, among others, UN-ECLA, The Process . . ., "Income . . .," and Estudio . . .; M. Singer, Growth, Equality and the Mexican Experience [Austin: University of Texas Press, 1969]; and P. González Casanova, La democracia en México [México DF, 1965]).

[78]For Brazil (data on purchasing power of Sao Paulo workers), see the publications of the Departamento Intersindical de Estatistica e Estudos Socio-Economicos (DIEESE). For Argentina, see Ministerio de Economía, Informe Económico, several issues since 1967.

[79]The distinction between psychological, utilitarian, and coercive power assets has been proposed by Amitai Etzioni, A Comparative Analysis of Complex Organizations (New York: Free Press, 1961), and W. Gamson, Power and Discontent (Homewood: Dorsey Press, 1968).

owned industry in achieving more vertical integration, and in the overwhelmingly foreign ownership of those private firms that have the necessary technology and financial backing.[80] The implementation of "efficientist," "denationalizing" policies was bound to meet most resistance precisely in the two most modernized South American countries in which domestic industry had spread furthest, insofar as these policies threatened to eliminate domestic entrepreneurs from the more attractive industrial and financial activities. Some military officers and civilian governmental técnicos sought to strengthen the public sector--in part to increase control over other political actors, in part as a way out of the industrialization dilemma. For many reasons that need not be considered here, this effort had very little success as a solution to the industrialization dilemma, but its effects in terms of further centralization of decision-making and further bureaucratization accentuated the isolation of the ruling coalition from most of the other social sectors. The attempts to enlarge the size and the role of the public sector have been a source of serious strain among the set of incumbents of technocratic roles: they have clashed with the demands of big business representatives for further "liberalization" of the economy that would make possible its more complete domination by the more "efficient" producers.

As a consequence, the situation of the peripheral regions, of the popular sector, and of parts of the middle class deteriorated. In addition, the domestic capitalist sector decreased its participation in many activities. The fairly broad initial support for the governments that immediately followed the 1964 and 1966 coups eroded pari passu. The period after the exclusion of the popular sector promoted growth mostly through the hypertrophy of a limited private sector attempting to supply an increasingly skewed composition of consumers' demand.

A record of performance that is at best mixed, the accentuation of an unfortunate distribution of resources, the lack of ideological and international legitimation, the long-range consequences of economic concentration, and the failure to create

---

[80]It is worth noting that this issue became genuinely salient only in the two South American countries that had advanced furthest in modernization, as a quick perusal of Argentine and Brazilian publications since the late 1950's and early 1960's reveals. See the discussion of the problem "estatismo-gran empresa" in Cardoso and Faleto, pp. 116ff. For official publications and reports of planning commissions that discuss this problem (with very inconclusive results), see, e.g., "Introducción," Plan Nacional de Desarrollo, 1970-1974 (1970, mimeo); J. Villanueva, "El problema del desarrollo industrial dependiente," CIAS, December 1969; and A. Canitrot, "Nuestro desarrollo económico: Conflictos e interrogantes," Criterio, No. 1606 (1970).

viable political institutions--all these factors raise basic questions about the evolution of these political systems.

This is perhaps a good point to note that there have been considerable differences in the performance and evolution of the Argentine and Brazilian political systems. While there is little doubt that in Argentina the post-coup political experiment has been a failure in all possible senses (including from the point of view of the ruling coalitions), in Brazil in recent years there has been a decline in active opposition, along with high yearly rates of aggregate economic growth, reduced inflation, and indications that part of the huge concentration of wealth that has been generated has spilled over into some segments of the urban middle class. Both countries have seen attempts by some military officers to appeal to domestic entrepreneurs and organized labor, using nationalistic pleas and promises of protectionist and more distributionist policies, in their efforts to reconstruct the political system along populist lines. These attempts have failed-- and if the theses of this study are correct, their chances for success are slim.

Until now the focus of my analysis has been on the factors that in Argentina and Brazil led to the military coups that attempted (and, at least in the short term, achieved) the implantation of bureaucratic-authoritarian political systems. For such a focus it has seemed sufficient to use a set of concepts and variables at a fairly high level of generality which reflected important similarities in the Argentine and Brazilian centers. A different problem (or, to use the jargon, a different "dependent variable") is to explain the differences in the performances and degrees of consolidation of these two political systems. This task cannot be undertaken here, but I cannot resist the temptation to speculate briefly about the main reasons for these differences. In terms of strategy of analysis, what is required for such an explanation is the examination of factors more specific than those used for establishing the typological similarity of Argentina and Brazil. More specific analyses would enable us to make distinctions among units within the same general type. The preliminary typological task undertaken here is useful for such purposes in a double sense--first, for drawing marked distinctions across types (e.g., Argentina and Brazil vis-à-vis the other two groups of South American countries); second, for underscoring subsequent identification of specific differences among countries of the same type, which facilitates comparative analysis within the same type.[81]

---

[81]Gerschenkron makes some illuminating comments on this methodological issue. His strategy of analysis is analogous to the one

In this matter it is necessary to stress again the crucial importance of governmental coercion for bureaucratic-authoritarian "success" in excluding and deactivating the popular sector, as well as for enforcing decisions tending to facilitate economic concentration in the more "dynamic" or "efficient" sectors, and for repressing the opposition of intellectuals and university students. For reasons to be spelled out below, the crucial period for the use of coercion seems to be the period closely following the inauguration of the bureaucratic-authoritarian system.[82]

---

used here: first, a discussion of what the author thinks is the erroneous conception that there is only one basic process of industrialization (in the present study, the assumption that equivalent causal processes lead toward political democracy); second, the proposal of various distinctive types or patterns extracted, at a high level of generality, from the historical experience of several countries. Gerschenkron comments: "Once the dogmatic belief in the unavoidable similarity of the processes of industrialization has been discarded, the discovery of a certain amount of variation requires little effort. In fact, the problem consists in restraining oneself from finding too much variation" (Continuity in History [Cambridge: Harvard University Press, 1968], translated by this author from the Spanish edition [Ediciones Ariel, 1970], p. 173). This point is well taken. Once the simplifying assumption of one fundamental pattern is discarded, it becomes a crucial analytical problem to decide at what level of generality similarities among units can be established which will allow them to be classed within general types. Otherwise, the tendency would be toward an inventory of country-by-country specifics, with no criteria for comparison to guide future analysis. As a consequence, each case would be one type, the criteria for defining each case would not be homogenous across all units of analysis, and comparisons of the units (or countries, in this case) qua units would be impossible. The use of criteria at a level of generality that makes possible the inclusion of several cases within the same general type permits comparative work at the same level of generality as the types established (the strategy followed here), and is a useful preliminary for highlighting and controlling the more specific factors that, at a lower level of generality, facilitate study of the differences that distinguish the units that have been classed within the same general type.

[82] Even though the events that preceded the inauguration of the Spanish bureaucratic-authoritarian system were different in many important respects from those in the cases being considered here, the regime took full advantage of the destruction of opposition and widespread political apathy that resulted from the Spanish Civil War. The Greek case needs no comment in this respect.

At that point the use of coercion (especially that geared to effectively exclude and deactivate the popular sector) is required for achieving the extreme concentration of wealth and power epitomized in the socio-economic policies of Ministers Campos of Brazil and Krieger Vasena of Argentina. The Brazilian bureaucratic-authoritarian system was able (and willing) to apply the degree of coercion required to achieve the complete political exclusion and deactivation of its popular sector. On the other hand, the Argentine bureaucratic-authoritarian system implemented its policies in a context in which the popular sector retained a high level of political activation, even though the sector's main channels of political access were suppressed.

To determine what may have led to this difference, it is necessary to recall a factor that was alluded to when discussing the fact that both Argentina and Brazil belong to the "South American high modernization" type--i.e., the different degrees of intra-country heterogeneity. The big "peripheral" area of Brazil has always provided a huge labor supply that has had very debilitating effects on its labor unions. On the other hand, the Argentine economy has functioned for long periods with full employment.[83] Thus, even though both countries have a similar concentration of unionized and industrial workers in the big urban centers, a careful examination shows that in their pre-coup periods there were already important differences in the strength and autonomy of the political activation of their popular sectors. As a consequence, it could be assumed that to achieve similar results in the political deactivation of the popular sector, the Argentine bureaucratic-authoritarian system would have to apply a significantly higher degree of coercion than the high degree applied in the Brazilian case.[84]

---

[83]This was true until 1959-1960; since then there has been a permanent pool of urban unemployment in Argentina. This has had a debilitating effect on labor unions, but it does not seem to have resulted in an elimination of the national differences being commented upon here.

[84]One can only speculate about the extreme repressiveness that would have been necessary to achieve the political deactivation of a popular sector with a comparatively high degree of strength and autonomy. It should be noted that (as I argue further below) the Brazilian "success" entailed the always huge social costs of high repression, which would have increased pari passu with the significantly higher degree of coercion "required" by the Argentine situation. These increased costs would soon have reached a critical threshold where the degree of social dislocation they produced would have made it very unlikely that the Brazilian type of "success" could have been achieved.

Another factor seems to have contributed to the initially different degrees of coercion applied by the Argentine and Brazilian bureaucratic-authoritarian systems. The political activation of the Brazilian urban popular sector increased at a very rapid rate during the years preceding the 1964 coup. In the Argentine case, though the rate of increase of urban political activation was not as rapid as in Brazil in the period immediately preceding the 1966 coup, the level of such activation apparently was higher. Both countries shared the high-modernization characteristic of the presence in the big cities of a large number of politically activated individuals composing the urban popular sector. But it seems likely that in Argentina it was the level, while in Brazil it was the rate of increase, of urban political activation that contributed most to the defensive political reactions that led to their coups. This seems to be a reflection of the different sources of the main Argentine and Brazilian pre-coup popular political activation. In Brazil the inducement of popular political activation "from above" (especially by the Goulart government) played an important part. In Argentina the impulse came mainly "from below" (unions and Peronismo), with the governing Radicales definitely not encouraging it. In this respect, the nature of the political system change in Brazil must have exerted a more marked deactivating effect on the popular sector than in the Argentine case.

Finally, the Peronista allegiance of most of the Argentine popular sector was perceived as relatively less threatening by the more established sectors than the suggestion of socialist tendencies among some of the Brazilian governing personnel prior to the 1964 coup. In the latter case the perception of a more immediate threat to the existing social system may have fostered an initially tighter degree of cohesion in the ruling coalition, as well as increased the influence of its more "anti-subversive" and "efficientist" members. Another possible factor in determining the different degrees of coercion initially applied in the two coups is that while by and large the Brazilian urban popular sector supported Goulart, the unions and Peronistas were strongly opposed to the pre-coup Radicales Argentine government. The unions and Peronistas welcomed the 1966 coup for the short period of time that it took for the policy implications of the new political system to be spelled out; this delayed and lessened the degree of coercion applied. In contrast to the Brazilian case, the Argentine bureaucratic-authoritarianism did not begin with the more influential leadership of the popular sector in a markedly antagonistic position.[85]

Obviously, these are only hypotheses about what seem to be important factors for explaining the differences in the degrees

---

[85] The reasons for this peculiarity of the Argentine case will become apparent in Chapters III and IV below.

of coercion initially applied in the Argentine and Brazilian
cases. These hypotheses cannot be tested here; the point to be
stressed is that the different degrees of coercion that were applied (and the different degrees of coercion that each case apparently "required") seem to have been influential factors in the
deactivation of the popular sector achieved in the Brazilian case
and the retention of the relatively high level of political activation by the Argentine popular sector. When the socio-economic
implications of the "bureaucratic-authoritarian" systems became
fully apparent, they triggered "social explosions" in the Argentine modern areas, while they aroused no significant opposition
in Brazil. This may be a basic reason for the different degrees
of present-day (July 1971) consolidation of the two systems.

I have hypothesized that the "maps" of social reality of
incumbents of technocratic roles tend to emphasize those aspects
that secondary socialization has best taught them to measure and
deal with. Reality may be confounded with that which is indicated
by easily available, "hard" data. In such cases, performance (including a political system's performance) will tend to be measured
by these types of indicators and what they reveal, to the neglect
of hard-to-decode information coming from the "noisier" channels
for the expression of popular preferences.[86] Thus, growth in
GNP, diminished inflation, and fewer strikes may be achieved at
a huge cost in terms of repression, income redistribution, elimination of national entrepreneurship, liquidation of political
institutions, increased poverty of the urban and rural popular
sectors, and alienation of intellectuals and students. But it
is the former set of indicators that the technocratic outlook is
inclined to emphasize. If this set of indicators shows "satisfactory" performance, political rule based on a technocratic outlook
will be easily rationalized, the technocratic roles' coalition
will be consolidated, and the technocrats' assessment of their
capabilities for "solving" social problems will be reinforced.

I suspect that this is the single most important factor
for understanding why, in the Argentine case, influential members
of the original ruling coalition seem willing to attempt a "return to democracy," whereas the Brazilian system has hardened,
and its rulers intend to continue in power for a long time. In
Argentina the "failure" of the political system has been blatant,

---

[86]See on this point Apter's discussion of different types of
"political information" (esp. Choice . . .). Apter argues that
one important characteristic of a "bureaucratic system" is its
closure to the type of "political information" provided by the
expression of popular preferences.

even using the set of indicators that I have hypothesized would be preferentially monitored. This situation has weakened the cohesion of the original ruling coalition and its confidence in its capabilities--as is evidenced by the coups that deposed General Onganía and, more recently, General Levingston.[87]

As a consequence, there is less probability of long-term consolidation of a bureaucratic-authoritarian system in Argentina than in Brazil.[88] But if democratization is seriously attempted in Argentina, the high level of public disaffection will present serious problems. In particular, it will make it especially difficult to create a government built around "friendly" political parties that can successfully compete in the electoral arena. Rather, candidates are likely to win on the basis of appeals to the grievances that have accumulated against the disintegrating bureaucratic system among many sectors of the population. Among the military, the attempt to promote a "return to democracy" has a strong element of self-interest. As events in Argentina have clearly shown, direct rule and "unsatisfactory" governmental performance fractionalize the armed forces and make them the direct target of popular hostility. But the probability of a victorious "anti-system" government could be an even more serious menace to corporate interest (not only of the military).[89] Today (July 1971) it is far from clear what the outcome will be. If the "return to democracy" succeeds, one possibility is the tightly controlled elections in which, as a price for their authorization, political parties will agree to present candidates "suggested" by the military and to accept, when in power, severe constraints on their socio-economic policies. But once the "electoral" option has prevailed, the military's bargaining position vis-à-vis political parties (especially the major ones) would seem to be too weak

---

[87]The dynamics of this situation are spelled out in more detail in the "Excursus" below (pp. 106-109).

[88]In terms of my own values, the Argentine situation is more desirable than the Brazilian, but in neither case is an easy optimism warranted--Author.

[89]In a final revision of this work (October 1971) I have decided to leave this analysis and what follows unchanged. I feel that it emphasizes predicaments that, if anything, are more visible today than six months ago, when General Lanusse had just ousted President Levingston. Also, the deep concern of many business leaders is visible with what they perceive as "demagogic" socio-economic policies that would be unavoidably entailed by the reinstitution of electoral processes. And within the armed forces it is evident that the decision for "democracy" has met strong resistance.

for extracting such a price. But more important, this would create a situation similar to the one to be studied in Chapter IV, with a huge "vacant" electorate willing to vote for independent candidates and support new socio-economic policies. Such an electorate would constitute such a strong temptation for political parties to appeal to its preferences that the effectiveness of any agreement would seem to be very unlikely.[90] If, on the other hand, the continuista option prevails, there is little doubt that there would be an attempt to "deepen the revolution" along the Brazilian model. The problem in that case would be that a bureaucratic-authoritarian attempt to deactivate the popular sector would require an even greater degree of coercion than in 1966, when such an attempt "failed." If we consider that in Argentina in 1966 the degree of coercion "required" was significantly higher than that applied in Brazil in 1964, it is obvious that a new attempt to politically deactivate the Argentine popular sector would entail frightful social costs, with very little chance of success.

This prospect, combined with the disintegration and loss of confidence in their capabilities of the 1966 coalition, may act as a deterrent to the manifold tendencies operating in a continuista direction. The option seems to be between continuismo and truly open elections, given the unlikely possibility of controlled elections. The great risk in the continuista option is the huge social costs it would entail, but it is the open elections option that raises the most serious concerns, and most deeply divides, the sectors now in power.[91]

The Argentine case highlights the enormous difficulties to be faced in democratizing a bureaucratic-authoritarian system. Unable to solve the salient social problems and developmental bottlenecks, and to institutionalize itself, the Argentine political system must try to find its way through the vacuum left by the destruction of its deteriorated political institutions. After a 1966-1969 "truce," mass praetorianism has re-emerged in Argentina. If the many obstacles to political democratization that remain can be overcome, the new political system will still be instituted under very unfavorable circumstances. The renewal of mass praetorianism can only hinder its problem-solving capabilities and induce many established sectors to consider new authoritarian experiments. The great question would be to what extent

---

[90]See Chapter IV below for an analysis of this type of situation.

[91]Consider the many expressions of concern (again) from the established sectors raised by the possibility of a future Peronista electoral victory.

105

the social learning provided by the bureaucratic-authoritarian period had promoted changes in the attitudes of the crucial political actors, and persuaded them to forgo praetorianism and seek better ways to deal with the still unsolved "problematic space" within a democratic framework.

EXCURSUS: A Sketch of the "Political Game" under a Bureaucratic-Authoritarian Political System

In Chapter IV I will propose a more elaborated "political game," and there a more adequate discussion of this analytical undertaking will be possible. Here it suffices to say that, using the analogy of a game-situation, political action can be seen as action in a situation (policy issues, type of political system and rules of competition, and set of players) that must be taken into account by "players" trying to achieve goals.

In a highly simplified representation of the situation under bureaucratic-authoritarianism in contemporary South America, the main elements are:

(1) Incumbents of technocratic roles measure governmental performance from the perspective of a biased set of indicators.

(2) These indicators are: growth in GNP; growth in the "efficient" sectors of the economy, where most of these incumbents are located; low level of social unrest (strikes, demonstrations, riots); low rate of inflation; favorable external balance-of-payments and movements of international capital.

(3) Whatever other indicators may show, the performance of the government under a bureaucratic-authoritarian system will be considered "satisfactory" by incumbents of technocratic roles if the biased set of indicators shows significant improvement in comparison to the performance of the previous political system, and if the indicators show a tendency toward further improvement. If improvements are not observable, the performance will be considered "unsatisfactory," and the incumbents of technocratic roles will promote the ousting of the government.

(4) Governments of bureaucratic-authoritarian systems cannot count on the support of sectors of the population other than those densely penetrated by incumbents of technocratic roles. Hence, to survive in office governments must perform "satisfactorily" according to the indicators that these incumbents monitor.

(5) Achievement of "satisfactory" performance requires, at a minimum, negative redistribution of income, neglect of

popular consumption demands, and elimination of inefficient producers from the economy. These policies encounter strong resistance from the deprived sectors; the government must be able to meet this resistance with coercive force.

NOTE: At this point the analysis branches in two directions, depending on whether the government has been "successful" or "unsuccessful" in applying the "required" coercion.

(6) If the government has been "successful" in applying coercion, it will receive support from the incumbents of technocratic roles, but its policies will deeply alienate the deprived sectors--i.e., the popular sector, as well as some segments of the middle class and some domestic entrepreneurs who had originally supported the inauguration of the political system. Thus "success" in the use of coercion and "satisfactory" performance according to the biased set of indicators trades off support from incumbents of technocratic roles with further isolation from many of the remaining social sectors.

(7) Since the government thus becomes more dependent on the narrow coalition based on the incumbents of technocratic roles, the only policy options are more of the same. Severely imbalanced growth and further isolation of the government result. Some members of the ruling coalition who may become aware of the huge social costs of imbalanced growth and political isolation may attempt to change policies, but this requires effective support "outside" the ruling coalition, which cannot be obtained because coercion has destroyed most or all of the autonomous bases of political power. Besides, outside support is not readily given to personnel who have previously ostensibly participated in coercive policies. Hence, the chances of dissidence within the coalition are minimal.

(8) The continuation of "satisfactory" performance according to the biased set of indicators increases social costs. While the indicators are salient for the ruling coalition, the social costs are salient for the deprived sectors. Thus, the very different "maps" of social reality of the two groups are reinforced, leading to further repression and easy rationalization of the repression by the rulers. This process stops only if and when the increasingly skewed distribution of resources prevents further improvements even in the biased set of indicators, but by then the bureaucratic-authoritarian system has drastically changed the social context existing at the time it was inaugurated. Consequently a new problematic space is created (one in which the accumulated social costs probably will weigh heavily), and an entirely new "political game" is initiated.

(9) If, on the contrary, the government has been "unsuccessful" in applying coercion, very different consequences follow. The government must try to attain the goals listed in (5), but the popular sector and domestic entrepreneurs can effectively resist.

(10) More specifically, the popular sector retains its capacity to strike, demonstrate, and riot. This is a very effective weapon against a political system that has emerged as a "law and order" reaction to mass praetorianism.

(11) Hence the government must negotiate and grant concessions to placate the more threatening political actors. But this adversely affects its performance according to the indicators monitored by the incumbents of technocratic roles, on whose support the government depends. In order to "survive," the government must continue to try to implement the policies that will produce "satisfactory" performance. This generates renewed resistance and threats from the deprived sectors, now more extensive because of the previous demonstration that the government is unable to apply the "required" coercion. In other words, mass praetorianism and political instability have fully reemerged under the bureaucratic-authoritarian system.

(12) As a consequence, the ruling coalition becomes profoundly split. One subcoalition will argue that its preferences have not received proper consideration (the government has been too vacillating and "soft"), and that what is required is serious implementation of the policies listed in (5). But this continuista subcoalition is weaker than the original coalition, at a time when much more coercion is needed to achieve the same goals (if only to a minor degree).

(13) Another subcoalition will conclude that the bureaucratic-authoritarian attempt has irremediably failed. On the assumption that open participation in a failed political system damages their interests, the members of this subcoalition will choose to extricate themselves rapidly, handing over to other sectors the responsibility for dealing with the problematic space. Insofar as their attempt to disengage "reopens the game" to other political actors, it can obtain more "outside" support than the continuista option.

(14) But outside support for the extricating subcoalition is limited because its motives are suspect and because the bureaucratic-authoritarian policies have produced intense disaffection among the sectors whose support is now sought. More important, since successful extrication requires collaboration and restraint from political actors (the popular sector and party personnel) whom the bureaucratic-authoritarian

108

political system had attempted to exclude, the bargaining position of the subcoalition is quite weak. Hence the still uncommitted members of the bureaucratic-authoritarian coalition are not convinced that they will benefit more from the extricating than from the continuista option.

(15) Thus, "unsatisfactory" performance leaves the social context and the "problematic space" existing prior to the inauguration of the bureaucratic-authoritarian system basically unchanged, but it polarizes the original coalition into advocates of more coercion and advocates of rapid extrication. If the continuistas prevail, the sequence of (6) to (8) will be attempted again, but at this later stage the social costs will be much higher and the chances of generating "satisfactory" performance much slimmer. Otherwise the outcome will be a return to a system of political democracy that (again) will have to operate under an unfavorable legacy of mass praetorianism. The circumstances under which it could avoid praetorianism and achieve greater problem-solving capacities (thereby diminishing the likelihood of a new authoritarian breakdown) are beyond what can be determined from an examination of the bureaucratic-authoritarian "game."

A Brief Overview of Other Contemporary South American Political Systems

So far I have analyzed the socio-economic correlates of South American political systems on three levels: (1) social structure, focusing on the productive-industrial base of "modern" areas and on social differentiation, with its correlates of political pluralization and activation; (2) the agenda of salient social problems and developmental bottlenecks that define the problematic space within each country; (3) the penetration of technocratic roles. These are all dimensions of the overarching concept of modernization, and at each level of modernization significant differences can be seen in them.

A fourth important dimension has been mentioned only in passing--i.e., the present position of South American countries in the international context. All the South American countries have very limited influence in international affairs; at most they can hope only to attenuate the internal effects of international events and the decisions of the great powers. They all lack market power in international trade; they are all subject to the virtually undisputed military, political, and economic hegemony of the United States; they are all dependent on scarce foreign capital; and they are all dependent on technologies that have originated in countries that are capital-rich and labor-scarce, and from which many of their role-models, consumption expectations, and ideological influences have been derived.

The particular ways in which these factors impinge on each South American country depend on their different levels of modernization. The problem of economic dependence, for example, is common to all, but it is expressed in Argentina and Brazil in inter-industry cleavages, while in most of the other South American countries it is still centered around the expropriation of extractive enclaves and/or export-oriented foreign-owned firms. These similarities and differences must be taken into account in studying the problematic space within each country and in examining the ways different political coalitions deal with that space.

Argentina and Brazil are the most highly modernized South American countries. Combined with the factors deriving from their position in the international context, this modernization has created the problematic space with which their pre-coup and bureaucratic-authoritarian political systems have had to deal. Can we conclude that, as modernization proceeds in other South American countries, there will be similar "pulls" in a bureaucratic-authoritarian direction?

It is basic to the argument of this book that this is a significant question to raise (and one that can scarcely be formulated--if at all--from the optimistic assumptions of the basic "paradigm" discussed in Chapter I). But in the absence of systematic research, there are too many indeterminate factors to answer that question with any degree of assurance. First, although the general context is common, an assumption of the equivalence of causal processes (here, those of Argentina and Brazil vis-à-vis those of the other South American countries) may be as fallacious as the one discussed in Chapter I. Second, even if the tendency were toward bureaucratic-authoritarianism, purposive political action might be able to bring about a change in directions--particularly with the experiences of Argentina and Brazil to alert leaders to the possibilities and generate effective efforts to avoid them. Third, other factors might invalidate any simple attempts at extrapolation--e.g., the existence of solid political institutions in Chile, particularly well-organized, non-personalistic political parties, a working parliament, and effective democratic socialization; "system pride" of many Chilean and (apparently) still some Uruguayan political actors, heightened by the "political primitiveness" of their larger neighbors; a tradition of military non-intervention in Chile and Uruguay; Venezuela's hard currency income from oil extraction, exceptional by South American standards; the end of the "National Front" in Colombia, with its serious danger of a breakdown leading toward authoritarianism, but also with the opportunities it raises for achieving and instituting open political competition;[92] the exhaustion of

_____

[92]For a good recent analysis of the Colombian situation, see

"horizontal" industrialization at a lower level than in Argentina and Brazil, and greater difficulties to be faced in attempting vertical integration, which may induce institutional innovations in other South American countries that were absent in Argentina and Brazil.

All these factors are potentially very important, but it should be remembered that they have to operate in a severely strained context. Low levels of performance[93] and growing demands, increased political activation and penetration of technocratic roles, many salient social problems—these can only be seen as pushing societies away from political democracy and toward authoritarian breakdowns that, as modernization proceeds, are quite likely to be of the "bureaucratic" type analyzed in this chapter.

Lacking sufficient evidence for weighing all these factors, one must suspend judgment. But this being the case, suspension of judgment applies both to my speculations and to the more sanguine expectations derived from the basic paradigm. Reverting back to the discussion in Chapter I, it can be reasserted here that clarification of the main historical tendencies in operation can hardly be obtained under the assumptions of linear democratization.

The Vargas and Perón periods have already been referred to as populist authoritarianisms; another case that belongs in this category is the contemporary Peruvian political system. It is ruled by the same type of coalition; it has the same "enemies"; its policies are the same combination of expansion of the domestic market based on a still homogeneous industrial sector, weakening of the traditional ruling sectors, and expropriation of the most visible symbols of foreign presence. It has the same mixture of radical policies that irreversibly change society, leaders with conservative ideologies, and regressive policies in some important areas. Furthermore, as in the Argentine and Brazilian populist experiences, the Peruvian system is attempting the political activation and incorporation of segments of the popular sector "from above"--i.e., from the government--while trying to maintain tight controls over the process. In terms of my analysis, its lower levels of social differentiation, political activation, and

---

C. Rama, "El sistema político colombiano: Frente Nacional y ANAPO," Centro Paraguayo de Estudios Sociológicos, 1970.

[93]Even in the otherwise particularly favorable case of Venezuela, the growth record has been very poor. See James Petras, "Una década de democracia capitalista en Venezuela," Estudios Internacionales, IV, No. 12 (1970).

penetration of technocratic roles prevented the emergence in Perú of a bureaucratic-authoritarian system and its supporting coalition.[94] These circumstances, together with the concomitant possibilities of further "horizontal" industrial expansion and the prevalence of foreign-owned firms in the export-oriented sectors, permitted the grand coalition typical of populism. There are important differences between the Peruvian populist authoritarianism and the bureaucratic authoritarianisms inaugurated in Brazil in 1964 and in Argentina in 1966. The fact that in all three cases the military appear to hold governmental power is typologically inconsequential.[95] What matters most are the policies of each system and the social problems to which it responds, the coalition on which it is based, and whether or not it attempts to exclude and deactivate the popular sector. Perhaps the most significant difference between the Peruvian and the older populisms is that the former emerged during a period in which U.S. policies had induced substantial changes in military organization, but it remains to be seen if this will finally result in a better record.

Bolivia and Ecuador also have been going through a period of authoritarian expansion of their political systems. These populisms, however, are following very erratic paths. Constraints derived from the extremely small size of their domestic markets[96] have kept their "horizontal" industrial expansion at a lower level than Perú's. Thus the driving force of the populist policies has been weak, and a crucial element of the coalition (domestic market-producing industrialists) has had to play a lesser role than in countries that have started from a more favorable base.

Finally, in Paraguay is the only survival of traditional authoritarianism in South America. A small and quite homogeneous elite rules over a largely politically inert and scarcely differentiated population. The foreign export-oriented sector is dominant, and there have been no serious attempts to subordinate it to domestic industrial and market expansion.

---

[94] For good recent analyses of the Peruvian case, see J. Cotler, "Crisis política y populismo militar en el Perú," Estudios Internacionales, IV, No. 12 (1970), and F. Bourricaud, "Los militares: ¿Por qué y para qué?" Aportes, No. 18 (1970).

[95] The linkages established with military institutions (particularly CAEM) in Perú tended to be with left-of-the-center intellectuals rather than with the technocratic-right civilians of Argentina and Brazil.

[96] See data in Chapter I.

TOWARD AN ALTERNATIVE CONCEPTUALIZATION

The Proposed Classification

The preliminary classification of Chapter I can now be completed. In Table 19, South American countries, clustered by levels of modernization, are paired with political system types according to the criteria and the definitions set forth in this and the preceding chapter. The differences between the classification proposed here and the studies analyzed in Chapter I need not be repeated; but it might be useful to note what this proposed classification and those studies have in common. All involve ordering cases along two dimensions (socio-economic and political, albeit differently defined) and then asking the question "What goes with what?" All stress unidirectional effects--those produced by socio-economic factors on the political "side."[97] All are preliminary operations before the really important theoretical task of specifying the relationships that determine the interactions between these dimensions. If these relationships could be specified, a powerful explanatory theory could be formulated, and more reliable predictions about future trends would be possible.

All this serves to underline the common shortcomings of those studies and the present one. But strongly influenced by the view that explanation can only be approximated by consideration of dynamic, time-bound processes, I have taken more steps than are customary in a study of this type.[98] The first step, common to all studies, consisted in establishing a pairing--in this case between levels of modernization and political system types. The second step focused on Argentina and Brazil, attempting to bring forth elements to provide a genetic explanation of the implantation of contemporary South American bureaucratic-authoritarian systems. There we examined the main characteristics of the Argentine and Brazilian political systems, and tried to place them in comparative perspective vis-à-vis European bureaucratic-authoritarian systems and other South American authoritarianisms. A brief third step, highly speculative, consisted of attempting to assess some trends.

---

[97] This is the best indication of the incompleteness of these efforts. I believe that the truly important question is what effects political action can have on socio-economic factors. But these preliminary efforts may be useful for providing better "maps" of the social reality with which purposive political action will have to deal.

[98] These "steps" include the three stages (static-correlational, explanatory, and predictive, each one unfortunately more tentative and speculative than the preceding one) that underlie my analysis. In the preceding pages, for the sake of better exposition, it has seemed unavoidable to enter into digressions, and on a few occasions, to partially alter this ordering.

Table 19

A CLASSIFICATION OF CONTEMPORARY SOUTH AMERICAN POLITICAL
SYSTEMS BY LEVELS OF MODERNIZATION

Level of Modernization	Political Democracy?	Excluding System?	Resulting Political Type
High			
Argentina	No	Yes	Bureaucratic-
Brazil	No	Yes	Authoritarian (Modal Type)
Medium			
Chile	Yes	No	
Colombia	Yes	No	Political
Uruguay	Yes	No	Democracy
Venezuela	Yes	No	(Modal Type)
Perú	No	No	Populist- Authoritarian
Low			
Bolivia	No	No	Populist-
Ecuador	No	No	Authoritarian (Modal Type)
Paraguay	No	No	Traditional- Authoritarian

On the basis of this analysis, several points can be made
with some confidence. First, the higher levels of contemporary
South American modernization are not associated with political
democracies. Second, the Argentine and Brazilian bureaucratic-
authoritarianism systems can hardly be conceived as having increased the probabilities of establishment and consolidation of
political democracies in these countries. Third, until much more
solid and better focused evidence is brought forth, there are no
reasons to believe that the chances of the survival of the existing South American political democracies are significantly higher
than those of their breakdown in an authoritarian direction.
Fourth, as modernization proceeds there is an indeterminate but
considerable probability that such authoritarian breakdowns will
fall within the "bureaucratic" category analyzed here. Fifth, the
basic paradigm and its underlying assumption of equivalence of
causal processes are not supported by the South American cases.

In the following two chapters of this book the subject-
matter shifts to the study of specific aspects of the Argentine
political experience. These will illustrate in more detail, and
present more detailed data concerning, the processes that led to
an attempt to inaugurate and consolidate a bureaucratic-authoritarian political system.

Chapter III

ARGENTINA, 1966: THE INAUGURATION OF A
BUREAUCRATIC-AUTHORITARIAN POLITICAL SYSTEM

On June 28, 1966, military officers "acting as representatives of the Armed Forces" ousted Arturo Illia, the constitu-
tionally elected President of Argentina. They did not bother to
take the "usual" steps for prevention of popular disorder--which
did not occur. Foreign correspondents reported a surprising lack
of opposition from the public-at-large.[1] Their impression was
confirmed by survey data, which showed that 66 percent of the
respondents approved of the coup and only 6 percent disapproved.[2]
All major groups (except the ousted political party and a few
minor parties, as well as university students) expressed support
for the coup and for the new military government. The Junta
Revolucionaria, formed by the Chiefs of Staff of the Army, Navy,
and Air Force, ousted the President and the Governors of the
States, dissolved Parliament, dismissed the Judges of the Supreme
Court, and enacted an Estatuto Revolucionario whose regulations
prevailed over the national Constitution. All "political activities" were banned, political parties were dissolved, and elections were postponed sine die. The junta appointed retired General Juan Carlos Onganía as President. Communiques of the junta
and of the new President stated the "reasons" for the coup. The
most important of these were: (1) the lack of harmony and soli-
darity in and among the major social groups, which had led to
anarchy, subversion, and neglect of the public interest; (2) the
incapacity of previous civilian governments to solve the nationa
problems of economic stagnation, inflation, lack of authority,
widespread social unrest, and loss of international prestige;
(3) the unrepresentativeness of the leadership of the political

---

[1]See, e.g., The Washington Post, June 30, 1966.

[2]Survey [sample and methodology unknown] taken by Primera Plana,
reported in C. Astiz, "The Argentine Armed Forces: Their Role and
Political Involvement," The Western Political Quarterly, XXII, No.
4 (1969). This article provides useful information and analysis
complementary to this chapter. In another survey (n = 1,000 respondents of the Greater Buenos Aires area), to the question "Do
you think that the revolution of June 28th [1966] was necessary?,"
77 percent answered "Yes" (Correo de la Tarde, June 6-12, 1967;
survey taken in July 1966, methodology unknown).

parties and of most organized groups; (4) the irresponsible behavior of political parties, which had led to the polarization of
public opinion and inefficient governmental performance; and
(5) the danger of a breakdown of the cohesion of the Armed Forces,
the only solid institutions remaining after a long period of
national crisis.[3]

This was certainly not the first coup in Argentine history.[4] But it differed from all the others in that it was the
first time that the Armed Forces, with a high degree of internal
cohesion, had decided to take political power directly in their
own hands for a long and indefinite period, and with no intention
of convoking elections or returning government to political parties in the foreseeable future. The preceding 1955-1966 period
had been punctuated by numerous attempts (successful and unsuccessful) at military coups, but none of these changed the type of
political system existing during the period. Rather, the continued political instability of that period was a characteristic
feature of the workings of a pseudo-political democracy that
denied electoral access to the first plurality (i.e., the largest
single political party--or bloc--in a multi-party system) of the
electorate.[5] The importance of the June 1966 coup is that it was
a conscious effort to change the existing political system by the
inauguration of a bureaucratic-authoritarian regime. This "cul-
minating" (in terms of the focus of this chapter) event was the
result of manifold factors, among them the recurrent political
instability of the 1955-1966 period.

It is important to bear in mind here certain important
distinctions. This chapter is intended to contribute to the

---

[3]See, among others, the following official publications: "Men-
saje de la Junta Revolucionaria al Pueblo Argentino" (1966);
"Mensaje al País del Presidente de la Nación Teniente General
Juan Carlos Onganía" (1966); "Mensaje del Teniente General Juan
Carlos Onganía con motivo de asumir la Presidencia de la Nación"
(1966); and "Mensaje del Presidente de la Nación en la reunión
de camaradería de las Fuerzas Armadas" (1967)--all printed by
Presidencia de la Nación, Argentina.

[4]The best analyses of Argentine civil-military relations, although they do not cover all the main historical events, are the
works by Dario Cantón, La política de los militares argentinos:
1900-1971 (Siglo XXI, 1971), and Robert Potash, The Army and Politics in Argentina (Stanford: Stanford University Press, 1969).

[5]This question will be considered in more detail below. From
a different point of view, it will also be discussed in Chapter
IV.

explanation of the 1966 change in the Argentine political system by an analysis of the crucial step that brought about that change. Thus it is not focused on the examination of the 1955-1966 political instability, except insofar as this seems to have contributed to the final 1966 breakdown.

It is always difficult to decide how far one should "go back" in examining the factors that seem to have had an effect on the event or phenomenon that is the "dependent variable" being analyzed. In the present case it is evident that it would be too restrictive to limit the examination to the factors that were immediately related to the 1966 coup, such as the military's decision to intervene, the high degree of cohesion among the coup leaders, and the goal of inaugurating a different type of political system. Consideration of these factors immediately raises questions concerning the reasons for the military decisions and the lack of opposition from the public to the coup.

In this way the focus of analysis is broadened; but such a broadened perspective involves problems. First, the conceptual neatness of an explanation centered on only the most immediate factors is sacrificed. Second, it is impossible to avoid simplifying the broad historical and social factors that are thought to have exerted an important influence on those more immediate to the coup. Why did the military change the goals of their intervention in 1966? Why was this coup decided upon by military officers who had shortly before taken a very explicit legalista (i.e., anti-coup) stand? Why was the 1966 coup executed with such an unusual degree of cohesion among the Armed Forces? Why did most organized groups in Argentine society hasten to express support for the coup and the military government? And in what ways did these circumstances relate to the attempt to inaugurate and consolidate a new type of political system in Argentina?

However, even with its pitfalls, a broad analytical perspective is desirable because only it will allow a search for answers to these questions. The strategy I intend to follow here consists, first, of a brief examination of some aspects of Argentine history. Second, I will study aspects of the general social context of the 1955-1966 period. The first phase will provide the main outlines of a "longitudinal" perspective, while the second will give a detailed picture of the Argentine background that immediately preceded the 1966 coup. These two sections will establish the coordinates within which the factors most directly related to the coup will be studied--in the final section of the chapter.

Some Aspects of Argentina's Historical Legacy

The analysis here of the historical aspects that preceded (some of them by many years) the 1966 coup will of necessity be very selective. There is no pretense here to write history. The aim is to identify some social problems emerging during certain historical periods which have remained as "constants" in Argentine society. The historical discussion will be limited strictly to those developments which seem indispensable for this purpose.[6]

"Constants," as used here, are characteristics of Argentine society that have remained as persistent problems or constraints limiting the possibilities of political action. The persistence of certain historical constants and the emergence of new ones is, during each historical period, a major part of the constellation of problems that must be faced. Each such constellation is made up of the "constants" and the cluster of more specific problems that confront the political actors in each particular period. These constants could have been "eliminated," but the fact that they have not has--to borrow Weber's analogy-- loaded the dice more and more against an effectively working political system in Argentina. This failure has in turn fostered the persistence and accumulation of an increasing number of constants.

National Unification and the Landed Oligarchy. Two constants have persisted from a very early period. One is a high degree of incongruence between actual political behavior and political behavior as prescribed by formal institutions and dominant ideologies.[7] The second is a strong disaffection of vast sectors of the population vis-à-vis the existing political system and the holders of political power, based on salient cleavages around issues of high significance and on a very unequal distribution of political resources.[8]

During Spanish colonial rule two very different patterns of settlement prevailed in what would later be Argentina. The central and northern regions were economically part of the

---

[6]For greater detail, the reader is referred to the various sources hereafter cited. An excellent general political history of Argentina is C.A. Floria and C. Garcia Belsunce, Historia de los Argentinos (2 vols.; Editorial Kapelusz, 1972).

[7]It scarcely need be noted that this discrepancy has been repeatedly observed by students of Latin American history; see, for example, Stanley Stein and Barbara Stein, The Colonial Heritage of Latin America (New York: Oxford University Press, 1970). For an assessment of more recent evidences, see Federico Gil, Instituciones y desarrollo político en América Latina (INTAL, 1966).

[8]On "political resources," see Dahl, Modern Political Analysis (Englewood Cliffs: Prentice-Hall, 1969).

Peruvian Viceroyalty, and the conquistadores established a patriarchal rule over largely self-sufficient societies, which they
found fit quite well with the hierarchical world-view they had
brought from Spain. In contrast, Buenos Aires was a very secondary settlement; the lands around it were sparsely populated by
nomadic Indians and lacked any economic value. The village, although a port, was too distant to benefit from the more affluent
Peruvian region, and it had been prohibited by Spain from engaging
in international trade. But the expansion of British commerce
brought Buenos Aires into conflict with Spain, and soon it became
a major center for smuggling. The legislation that the Spanish
enacted to prohibit commerce and smuggling in Buenos Aires was
utterly ineffective (as was the legislation to protect the
Indians of the "Peruvian" regions). The famous dictum that "the
will of the King is obeyed but not executed" accurately reflected
the reality.

The movement toward independence from Spain, which originated in Buenos Aires, triggered sixty years of convulsion and
anarchy. The wars of independence were almost one continual civil
war. On one side of the struggle were the unitarios, based in
Buenos Aires and heavily involved in international trade. Eager
to absorb all European ideological currents, they drafted laws
and constitutions for a nation that did not yet exist and that
successfully resisted their claims to rule. Their opponents, the
federales, based in the central and northern regions, sought to
preserve their patriarchal, pre-capitalist way of life. At stake
were two very different mentalities and economic interests: the
philosophy of the Enlightenment as opposed to that of late Spanish
scholasticism, the incorporation of Argentina into the world market as opposed to the persistence of the closed subsistence
economies of the interior. After independence the Spanish colo-
nies were, as Richard Morse puts it, "a decapitated patrimonial
state"[9] in quest of a legitimacy formula. For the unitarios,
outward-oriented and without traditional legitimation, government
"had" to be some form of constitutional government in the fashion
of the Western European or the U.S. models. The obvious difficulty was that the context in which the newly independent Spanish
colonials operated was not at all the type of society presupposed
by those models. The difference between the actual social conditions and those presupposed by the models was too great to be
ignored. One possibility would have been to try to establish
institutions better adapted to the actual conditions, but many
unitarios believed that imposing, for the sake of "progress" and
at any cost, the forms of constitutional government would necessarily push the social reality toward resembling the model

---

[9]"The Heritage of Latin America" in L. Hartz, ed., The Founding
of New Societies (New York, 1966).

119

societies. "Transplanted" institutions would shape a social reality that would be compatible with them. After many failures,
a Constitution was enacted in 1852 that has endured (at least
nominally) until the present. The representative who formally
proposed the text to the Constitutional Convention said:

> There are only two ways of building a nation: to take her
> behavior, her character and her habits as they are, or to
> give her the code that must create the proper behavior, char-
> acter and habits if the country does not have them. Since
> this is the case, since the country is in chaos, this consti-
> tutional project is the only way to save her.[10]

During the civil wars the words "constitution," "liberal-
ism," and later on "democracy," belonged to the unitarios; but the
incongruence between institutional and formal prescriptions of
behavior and the actual performance of government was as great as
during Spanish rule. In addition, these terms became the symbols
of a minority that denied the traditional culture and destroyed
the social structures and forms of government of a large proportion of the population.[11] The privileged location of Buenos Aires
as a port meant that its inhabitants could act as middlemen for
the introduction of European (mainly English) manufactured goods.
Because the craft industries of the interior could not compete
with these imports, the territorial expansion of Buenos Aires'
hegemony resulted in the extinction of many domestic economic
activities. This helps to explain the stern resistance of the
interior against Buenos Aires and its unitarios.

When the pace of the industrial revolution accelerated in
England during the second half of the nineteenth century, Buenos
Aires was able to acquire economic resources and warfare technology that firmly established its hegemony over the interior. But
even after 1870, when the country was relatively pacified, the
transplantation of "democratic" political institutions continued to create major problems. In particular, it required that
elections be held, when the supporters of the central government
frequently were a minority. Since there was no possibility of
allowing "the barbares" to rule, electoral fraud, as well as

---

[10]Speech by José M. Gutiérrez to the Constitutional Convention.

[11]This temporal sequence of national unification is very different from that of earlier European modernizers. In those countries
the harsh task of national unification had been largely completed
before constitutionalism and democracy became an issue. Significantly, the only clear-cut South American exception to the sequence depicted in the text is Chile.

violence and openly arbitrary exercise of the central government's powers, became a frequent occurrence.

At this point a third Argentine "constant" became clearly evident. The democratic "rules of the game" were to be given only limited and conditional adherence by the ruling sectors--the application of these rules was subject to the proviso that it produce the "correct" government.[12] If this requirement was not met, the rules were suspended to the extent and for the period necessary to assure that the "correct" government was in power. As would happen in succeeding periods, since "playing democratically" endangered "democracy" (as defined by the ruling sectors), the only solution was to act in a blatantly undemocratic fashion while asserting that it was necessary "for the sake of democracy." Given the consistently high level of popular disaffection toward rulers and institutions, it is not difficult to understand how this constant bred cynicism, instead of helping to establish the legitimacy of the system and its institutions.[13]

At the end of the nineteenth century the ruling sectors eagerly adopted the new ideas emanating from Europe, mixing positivism with Darwinian and Spencerian concepts. The struggle previously defined as "civilization against barbarism" could now be "scientifically" interpreted. It was maintained that there was no hope until the remnants of Spanish culture and the "degraded races" were replaced by European migration.[14] During a

---

[12]Other authors have observed this "constant" in Argentine society; see C.A. Floria, "Una explicación política de la Argentina," CIAS (1967); Dahl, Polyarchy . . ., pp. 132-140; E. Kenworthy, "The Formation of the Peronist Coalition," unpublished dissertation, Yale University, 1970.

[13]An excellent theoretical analysis of legitimacy is N. Botana's La Légitimité: Probleme politique (Louvain, 1968). See also his "La crisis de legitimidad en la Argentina y el desarrollo de los partidos políticos," Criterio, No. 1604 (1970).

[14]This has been labelled the "period of self-incrimination" by A. Hirschman ("Introduction" in Hirschman, ed., Latin American Issues [New York: Twentieth Century Fund, 1960]). But the incrimination was one-sided: it was directed by the ruling sectors at the majority of the population. Naturally, the response was bitter. The ruling sectors' perception of the rest of the population was partly a process of selective borrowing; after a visit to Argentina Lord Bryce noted: "The books most popular among those few who approach abstract subjects are those of Herbert Spencer. [Argentines] are unwilling to believe that he is not deemed in his own country to be a great philosopher" (cited

period of rapidly growing need for labor because of export expansion, the national governments at the turn of the century actively encouraged Europeans to migrate.[15]

Another "constant," with initially favorable consequences, manifested itself in this period--i.e., the marked dependence of the Argentine economy on international trade and capital movements, with limited capabilities for domestic control of their effects. Since the end of the eighteenth century, a basic tenet of the unitarios had been free trade, under which Argentina would export agrarian goods and import most of the industrial products it needed. When around 1870 British industry expanded rapidly, so did its need for the exports that Argentina was in a particularly good position to provide. The vast pampas around Buenos Aires which could provide the cereals (and later also the beef) for export became essential in the new international trade situation--and the economic center in Argentina shifted decisively from the central and northern regions to Buenos Aires. Great efforts were exerted to establish the financial and transport structure required to open the pampas to capitalist exploitation. The extent and rapidity of this expansion into the pampean land can be seen in the data presented in Table 20.

Under this external inducement the Argentine economy grew rapidly in the 1870-1914 period. The country won an international reputation for prosperity. The standard of living--at least in the Buenos Aires area--was high as a result of the advantages that Argentina enjoyed in the international market for the exportation of cereals and beef. But the rest of the country lagged far behind the Buenos Aires-pampas region. Furthermore, millions of hectares of the best pampean land were appropriated by a tiny sector: Argentina never had an open frontier.[16] The

---

by A. Whitaker, Argentina (Englewood Cliffs: Prentice-Hall, 1964), p. 61.

[15]On the great wave of European migration of this period, see G. Germani, Política . . ., pp. 179-216; O. Cornblit, "European Migrants in Argentine Industry and Politics" in C. Véliz, ed., The Politics of Conformity in Latin America (Oxford: Oxford University Press, 1967); and C. Solberg, Immigration and Nationalism: Argentina and Chile, 1890-1914 (Austin: University of Texas Press, 1970).

[16]For a description of this situation and analysis of the factors that led to it, see H. Giberti, El desarrollo agrario argentino (Eudeba, 1964); James Scobie, Revolution on the Pampas (Austin: University of Texas Press, 1969); R. Cortés Conde and E. Gallo, La formación de la Argentina moderna (Paidós, 1967); and R. Cortés Conde, "Algunos aspectos de la expansión territorial

Table 20

SELECTED ECONOMIC INDICATORS: ARGENTINA, 1870-1914

	1865-1869	1890-1894	1910-1914
Total Length of Railroad Track (Kilometers)	503	N.A.	31,104
Total Merchandise Exports (Millions of gold pesos)	38	N.A.	410
Total Area Sown with Crops (Millions of hectares)	0.58	N.A.	20.62
Total Wheat Exports (Annual averages, millions of gold pesos at 1910-1914 values)	0.2	28.1	78.1
Total Corn Exports (Same measure as wheat)	0.3	6.0	72.4
Total Frozen Beef Exports (Same measure as wheat)	0.0	0.1	49.7

Sources: Alejandro, Essays . . ., pp. 2-5, and Ernesto Tornquist and Co., The Economic Development of the Argentine Republic in the Last Fifty Years (Buenos Aires, 1919), pp. 26, 116-117, 139-140.

resources from which Argentine prosperity derived were monopolized by very few, the beneficiaries taking for granted that this was the road to progress. As one President of the period, Juárez Celman, stated: "With latifundio we have achieved the present progress and our outstanding economic and productive capacity. The system of big property has made us rich."[17] Perhaps more important, this privileged stratum consisted, by and large, of less than efficient entrepreneurs[18] who showed very little interest

---

en Argentina en la segunda mitad del siglo XIX," Desarrollo Económico, 29 (1968).

[17]Cited in O. Cornblit, E. Gallo, and A. O'Connell, "La generación del 80 y su proyecto: Antecedentes y consecuencias" in T. di Tella et al., eds., Argentina: Sociedad de masas (Eudeba, 1965), p. 54. This is an excellent monographic study of the period under consideration here.

[18]See Scobie.

in industrial activities.[19] These factors combined to restrict what would otherwise have been an unusual opportunity for building a solid economy and a more open society.

The Middle Class. By the end of the nineteenth century (especially in Buenos Aires), the expanding economy had created an important middle sector, formed by merchants, professionals, civil servants, and owners of the primitive industries that have typically appeared in the large export-sites of agrarian-export economies. Recent investigations have shown that sheer distance and some tariff protection for certain products stimulated the growth of some industry, but such industry was owned largely by foreign nationals. This, combined with a preference on the part of the government and ruling sectors for open trade policies, prevented the emergence of a numerically important and politically active national industrial bourgeoisie. Instead, within the middle class the salaried, non-entrepreneurial sectors prevailed overwhelmingly. This middle class fully accepted the existing socio-economic policies and, if anything, were more anti-industry and more pro-free trade than the oligarchy. Their political demands were limited to fair elections and open access to high-ranking national government positions.[20] However, their road to political power was not easy. Only after three unsuccessful civil-military revolts was a law passed providing for honest electoral registrations, secret ballots, and custody by the military of the urns in which the ballots were deposited.

This long delay in the admission of the middle class into the political arena reflects another "constant": the strong resistance by established political actors to the expansion of political participation to include new actors, even when favorable economic circumstances and almost total policy consensus minimized

---

[19]Only a small proportion of the industrialists were Argentine. A very small proportion of European migrants opted for Argentine citizenship, and most of them were politically inactive. See Cornblit; Germani, Política . . .; and Alejandro, Essays . . ., Chapter I, for valuable data and good analyses.

[20]On the socio-economic background and policy preferences of this middle sector and its main political expression, the Radical party, see Cornblit; E. Gallo and S. Sigal, "La formación de los partidos políticos contemporáneos: La Unión Cívica Radical (1880-1916)" in di Tella et al., eds.; and Peter Smith, Politics and Beef in Argentina (New York: Columbia University Press, 1969).

the "risks" of such expansion. When later these favorable circumstances changed, and new political actors sharply disagreed
on policy matters, outright opposition to further expansion became
the rule.

As Peter Smith argues, neither the oligarchy's concession
to the claim for clean elections nor the election in 1916 of the
Partido Radical leader, Hipólito Irigoyen, meant genuine commitment of the oligarchy to democratic rules of the game.[21] The new
government operated under conditions of "uncertain legitimacy,"[22]
subject to a "satisfactory" (as defined by the old rulers) handling of national affairs. The oligarchy retained control of
crucial political resources--social prestige, economic power, influence on the Army, control of the press and the University.
Throughout the Radicales period the old rulers showed their contempt toward the parvenus, whom they saw as inefficient and unreliable people who, after all, were only following the ruling
sectors' old socio-economic policies.[23]

The Radicales governments were not entirely free of fraud
and arbitrary interventions of the central government into states'
affairs, but on the whole they made remarkable progress in electoral practices and in extending the rule of law. It was particularly unfortunate for Argentina that the British economy began
to decline after 1914. Because of this decline and less than
skillful government policies, economic growth slowed in comparison
to the rates achieved before 1914. Finally, with the impact of
the world crisis beginning in 1929, the economic situation became
very serious. The oligarchy saw in these conditions a confirma-
tion of their never-abandoned belief that only they could govern.
In 1930 an oligarchy-backed military coup ousted the Radicales
government.

The old oligarchy, then generally called the Conservadores, attempted to govern in the midst of the economic crisis.
They undertook a program of industrialization designed to save
badly needed international currency and provide an internal market
for agrarian production.[24] The severe impact of the crisis in

---

[21]"The Breakdown of Democracy in Argentina, 1916-1930," paper
presented to the World Congress of Sociology, Varna, 1970.

[22]The expression is from Floria.

[23]For expressions of this contempt, see D. Cantón, El parlamento
argentino en epocas de cambio: 1880, 1910 y 1946 (Editorial del
Instituto, 1966).

[24]For an excellent analysis of these economic policies, see
Alejandro, Essays . . . . A review of the pertinent literature

the interior of the country, combined with the efforts to indus-
trialize in Buenos Aires, drew large numbers of people into urban
life.[25] These new migrants were to form the basis of a large urban proletariat, remaining close to their agrarian origins and
bringing with them a long record of grievances against the central
government. The Conservadores were faced with the old predicament: since they were "democratic," sooner or later they had to
call elections. They first tried a gubernatorial election in
Buenos Aires State in 1931, which resulted in a Radicales victory.
Since the "correct" candidate had not won, the election was annulled, and a federal delegate appointed instead of the elected governor. Later, when former Radical President Marcelo de Alvear
tried to run in presidential elections, his candidacy was vetoed
by a decree. As a result, under the motto of "Intransigence," the
Radicales abstained from electoral participation and organized
several unsuccessful civil-military rebellions. Even with the
Radicales abstention, the Conservadores could not risk honest
elections. Systematic "patriotic fraud"[26] was practiced, on the
grounds that it was the only way to avoid the disasters that would
follow if a majoritarian government were elected. To quote from
A. Whitaker:

> As the Presidential election of 1937 approached, the rising
> Radical tide made Justo [the President, elected by fraud in
> 1932] himself uneasy over the chance of passing electoral
> control to the right people. Accordingly, he and his follow-
> ers simply stole the elections by fraud and force . . . . For
> the political health of the country the effect was disastrous.
> Coming on top of all that had gone before, it seemed to con-
> firm what non-conformists had been saying for years past:
> that in Argentina democracy was only a snare to facilitate
> dominion and exploitation of the nation by a privileged few.[27]

---

and an analysis of the socio-political implications of the policies can be found in M. Murmis and C. Portantiero, "Crecimiento
industrial y alianza de clases en Argentina, 1930-1940," Instituto
Torcuato di Tella, Centro de Investigaciones Sociales, Documento
de Trabajo, 1968..

[25]Using Karl Deutsch's concept, Peter Smith argues that "social
mobilization" took place in Argentina during this period ("Social
Mobilization, Political Participation and the Rise of Juan Perón,"
The Western Political Quarterly, XXXIV, No. 1 [1969]).

[26]This expression was coined by M. Fresco, a Conservador Governor of Buenos Aires State, elected by fraud in the 1930's.

[27]A. Whitaker, Argentina (New York: Prentice-Hall, 1963).
For valuable information on Argentina from the 1930's until 1963,
see T. Halperin Donghi, Argentina en el callejon (Editorial Arca,
1964).

For the <u>Radicales</u> and for the still inarticulated groups emerging from rapid industrialization and urbanization, this was the "infamous decade." This label reflected, among other things, the outrage produced by the huge concessions that the <u>Conservadores</u>, attempting to preserve part of the original export market, made to British interests. Nationalist sentiment grew against both <u>Conservadores</u> and British influence.

The 1930's saw sweeping political and social changes. The new import-substituting industrialists sought to increase their influence in government decisions. The military saw industrialization as the path to international power, and British influence as the major obstacle to industrialization. Ideological alternatives to democracy were being tried in Europe in the 1930's by apparently successful regimes. Moreover, the Church, particularly after the beginning of the Spanish Civil War, was ready to grant ideological legitimacy to anti-democratic movements. From all these elements a nationalist-industrialist ideology with strong authoritarian components began to develop. It had a wide appeal against which the old ruling sectors could oppose only a mockery of democracy and a dependent association with England.[28]

The Urban Popular Sector. During the 1930's the urban popular sector (i.e., the working class and segments of the lower middle class) went through a process of rapid political activation. But none of the existing political parties was willing to absorb a sector that was formed largely by recent rural migrants-- not even the Socialists and Communists, whose basic constituencies were skilled workers and European migrants.[29] World War II further complicated the domestic political situation. The demands

---

[28]The perception by the growing numbers of urban workers of the "democracy" they saw in operation could only reinforce their assessment of the political system and the ruling sectors.

[29]The more established sectors referred to the new migrants as "the shirtless," "the blackheads," "the zoological landslide," and other intentionally derogatory terms. Perón wisely responded by appropriating most of these terms to underline the popular character of his following. This was primarily the language of <u>Conservadores</u> and <u>Radicales</u> supporters, but the reactions of Socialists and Communists toward the new and increasingly active migrants were not noticeably better; see, among other discussions of the reactions of the "traditional" Argentine left, J.A. Ramos, <u>Revolución y contrarevolución en la Argentina</u> (La Reja, 1961), and A. Hernández Arregui, <u>La formación de la conciencia nacional</u> (Hachón, 1964). For a general analysis of this period, see A. Ciria, <u>Partidos y poder en la Argentina moderna (1930-1946)</u> (Jorge Alvarez Editor, 1964).

for autarchy and industrialization, as well as the diffusion of pro-Axis ideologies, clashed with British interests and with the pro-Ally international policies that most of the established sectors favored. Like the rural migrants, the new industrialists and many military officers could find no political parties through which to channel their preferences. The new issues and ideologies had a profound impact on the military, and for the first time the oligarchy could not count on their firm allegiance. In 1943, when it became evident that the 1944 elections were to be decided by "patriotic fraud," the military ousted the Conservadores government. In the resulting military government, Colonel Perón emerged as the leader best able to pull together all the dissident elements that the Conservadores period had generated.[30] Against this coalition, the Radicales, Conservadores, Socialists, and Communists formed a "Democratic Union," but they were defeated (in honest elections) by Perón in 1946.[31]

This is not the place for a study of Peronismo.[32] It included authoritarian components which were a blend of the ideologies of the 1930's, with a traditional (for Argentina) style of leadership.[33] Perón's policies of income distribution in favor of industry and the popular sector, the enactment of comprehensive labor and welfare legislation, and the introduction of numerous economic controls gained an enthusiastic response from the popular sector, but were very much at odds with the preferences of the recently displaced ruling sectors. As a consequence, and for the sake of "defending democracy," very early in Perón's government the old parties engaged in "disloyal opposition,"[34]

---

[30]Kenworthy, "The Formation . . .," provides an interesting analysis of the formation of the populist Peronista coalition.

[31]As an indication of (to say the very least) the degree of misperception of the national mood by the "Democratic Union," the Union allowed S. Braden, the U.S. Ambassador, to openly campaign for them. Perón capitalized on this fact, presenting the election as a choice between "Braden or Perón."

[32]A useful survey of interpretations of Peronismo is C. Fayt, La naturaleza del Peronismo (Editorial Viracocha, 1967).

[33]On the ideology of Peronismo during the period in which the movement was in power, see A. Ciria, Perón y el justicialismo (Siglo XXI, 1971).

[34]This concept is from J. Linz, "The Breakdown of Democratic Regimes," paper presented at the World Congress of Sociology, Varna, 1970. From the beginning the opposition tried to oust Perón illegally and engaged in very obstructionist parliamentary strategies.

reinforcing Peronismo's authoritarian tendencies. The massive appeal of Perón's and his wife's personalities had won Perón wide support, particularly among urban and rural workers. In addition, during Perón's government the standard of living of these sectors rose significantly, many labor rights were effectively protected, and workers could feel that they had gained some influence in national affairs. When attacked, Perón did not miss an opportunity to emphasize his opponents' past behavior to support his argument that the "return to democracy" they advocated was a trick for establishing a dictatorship to oppress the people. To say the least, Perón had a strong point when he observed that his opponents had never practiced the liberal advice they were now giving.

The effect of these developments was to increase the conflict between Peronistas and anti-Peronistas, and to decrease the chances that the formally democratic institutional framework could operate. Both "sides" helped in creating a situation that is well summarized by Floria:

> Perón's period was not only the period of Peronismo; it was also the period of anti-Peronismo. This polarization, as it was afterwards called, was the result of the articulation of power and opposition according to rules that were not shared. There were not two parties; there were "two countries": one whose inhabitants could only conceive of Argentina with Perón, and another that could only accept Argentina without Perón and, in terms of power, without Peronismo.[35]

By 1950 the broad coalition that Perón had formed began to disintegrate. Crop failures, misallocation of resources, unfavorable trends in international trade, and the increasing need for foreign currency to sustain advancing industrialization led to an economic crisis. Though unwilling to oppose agrarian interests by pursuing a program of land reform, and unwilling to force industry to absorb the costs of the economic crisis, Perón's government had to protect the gains achieved by the urban workers, its staunchest supporters. In this predicament the "easy" solution was to trigger the inflation that began to plague the Argentine economy. After 1949 the industrialists started to withdraw their support and align themselves with the opposition, and in 1954 Perón became involved in a serious conflict with the Catholic Church. The Armed Forces also began to waver in their support, and when, after two abortive attempts to stage coups in 1951 and June 1955, they found that the only remaining solid support for Perón came from the popular sector, they finally ousted him in September 1955.

---

[35] Floria; translated from Spanish by this author.

During the Provisional Government of General Eugenio
Aramburu (1955-1958), with the support of the now bitterly anti-
Peronista Armed Forces the old leaders of the old parties returned
to power. The point to be emphasized here is that by 1955 two
fundamental and overwhelmingly salient cleavages had coincided:
the political division of Peronistas and anti-Peronistas, and the
socio-economic division of the popular sector (constituted largely
by the working class) and the labor unions against the rest of
society. The result was intense and cumulative polarization.[36]

After 1955 a program of "democratization" was undertaken
which resulted in a drastic decrease in the share of wage income
in the GNP, numerous attempts to weaken labor unions, and the
electoral proscription of the Peronista party. If to these are
added the effects of economic stagnation and inflation,[37] it is
hardly surprising that the Peronistas maintained their allegiance
to Peronismo. The fact that the legal road to political power
was closed to them, the memories of recent times in which they
were much better off, the need to fight constantly for their
shares of income, the vengefulness of the Provisional Government's
policies--all hardened the Peronistas' opposition. Widespread
social unrest followed.[38]

For anti-Peronistas any return to the pre-1955 political
situation was totally out of the question. This view was shared

---

[36]The concept of polarization is discussed in R. Dahl, "Some
Explanations" in Dahl, ed., Political Oppositions in Western
Democracies (New Haven: Yale University Press, 1966), pp. 380ff.;
it is further analyzed in Chapter IV below. For a sense of the
saliency of this cleavage, see (among many others) D. Cúneo, El
desencuentro argentino (Pleamar, 1965); Floria; M. Grondona,
Argentina en el tiempo y en el mundo (Editorial Primera Plana,
1967); A. Morello and A. Tróccoli, Argentina ahora y después
(Editorial Platense, 1967); G. Merkx, "Politics and Economic
Change in Argentina from 1870 to 1966," unpublished dissertation,
Yale University, 1968. For evidence from survey data, J.L. de
Imaz, Motivación electoral (IDES, 1962), and P. Snow, "Argentine
Political Parties and the 1966 Revolution," Laboratory of Polit-
ical Research, University of Iowa, 1968.

[37]For the relevant data on the economy, see Tables 21-26
below.

[38]For information concerning the high degree of domestic political violence in Argentina, as indicated by data from this period,
see B. Russett et al., World Handbook of Political and Social
Indicators (New Haven: Yale University Press, 1964). See also
Baily and Rotondaro.

by the Armed Forces, where all officers suspected of _Peronista_
leanings had been purged. The military leaders had not forgotten
that, shortly before being ousted, Perón had seemed determined
to organize workers' militias. When a rebellion by _Peronistas_
failed in 1956, the anti-_Peronista_ military officers, breaking
an unwritten rule, ordered the leaders of the rebellion to be
shot, thereby increasing the existing polarization.

All the "constants" described above were still very much
present in Argentine life. The _Peronistas_ had been removed from
government in the name of "democracy." This meant elections would
be necessary, but the "wrong" party--_Peronismo_--controlled the
largest share of electors. Under these circumstances, political
activity was severely constrained: it could not serve as means
for the return of _Peronistas_ to government, nor as a channel for
the implementation of socio-economic policies favored by _Peronis-
tas_ and the labor unions.[39] The discrepancy between the outwardly
expressed democratic beliefs of the ruling sectors and the actual
workings of the political system was almost beyond measure. In
addition, the severe socio-economic crisis (which will be analyzed
further below) had accentuated the manifold rigidities in the
social structure, and was creating new patterns of stagnation
and dependence. Finally, no matter how great the economic, social, and political costs, the established sectors were determined
to close any significant political access to a politically activated urban popular sector.

Here I have tried merely to underline political and social
constants "extracted" from historical sequence, without attempting
the (here) impossible task of explaining their emergence. Despite
the pitfalls that are unavoidable in highly condensed descrip-
tions, it was essential to discuss these "constants." They refer
to historical factors that are difficult to measure in their more
immediate effects, whether on the social processes studied in the
section immediately following or on those connected with the 1966
coup that are the subject of the final section of this chapter.
But insofar as they determine a persistent and pervasive "political climate," these "constants" form the broad base of reference
without which it seems impossible to achieve an understanding of
more specific factors.

The focus of this chapter turns now toward a more "horizontal" perspective: an analysis of the social context of the
1955-1966 period. This analysis is provided on the assumption

---

[39]This theme is examined in much more detail in Chapter IV
below.

that this context, to a large extent influenced by the historical "constants," exerted a direct influence on the military intervention of June 1966.

The Social Setting of the 1966 Coup

In 1966 Argentina's per capita income was $818 in U.S. 1966 dollars.[40] In 1960 the number of unionized workers was around 2,600,000.[41] The contributions to the GNP of agriculture and industry were 16.6 and 34.0 percent respectively, while the percentage of working age population employed in agriculture was 21.4 and in industry, 28.0.[42] Clearly, Argentina was far advanced beyond the situation associated with "underdeveloped" agrarian, "traditional" societies. But these data must be considered from the perspective of a long period of slow growth.[43] In 1929 Argentina's per capita income was about 700 U.S. 1960 dollars.[44] At that time the Argentine per capita income was slightly below that of Australia, a country remarkably similar to Argentina in terms of production and relations with the world market. Today, Australia's per capita income is almost twice that of Argentina.

From 1925-1929 to 1961-1965 the average per capita growth rate in Argentina has been 0.8 percent yearly. Alejandro offers this description of the situation:

---

[40] University of California, Statistical Abstract for Latin America, 1966.

[41] Needler, Political Development . . ., p. 96.

[42] International Labour Organization, Yearbook of Labour Statistics, 1967.

[43] In my examination of economic aspects, I have relied heavily on the excellent Essays . . . of Alejandro. Other important sources are C. Díaz Alejandro, Exchange Rate Devaluation in a Semi-Industrialized Country: The Experience of Argentina 1955-1961 (Cambridge: The MIT Press, 1965); A. Ferrer, La economía argentina: Las etapas de su desarrollo y problemas actuales (Fondo de Cultura Económica, 1963); G. di Tella and M. Zymmelman, Las etapas del desarrollo argentino (Eudeba, 1967); J. Villanueva, La inflación argentina (Instituto Torcuato di Tella, 1964: mimeo); UN-ECLA, El desarrollo económico de la Argentina, 5 vols. (New York, 1959: mimeo); UN-ECLA and Consejo Nacional de Desarrollo (CONADE), Distribucion del ingreso y desarrollo económico en la Argentina (New York, 1968).

[44] Alejandro, Essays . . ., p. 55.

Since 1930 . . . the growth rate has been so small, the
cyclical fluctuations so violent, and the swings in income
distribution so pronounced that it is easy to believe that
during some years several groups have been worse off than
they, or their parents, were during 1925-1929. Furthermore,
in some public services (e.g., telephones, railroads, the
post office, statistical services) and in some import-substituting manufactures, quality has deteriorated so that a
quality-corrected growth rate would be even smaller . . . .
Although time-series for the Argentine terms of trade are
of doubtful reliability, it is likely that they declined
between 1925-1929 and recent years; correcting the growth
rate for this decline would further shave it.[45]

Taking the Perón period (1946-1955) as the baseline, the
per capita income reached in 1947 was not surpassed until 1965,
and the per capita real wages of 1947 were surpassed only in
1958 and in 1965, to fall below the 1947 level in the following
years.[46] The characteristics of this arrested development require
closer examination:

(1) When the GNP time-series since 1946 are considered, it
can be seen that, within the average low growth rate, wild
fluctuations have taken place from year to year. As column
(1) of Table 21 shows, in the years 1948, 1949, 1950, 1952,
1956, 1959, 1962, 1963, and 1966 net losses in per capita
income were registered--in some cases of substantial magnitude.

(2) The average 1946-1966 inflation rate has been 26.5 percent annually, but it was substantially higher in the 1955-
1966 period and in the years of negative growth (see column
(2) of Table 21).

(3) After reaching a maximum of 46.9 percent in 1952, the
salary and wage share in the GNP declined to 39.8 percent in
1965 (see column (3) in Table 21), even though the productivity per worker in 1961 was 23 percent above the 1953 level.[47]

(4) During the 1949-1966 period Argentina suffered a chronic
foreign exchange shortage (see column (4) of Table 21), which
was aggravated in the years of economic recovery.

---

[45] Ibid., pp. 69-70.

[46] Computed from Banco Central de la República Argentina, Boletín
Estadístico, several issues.

[47] UN-ECLA and CONADE, p. 193.

Table 21

ANNUAL MEASURES OF VARIOUS KEY ECONOMIC INDICATORS: ARGENTINA, 1946-1966

Year	Annual Changes of Gross Domestic Product per Capita (percent of previous year level; in constant pesos) (1)	Yearly Percent Inflation (2)	Wages and Salaries as Percentage of Gross National Product (3)	Change in Net Foreign Exchange Reserves (in million current U.S. dollars) (4)
		Perón's Government		
1946	6.4%	17.7%	38.7%	
1947	11.9	13.5	37.3	
1948	-0.7	13.1	40.6	
1949	-6.5	31.1	45.7	-269
1950	-0.3	25.5	45.9	166
1951	2.1	36.7	43.0	-333
1952	-8.2	38.7	46.9	-173
1953	5.1	4.0	44.8	279
1954	1.9	3.8	45.6	-33
1955	5.0	12.3	43.0	-175

Table 21 (continued)

Year	(1)	(2)	(3)	(4)
		1955-1966 Period		
1956	-0.2	13.4	42.6	-19
1957	3.6	24.7	41.4	-60
1958	5.3	31.6	43.3	-217
1959	-7.7	113.7	37.8	113
1960	6.1	27.3	38.4	161
1961	5.1	13.5	39.9	-57
1962	-3.7	28.1	39.1	-234
1963	-5.5	24.1	39.1	202
1964	6.2	22.1	38.2	-11
1965	6.7	28.6	39.1	139
1966	-2.4	32.3	39.8	53

Sources: Column (1): Banco Central de la República Argentina, Origen del producto y composición del gasto
nacional: Suplemento del Boletín Estadístico, n. 6 (Buenos Aires, 1966), P. 18, and Alejandro,
Essays ..., P. 352; Column (2): Alejandro, Essays ..., P. 528 (Buenos Aires cost of living);
Column (3): UN-ECLA and CONADE, El desarrollo económico y la distribución del ingreso en la Argentina
(New York, 1968), P. 164; Column (4): Alejandro, Essays ..., P. 353.

Many economists agree that the foreign exchange shortage has been the single most important factor in retarding economic growth in Argentina. This shortage has been closely related to other factors. First, as Table 22 shows, the quantum index of Argentine exports declined from 1925-1929 to 1960-1964 not only in per capita but also in absolute terms, reflecting lagging agricultural productivity (see column (2) of Table 22). During most of this period the domestic terms of trade discriminated against agrarian products (see column (3) of Table 22). In addition, of the net increase in national capital stock between 1929 and 1955, only 1.0 percent went to the rural sector.[48]

Second, from the 1930's to almost the end of Perón's government, Argentine industry expanded "horizontally" by putting heavy emphasis on consumer-goods import-substitution. But the "exhaustion" of these "easy" stages of import-substitution placed serious strains on Argentina's declining import capacity.[49] Domestic industrial expansion was hindered by problems of high costs and distorted schedules of supply, as well as severe financial, technological, and managerial limitations. Under such conditions, the need for critical inputs of intermediate and raw materials, as well as of capital goods, grew at a time when exports were lagging. There were growing demands for capital and technology transfers from abroad, indicating a need (as well as the great difficulties to be faced) for making significant advances toward more mature--i.e., more vertically integrated, with a better structure of costs and supply--industrialization. Furthermore, increases in the domestic fabrication of capital goods were almost entirely at the level of relatively simple equipment, and Argentine production was not able to satisfy the growing demand for more complex equipment. The yearly average of machinery imports was 198 million U.S. dollars in 1951-1955, 352 million in 1956-1960, and 498 million in 1961-1965.[50] An observation made by Alejandro neatly summarizes this situation: The income elasticity of Argentine demands for imports was 2.6, which meant that, when and if national income grew by one unit, it generated a demand for 2.6 units of imported goods; therefore, the foreign exchange position of the country was worsened by positive rates of growth.[51]

---

[48]Alejandro, Essays . . ., p. 75.

[49]This subject has been examined in detail (with sources cited) in Chapter II above.

[50]Computed from Dirección Nacional de Estadísticas y Censos, Boletín Estadístico, several issues, and Alejandro, Essays . . ., Statistical Annex.

[51]Ibid., p. 356.

Table 22

ARGENTINE ECONOMIC INDICES: 1925-1964

Years	Quantum Indices of Argentine Merchandise Exports (1951-1954 : 100) (1)	Index of Agrarian Production (1960 : 100) (2)	Internal Terms of Trade (Ratio of Rural Prices to Industrial Prices) (1935-1939 : 100) (3)	
1925-1929	179	--	100	(1935-1939)
1930-1939	167	--	72	(1940-1945)
1940-1944	135	86	77	(1945-1949)
1945-1949	133	85	83	(1950-1955)
1950-1954	106	87	93	(1956-1958)
1955-1959	124	99	96	(1959-1961)
1960-1964	160	102	103	(1962-1964)

Sources: Column (1): Alejandro, Essays . . ., p. 76; column (2): Banco Central de la República Argentina, p. 36; column (3): Alejandro, Essays . . ., p. 89.

The effects of the factors cited--particularly the pressure of the growth years on the foreign exchange position of Argentina--led to drastic devaluations of the peso, usually combined with programs aimed at restricting internal demand and eliminating "marginal" industrial producers. By making imports and exportable agrarian goods more expensive, devaluations fed inflation, at the same time that the effects of internal policies drastically decreased output and demand. As can be seen in Table 21, the years of negative growth were usually also those of higher inflation and negative income redistributions. One major goal of devaluations was to increase, by the restriction of domestic demand and income transfers, short-run available exports and, in the long run, to improve agrarian productivity. These effects were supposed to be produced by improving the domestic agrarian terms of trade and the dollar-value of rural exportable commodities. But these policies meant severe income losses for the urban-industrial sector, which led to the intense social conflict that marked the 1955-1966 period. As a consequence of this conflict, the redistributive policies were soon relaxed, and the presumably beneficial consequences that would follow from them were never realized.[52]

An important effect of inflation and devaluations has been wild fluctuations in income shares. As a UN-ECLA and CONADE study says:

The effect of these devaluations on income distribution occurs in two stages. In the first, a horizontal distribution takes place when relative prices change in favor of agriculture, consisting of inter-sectoral income changes from the urban sectors to the agrarian sector or, more specifically, to agrarian producers. But since the effect of devaluation on relative prices is combined with policies of salary restriction or increased unemployment, to some extent the horizontal redistribution is transformed into a vertical redistribution. This means that, in the final analysis, the main income changes [produced by devaluations] are harmful to urban workers and beneficial to agrarian producers, while the relative position of urban entrepreneurs is damaged only to the extent that the effects of devaluation are more intense than the effects of salary [restriction] policies.[53]

In short, devaluations benefit the agrarian sector, but as inflation proceeds and no new devaluation takes place, the urban sector (however "its" share is allocated between workers and entrepreneurs) recovers its losses. At some point, the effects of devaluation are annulled or even reversed, domestic economic activity increases again, a new foreign exchange crisis is produced, and a new devaluation is made. The magnitude of the shifts of income for several Argentine sectors during 1958-65 can be seen in Table 23.

It is difficult to exaggerate the political consequences of this turbulent economic situation, particularly in a setting of a low level of political legitimacy and a high degree of popular disaffection. Note that the combination of constantly high inflation (aggravated in negative growth years) with drastic devaluations and slow or no growth meant that to remain at the same level of monetary income would have involved heavy real-income losses. Thus, gains made by all sectors were extremely unstable, and the zero-sum situation created by economic stagnation served to raise the stakes of the conflict.

---

[52]Analysis of these and related aspects of economic policy can be found in A. Ferrer et al., Los planes de estabilización en la Argentina (Paidós, 1969).

[53]UN-ECLA and CONADE, p. 264; translated from the Spanish by this author.

Table 23

INTERSECTORAL INCOME VARIATIONS EXPRESSED AS PERCENTAGES OF
THE INCOME PARTICIPATION OF EACH SECTOR: 1958-1965

	Average of Absolute Variations for Each Sector	Maximum Yearly Positive Variation for Each Sector	Maximum Yearly Negative Variation for Each Sector
RURAL			
Agrarian	12.1%	34.8%	-20.8%
URBAN			
Industry	4.8	10.1	-8.5
Construction	7.8	37.5	-11.1
Commerce	6.2	7.8	-22.0
Transport and Communications	4.4	12.7	-6.7
General Government	8.1	14.3	-17.0
Electricity, Gas, and Water	10.1	37.5	-20.0

Source: UN-ECLA and CONADE, p. 217.

Before going any further let us look at some more disaggregated data. As previously noted, the real wage income in 1965 was about the same level as in 1945. However, as Table 21 showed, the share of salaries and wages in the GNP decreased during the 1955-1966 period. This apparent discrepancy disappears at the level of more disaggregated data. First, the recurrent attempts to eliminate "marginal" industrial producers, combined with the introduction of more capital-intensive techniques,[54] produced a

---

[54]J.M. Katz, "Características estructurales del crecimiento industrial argentino," Desarrollo Económico, VII, No. 26 (1967). An excellent exploration of the socio-political consequences of these changes is in Cardoso and Faleto, pp. 130ff.

large pool of urban unemployed,[55] especially in the early 1960's. Since real wage data reflect only the incomes of those lucky enough to find work, they give only a partial picture of the income position of the popular sector. Second, among those employed, there were wide differences in the real income positions of those workers who were well organized and those who, belonging to the less dynamic sectors of the economy, lacked the degree of organization necessary to obtain satisfaction of their economic demands.

The source of data for Table 24 does not discriminate between wage and salary earners, but census data show that an important proportion of the "Industry and Mining" and "Construction" categories consists of blue-collar workers. The "Commerce and Finance" category is formed largely by white-collar workers, while "Services" (which includes government workers) is a very mixed category. It is important to note that while industrial workers fared relatively well, other blue-collar workers and apparently most white-collar employees did not. This circumstance surely underlay the disaffection shown by these latter groups during the 1955-1966 period, their initial willingness to support the military government, and their responsiveness to a "law and order" appeal. However, no matter how badly they fared, the non-industrial workers did better than those sectors even less capable of exerting effective pressure on the national government. As Table 24 shows, pensioners and _rentistas_ in particular were heavy losers.[56]

In other words, at the national level the economic "game" was definitely zero-sum, and the better organized (and perhaps in the short-run, economically more indispensable) sectors of urban entrepreneurs, agrarian entrepreneurs, and industrial workers could increase their real-income shares at the expense of other less organized, politically weaker sectors and regions.

The government as an institution was another loser. In terms of governmental resources (i.e., the pool of human and economic means at its disposal for the making and implementation of policies), there was a steady deterioration in the 1955-1966

---

[55] For discussion of this aspect, see UN-ECLA and CONADE, pp. 123, 193ff., and the "Introducciones" to the "Planes de Desarrollo" 1965-1969 and 1970-1974 (Consejo Nacional de Desarrollo, 1965 and 1970).

[56] Consistent with this general point, many regions of the interior, also incapable of exerting effective pressure on the national government, were also heavy losers (see Consejo Nacional de Desarrollo, "Introducción" [1970]).

Table 24

AVERAGE REAL-INCOME OF FAMILIES IN ARGENTINA IN SELECTED YEARS[a]
(1953 : 100)

	1946	1949	1953	1959	1961	1965
Salary and Wage Earners						
Industry and Mining	88	119	100	90	115	_146_
Construction	106	_137_	100	98	108	118
Transport and Communication	106	_128_	100	95	106	110
Commerce and Finance	85	_111_	100	94	_111_	_112_
Services	84	_113_	100	91	103	109
Entrepreneurs						
Agriculture	111	82	100	_143_	89	117
Industry, Mining, and Construction	115	_148_	100	124	135	143
Commerce	162	_175_	100	161	169	155
Transport	86	104	100	150	143	_170_
Services	109	_132_	100	98	105	109
Social Security Pensions	105	_130_	100	79	96	97
Rentiers	_150_	122	100	56	49	39
TOTAL	103	116	100	108	112	124

[a]Year of maximum real-income underlined.

Source: UN-ECLA and CONADE, p. 130.

period. In Lasswell's terminology, poor governmental performance and diminished resources resulted in a serious "power dis-accumulation" that hampered governmental problem-solving capabilities.[57] This reduced capability reflected the general social situation but also contributed significantly to its worsening and to the final 1966 breakdown.

In 1965 the tax revenues of the national government amounted to 13.2 percent of the GNP, which decreased to 11.9 percent in 1960, and to 10.9 percent in 1965. The income of the social security system amounted in the same years to 5.0, 3.5,

_____

[57]See Lasswell, "The Policy Sciences . . . ."

and 4.8 percent of the GNP.[58] (The deterioration of governmental income can be seen clearly in Table 25, where comparable data for other countries have been included.) The substantial decline in personal income taxes (see Table 26) was partially compensated for by increases in indirect tax collection, but the impact on income distribution was regressive. The drop in governmental income generated huge (and increasing) budget deficits, which were met by highly inflationary increases in the money supply.[59] The proportion of government expenditures allocated to public works dropped from 20.9 percent of the national budget in 1955-

Table 25

DATA ON TAXATION FOR ARGENTINA AND SELECTED OTHER COUNTRIES

	Percentage of Working Age Population Filing Income Tax Returns	Declared Income for Taxing Assessment as a Percentage of Total Personal Income
Argentina		
1953	10%	18%
1959	9	10
1961	5	9
Other Countries		
United States (1950)	89	77
England (1952-1953)	90	80
Australia (1958-1959)	80	68

Source: UN-ECLA, Economic Bulletin for Latin America, Vol. IX, 1 (April 1966).

---

[58] Computed from Consejo Nacional de Desarrollo, Plan Nacional de Desarrollo (1965). For useful data and analysis on this topic, see O. Ozlak, "Inflación y política fiscal en la Argentina: El impuesto a los réditos en el período 1956-1965," Instituto Torcuato di Tella, Centro de Investigaciones en Administración Pública, Documento de Trabajo (1970).

[59] For data on this point, see Oficina de Estudios para la Cooperación Económica Internacional, Argentina económica y financiera (FIAT, 1966), p. 366.

Table 26

DIRECT TAXES AS PERCENTAGE OF TOTAL GOVERNMENTAL INCOME
IN ARGENTINA: 1946-1964

Perón Government

1946	38.5%
1947	46.3
1948	49.8
1949	46.9
1950	47.3
1951	43.0
1952	47.3
1953	45.0
1954	41.7
1955	41.8

1956-1964 Period

1956	34.1
1957	37.9
1958	39.3
1959	29.1
1960	32.8
1961	33.0
1962	30.6
1963	30.6
1964	28.3

Source: Panorama de la Economía Argentina, No. 3, 1967.

1959 to 14.5 percent in 1965.[60] A partially overlapping catego-
ry--public capital investments--were 8.6 percent less during
1960-1965 than during 1955-1960.[61] Although the data are incom-
plete, it is very probable that real salaries of government employees declined throughout this period, partially recovering
during 1964-1966, but never returning to the 1949 level. Perpet-
ual political crisis resulted in a constant turnover of cabinet
members and high civil servants,[62] and in the few government

---

[60]See ibid., p. 351.

[61]UN-ECLA and CONADE.

[62]See E. Kenworthy, "Coalitions in the Political Development of
Latin America" in S. Groennings et al., eds., The Study of Coalition Behavior (New York: Holt, Rinehart and Winston, 1970).

activities which can be measured for productivity, a decline is evident.[63]

The general process can be summarized as follows: Devaluations benefitted agrarian producers and were "paid for" by the urban sector. This situation was reversed by the inflation and economic reactivation that took place between devaluations. Within the urban sector another "game" was played for the allocation of gains and losses among different categories of entrepreneurs and workers: the gains that could be appropriated by some of the organized categories were "paid for" by other less organized sectors and areas. Inflation meant that anyone could lose, on the average, one-fourth of his real income in a year.[64] From this situation a "catching-up game" developed, in which only a few sectors were able to influence public policies so as to keep them ahead in the constantly changing distribution of income shares. In this sense, a "powerful sector" was one that was able to maintain or improve (without serious lag) its real-income position by ensuring the implementation of favorable government policies--such as urban and rural entrepreneurs or industrial workers. (In this sense not even the government could be considered "powerful.")

An important aspect of this situation was determining strategies that would enable sectors to gain power. First, since inflation continued at a rapid rate, a sector that was trying to catch up had to do so in a relatively short time. Second, the focus of demands for policies that would permit "catch-up" was not in institutions such as Parliament, political parties, and state governments, which played at best a marginal role in the reallocation of economic resources. These demands were concentrated on the Presidency, with the result that it became increasingly unlikely that other political institutions could play a meaningful role. Third, the focus on the Presidency increased the importance of channels of access that enabled actors to exercise "power"[65] over the President. Thus, the military became

---

[63] See Oficina de Estudios . . ., pp. 351ff.

[64] This situation could be described as one of "fluid scarcity." It is certainly very different from that in more "traditional" and more "developed" societies, where income shares (albeit by different mechanisms) are more stable in the short run. The political correlates of fluid scarcity are not likely to be similar to those of more stabilized allocations of economic goods. (An interesting examination of this aspect of Argentine politics can be found in Merkx, "Politics . . . .")

[65] Used here in the sense defined by Harold Lasswell and Abraham

the most effective channel for the satisfaction of sectoral demands; civilian groups sought to influence military factions which could exercise power over the Presidency. This fractionalized the military, of course, and resulted in more and more numerous and changing demands being channeled through them.

The channeling of demands through the military involved a very real threat to the government of being ousted.[66] This danger was evident in the numerous planteos (demands by the military backed by the threat of using force if they were denied by the government), as well as in the many coups and attempted coups during 1955-1966. Those sectors that could induce threats of coups from the military had a definite advantage in playing the "catching-up game." These inducements could be obtained through direct access, as in the case of the urban and rural entrepreneurs. For the better-organized urban workers, indirect strategies could produce similar results. By promoting social unrest, as well as by paralyzing production through strikes and occupying factories, they could make governments appear unable to keep minimal law and order, and thus put them in immediate danger of being ousted. That is, the situation benefitted those workers in the better-organized and wealthier unions that could threaten governments with sustained disruptions. (This is reflected in the income figures in Table 24 above.)

It should be borne in mind that the legitimacy of the governments of this period was widely questioned, and that there was generalized political disaffection. Under these conditions threats were very real, and any government that valued survival in office could not ignore them. Hence, the governments tended to adopt whatever policies best satisfied the sector that was most threatening at a given time. But the zero-sum conditions meant that each such policy decision raised new threats from other powerful sectors. Frequent policy changes resulted from each governmental decision to placate one sector and the new threats that each such decision generated. (The fluctuations in the preceding tables reflect this pattern.)

Kaplan (Power and Society [New Haven: Yale University Press, 1950])--i.e., the ability to impose severe deprivations.

[66]Charles Anderson considers threat-capabilities a major asset in Latin American politics (Politics and Economic Change in Latin America [New York: Van Nostrand, 1967]), Chapter II. In a similar vein, see the interesting discussion of a "dual currency" (votes and control of means of violence) in Argentine politics by Kenworthy, "Coalitions . . ." and "The Formation . . . ."

The resulting situation is well described by Huntington's concept of mass praetorianism.[67] Where the primary political aim was control of the means for effectively threatening the survival of the government, political institutions designed for more consensual problem-solving could hardly survive. And where the "threat" strategy prevailed, the most effective way for a sector to have its demands met was to be more threatening than the other sectors. Thus, there was a tendency to escalate the levels of threats. The only effective strategy for each sector was to "play" according to the actual rather than to the institutionally prescribed rules. Otherwise, an "idealistic" sector would have lost heavily in a struggle in which, because of stagnation and inflation, the stakes were very high. A dynamic process begins that is very difficult to stop: praetorianism breeds more praetorianism until the conditions for systemic breakdown are reached.

Parallel to this trend, further complications were introduced by the changing lines of social differentiation. In particular, the new inter-industry cleavage (analyzed in Chapter II) destroyed the cohesion of the industrial entrepreneurs. To a certain extent, this cleavage had a similar effect on urban workers: they became differentiated into the obviously unemployed and various categories of employed working in industrial sectors of varying dynamism and financial strength. This social differentiation gave to Argentine politics characteristics that are typical of mass praetorianism at a high level of modernization. The propertied sectors agreed on the need to close political access to the popular sector and to refuse popular policy demands. This was accomplished mainly by severe constraints on the electoral arena.[68] The urban sector united to advance its common interests in opposition to the agrarian sector, and the differentiation within the urban social structure created shifting alignments of entrepreneurs and workers in the same urban subsector hostile toward other urban subsectors.[69]

Praetorian politics at high modernization become very complex in two ways. First, social differentiation leads to more, highly activated political actors playing--at several levels simultaneously--a "catching-up game" based on threats to the

---

[67] See Huntington, Political Order . . ., esp. pp. 192-237. For further discussion of this concept, see Chapter II above.

[68] This aspect is analyzed in detail in Chapter IV below.

[69] See M. Mamalakis, "The Theory of Sectoral Clashes," The Latin American Research Review, IV, No. 3 (1969), and G. Merkx, "Sectoral Clashes and Political Change: The Argentine Experience," same journal and issue.

government. Second, the combination of high stakes and weak constraints means that formally prescribed patterns become very poor indicators of actual political behavior. The influence of the "constants" identified earlier in the chapter created the initial conditions of dubious legitimacy, a high degree of popular disaffection, and intense rigidity of the established sectors. The Peronista period accelerated social differentiation and political demands well beyond social integration and social performance. Developmental bottlenecks diminished possible payoffs and made the competition for the allocation of social resources into a zero-sum game. Under these conditions, government personnel had little opportunity for effective decision-making and policy-implementation beyond what was demanded by the more threatening political actors. The steady deterioration of government aggravated the social situation. In the "catching-up game," most political actors and sectors pursued the vitally important goal of at least keeping pace with the inflation, using whatever strategies were most effective. Unfortunately, the most effective strategies for the individual actors were also the most damaging to overall social performance. Each actor was trapped in a situation he could not attempt to change by his own actions without losing heavily, and was forced to act in ways that led to even further deterioration of the social context upon which the satisfaction of his demands largely depended. Given the historical heritage, the zero-sum conditions, and the intensity of social conflict, it was very unlikely that these actors could have reached agreements among themselves that would have channeled their competition into less damaging patterns. This should have been accomplished by governmental action, but its low level of legitimacy and limited resources prevented any serious efforts by the government in this direction. The political actors were rational, in the sense that they pursued important goals with the most effective means at their disposal. But within a context where attempts to establish effective political institutions have failed and mass praetorianism has resulted, even individually rational actions can lead to major systemic crises. This is a classic problem with which political theory has been concerned from the very beginnings, but it is in a situation of high modernization that the likelihood of its emergence as a problem seems greatest.

The continued crises generated by this situation annul most individual and sectoral gains. But since there is no way for individuals or sectors to change the institutional parameters (the "rules of the game"), the only course is to continue along the same lines, hoping in each case that the social deterioration can be minimized. Slowly the possibility of another course emerges. After they have played a "loser's game" for some time, it becomes evident to most actors that most of them lose consistently while a few gain--but only to have most of their gains annulled shortly thereafter. Once this is perceived, the parameters of the situation are widely questioned. It is concluded

that the "rules of the game" ought to be changed, and with them
the political institutions that have been unable to conduct the
game in ways more beneficial to the participants. When this assessment becomes general, what might be termed a "ceiling consensus" is reached, and most sectors agree that the political system
should be changed and new parameters for competition established.
Of course, such a "consensus" is limited strictly to this point:
the actors disagree as much as ever about what the new rules
should be. Given a previous history of mass praetorianism, it is
likely--when the political system changes--that there will be an
authoritarian imposition of new "rules" by the coalition that
succeeds in gaining the governmental power.

A "ceiling consensus" eliminates the few remaining points
of support for the existing political system, which has failed to
overcome praetorianism in a way that would have created political
allegiance and improved social performance. From that point on,
it is only a matter of how long it will take for a winning coalition to emerge from the set of political actors represented in
the ceiling consensus.[70] A strong indication that this was the
case in Argentina is given by the broad initial support by most
organized groups for the 1966 coup.

Political Opinions and Attitudes. Observers find many
"paradoxes" in Argentine politics. For example, Kalman Silvert
finds the following "paradoxical" attitudes: (1) "zero-sum
mentality" and "lack of responsible entrepreneurship"; (2) "the
almost universal view . . . that no public measure can be good
for almost everybody"; (3) "the narrowness of loyalty horizons
. . . [and] the failure to accept the state as the ultimate ar-
biter of secular disputes."[71] I would argue that, while Silvert
is correct in his perception of attitudes, he is wrong in be-
lieving that these attitudes are "paradoxical." They may be so
from the point of view of Argentina's relatively high level of
development (gauged by static criteria that do not allow for consideration of the circumstances and processes analyzed in the
preceding pages), but these attitudes are hardly surprising given
the social context from which they stem.

Survey data, unfortunately scant, provide support for
Silvert's perceptions. In a nationally representative sample

---

[70]Of course, the patterns of coalition-formation are anything
but random. In Chapter II we examined the factors that lead to a
consensus based on the political exclusion of the popular sector.

[71]"Liderazgo político y debilidad institucional en la Argen-
tina," Desarrollo Económico, I, No. 3 (1963). (Also printed in
Silvert, The Conflict Society: Reaction and Revolution in Latin
America [American Universities Field Staff, 1966].)

148

(excepting the sparsely populated Patagonian states),[72] taken
three months before the 1966 coup, respondents were asked several
of the questions used by Almond and Verba in The Civic Culture.[73]
Table 27 shows the measure of one important component of political activation--political awareness--indicating that the impact
of government on daily life, as perceived by the Argentine respondents, is very high. Only 20 percent of the respondents declared
themselves supporters of a political party; 54 percent did not
even "lean" toward any party.[74] In another survey taken shortly
before the 1966 coup, to the question "Do you think that Argentine
politics need new men?", 83 percent answered "Yes" and only 4
percent, "No."[75] In Kirkpatrick's survey 42 percent agreed with
the statement "A few leaders would do more for the country than
all the laws and talk."[76] A similar percentage expressed the
belief that the government is controlled by influential people
and groups who do not care at all about people's needs--an atti-
tude reflected in perceptions of the social structure, as shown
in Table 28. The sectors perceived as most influential are the
least "acceptable" groups--i.e., 71.6 percent of the respondents
would not support a military-supported party, 58.4 percent a
Church-supported party, and 89.7 percent a landowner-supported
party.[77]

As these data indicate, economic concerns are by far
the most salient. The answers to the question "What do you consider the most important problems this country is facing at present?", reported in Table 29, clearly reflect this saliency.

The relationship of the concerns reported in Table 29 to
political opinions is evidenced by the 96 percent positive answers

---

[72]Kirkpatrick.

[73]Gabriel Almond and Sidney Verba, The Civic Culture (Princeton:
Princeton University Press, 1963).

[74]For other similar data, see Snow, "Argentine Political Parties . . . ."

[75]Gallup survey, sample of the Greater Buenos Aires area (n =
1,000); reported in Polls (1967), pp. 21-31.

[76]Snow reports a survey, taken in Buenos Aires before the 1966
coup, that showed 60 percent of the respondents in complete agreement with the statement "We have too many platforms and political
programs; what we need is a strong man to lead us!" Another 23
percent agreed more or less, and only 17 percent were in complete
disagreement ("Argentine . . .," p. 42).

[77]Kirkpatrick.

Table 27

PERCENTAGES OF RESPONDENTS FROM SELECTED COUNTRIES WHO SAY
THAT NATIONAL GOVERNMENT HAS GREAT EFFECT ON THEIR DAILY LIVES

United States	41%
Germany	38
England	33
Italy	23
Mexico	7
Argentina	41
Upper Class (n = 157)	52.2
Middle Class (n = 960)	40.3
Lower Class (n = 721)	39.9

Sources: For Argentina: Kirkpatrick; national sample: n = 2,000; for other countries, Almond and Verba.

Table 28

PERCENTAGES OF RESPONSES TO QUESTION "WHO HAS GREATEST
INFLUENCE OVER GOVERNMENT?"

Military	33.8%
Church	14.6
Landowners	10.0
Peronistas	8.3
Labor Unions	8.3
Entrepreneurs	4.5
Other and Don't Know	20.5

Source: Kirkpatrick; national sample: n = 2,000.

Table 29

PERCENTAGES OF RESPONSES TO QUESTION CONCERNING
ARGENTINA'S MOST IMPORTANT PROBLEMS

	Income Groups			
	All	Low	Medium	High
Socio-Economic Concerns				
High cost of living	35%	32%	38%	10%
Inflation, general economic situation	27	22	27	60
Housing shortage	7	6	7	10
Various social and economic problems	7	8	7	4
Wages (low, inadequate)	3	5	2	--
Pensions	3	5	2	--
Unemployment	7	12	4	--
Political Concerns				
Bad government, corruption in politics	7	8	7	4
Trade union, corporation problems	2	1	2	6
Other				
Other answers	3	3	2	17
No problems	2	2	2	--
Don't know; no answer	8	9	8	2

Source: Gallup Survey, Polls; open ended questions, multiple
answers allowed; n = 1,000, sample of the Buenos Aires
area.

given to a question asking if respondents would support a party
that "promised to stamp out corruption and inefficiency from
government," as well as by the answers given to the question "What
classes in your opinion profit most from the government of President Illia--laborers, middle classes, or upper classes?", shown
in Table 30. If one considers as "favorable" those responses of
Table 30 that indicate that the respondent's own sector plus "All"
benefit from the Illia government, less than 15 percent of the
low and middle income respondents express favorable opinions.
Even high income respondents are far less satisfied than would
be expected. (Note the sharp rise of "Nobody" answers among high
income respondents.)

With respect to the economic situation, there was broad
perception of the zero-sum conditions (see Table 31). As may be
obvious, a "Remain the same" prediction concerning the Argentine

151

Table 30

PERCENTAGES OF RESPONSES TO QUESTION "WHO PROFITS MOST FROM THE ILLÍA GOVERNMENT?"

	All Respondents (n = 1,000)	Income Group		
		Low	Middle	High
Laborers	3%	4%	2%	4%
Middle classes	6	4	8	4
Upper classes	53	63	50	27
All, everybody	7	5	7	15
Nobody	17	9	19	35
Don't know	14	16	13	14

Source: Gallup Survey, Polls; n = 1,000, sample of the Buenos Aires area.

Table 31

PERCENTAGES OF RESPONSES TO QUESTION "DO YOU THINK THAT ARGENTINA'S ECONOMIC SITUATION WILL IMPROVE, REMAIN THE SAME, OR DETERIORATE IN THE NEXT MONTHS?"

Improve	24%
Remain the same	19
Deteriorate	48
Don't know	9

Source: Kirkpatrick; n = 2,000, national sample.

Table 32

PERCENTAGES OF RESPONSES TO QUESTIONS CONCERNING GOVERNMENTAL PERFORMANCE

To the question "Do you think the government will be able to check inflation?"

Yes	20%
No	67
No opinion	13

To the question "According to the government, the recently authorized rise in prices will raise the cost of living only some two percent. Do you think this is correct or that it will be more?"

Correct	4%
More	86
No opinion	10

Source: Gallup Survey, Polls; n = 1,000, sample of the Buenos Aires area.

economy is a pessimistic view. The responses reported in Table 32 are a good indication of the perceived efficiency of the government for coping with major problems.

The data in Tables 28-32 reflect a politically informed population, conscious of the inefficiency of government, skeptical about political parties, hostile in their inter-sectoral perceptions, and aware of the "zero-sum" character of the national "pie." A very weak commitment to the survival of the existing political system--even when menaced by unpopular sectors--is indicated by the large proportions that agree on the desirability of "throwing the rascals out" and the need for a "strong man." Even though the military are unpopular, in 1966 the way was paved for a military takeover that would not meet resistance from the popular sector.

Unhappily, interview data are almost totally lacking for other social strata. Except for entrepreneurs, there are no interview data on the elite's political opinions and attitudes.[78] Not surprisingly, entrepreneurs show hostility toward labor and its leaders, fears of labor's eventual access to political power, and receptivity to "law and order" appeals.[79] Government is perceived by them as the epitome of red tape and inefficiency, and the major business organizations openly welcomed the ouster of Presidents Perón (1955), Frondizi (1962), and Illía (1966).

As has been suggested earlier in this chapter, discussion of the politics of labor unions is, to a very large extent, discussion of _Peronismo_. The events of 1955-1966 could hardly inspire labor union allegiance to government, and agreeing for the first time with the more established sectors (but for different reasons and with very different expectations), the unions and _Peronista_ leaders welcomed the 1966 coup.[80]

Very little is known about the underpaid and overstaffed government bureaucracy, but it seems evident that low salaries,

---

[78]The best study of the Argentine elite--de Imaz, _Los que mandan_--has no interview data.

[79]See S. Cúneo, _Comportamiento y crisis de la clase empresaria_ (Editorial Pleamar, 1967); Freels, _El sector industrial . . .;_ and Cardoso, _Ideologías . . . ._

[80]See, e.g., the enthusiastic remarks about the coup by union and _Peronista_ leaders in _La Prensa_, June 29 and 30, 1966. It became obvious very soon to these leaders that these remarks expressed only a "ceiling consensus" and some quite unrealistic hopes that they would have greater political access under the military government.

widespread abuses of patronage, and the lack of a civil service prevented the emergence of a public service that, in the midst of crisis, could have maintained a reasonably high level of problem-solving capabilities.

A general, socially diffuse factor should be mentioned which provides a common basis for the different attitudes of the various sectors. In contrast to what might be expected in a "developing" country, contemporary Argentina has lacked a feeling of "emergence"--a sense that the present, whatever its shortcomings, is better and more promising than anything that has been before. Argentina's history and literature and, more generally, its intellectual climate are pervaded by the memory (or imagination) of lost opportunities, and of periods in which the country is seen to have been better off than it is today. There is also a pervasive search for historical blame--for the identification of actors and sectors to whom the responsibility may be attributed for a history perceived largely as failure. Even today, the nineteenth-century struggles between _unitarios_ and _federales_ are recalled with bitterness. The failure to achieve a more congenial social context has led to the cynical belief that political and sectoral competition takes place within a Hobbesian world. This view was confirmed for Argentine intellectuals, on both the right and the left, by the problems described in the preceding sections, and what they had to say about the political and social situation made even more likely the final breakdown of the pre-1966 political system.

Due in part to the linearity of language, I have been able to provide only a very limited account of the highly complex interactions among the political history, the socio-economic context, and the attitudinal dimensions of pre-1966 Argentina, but what has been presented should suffice to indicate the general setting within which the factors immediately connected to the 1966 coup should be examined.

The Coup of 1966

As one Argentine sociologist has observed, at one time or another "Argentine politicans have all gone 'to knock on the door of the barracks'."[81] Between the overthrow of Perón (1955) and 1962, the Armed Forces were controlled by _gorila_[82] military officers, with various _gorila_ factions alternating in control, in

---

[81] De Imaz, _Los que mandan_, p. 84.

[82] The nickname _gorila_ was a derogatory allusion to the strong anti-_Peronista_ views of these military officers.

different moments and in different services, reflecting the high degree of fractionalization of Argentine politics. From these circumstances shifting alignments and intense internal conflict in the Armed Forces resulted. When there is conflict inside the military, it is essential to study the internal alignments, their origins, their connections with other political forces, and their political consequences. Only in this way is it possible to examine the military as a "political actor," subject to various inducements, but "processing" them in special ways that depend to an important extent on factors relating to military organization. This means looking "behind" public statements and into details of organization virtually inaccessible to empirical research. I cannot claim any substantial advantages over others in this matter, but on the basis of informal interviews I had with leading military officers during the 1955-1966 period, as well as published evidence, I propose the preliminary analysis that follows.[83]

---

[83]The prevailing trend in the study of civil-military relations in "developing" countries has been to endow the military with sets of attitudes and high decision-making capabilities which entail taking at face value its organizational charts and public statements concerning its ethos. The military is then assigned a crucial developmental role, and assertions that the military is the only group able to exercise effective governmental power in "developing" societies are "explained." A good example of this approach, applied to Latin American countries, is in John Johnson, The Military and Society in Latin America (Stanford: Stanford University Press, 1964). But, as Robert Price says in a good critique of this literature, the empirical evidence does not support these analyses ("A Theoretical Approach to Military Rule in New States," World Politics, XXIII, No. 3 [1971]). In contrast to this approach, several authors have argued (I think correctly) that the political behavior of the military can only be understood in relation to the characteristics of the society in which it operates. They further argue (again I think correctly) that the middle class in modernizing contexts has very different goals of expanding or contracting its participation in the political system, depending on whether it is still striving for its own political incorporation or has already achieved it. A link between these middle class attitudes and military behavior is presumed to exist because of the predominantly middle class origins of military officers. The most important statements of this interpretation are José Nun, "The Middle Class . . ."; Huntington, Political Order . . .; Needler, Political Development . . .; and E. Nordlinger, "Soldiers in Mufti: The Impact of Military Rule upon Economic and Social Change in the Non-Western States," American Political Science Review, LXIV, No. 4 (1970). But . . . according to this line of interpretation, the political behavior of the

In the ousting of Perón, undoubtedly a majoritarian dictator, the Armed Forces made appeal to the need for restoration and preservation of political democracy. Subsequently, their anti-Peronista stand was strongly reinforced by a climate of great social unrest and the effects of the Cold War and the Cuban Revolution. Peronista unions and the Armed Forces became the opposite poles of an intense social conflict. The poor performance of civilian governments created much dissatisfaction among gorila military officers. The Army Chief of Staff, General Toranzo Montero, said that the Armed Forces were "the guardians of the republican way of life against any extremism or totalitarianism" and were ultimately responsible, due to "the failure of civilian authorities," for solving the problems "caused" by Peronismo and "subversion" and for "restoring the values of national unity and public order."[84] This assumption of the role of custodian of "basic values" opened the door wide for a long series of planteos and coups, especially after President Frondizi came to power in 1958 by means of an electoral "covenant" with Perón. The military's definition of its own role made it the interpreter of the content of the "basic values" it was assigned to protect, as well as the interpreter of when and how the "basic values" were being threatened--opening the way for the electoral proscription of Peronismo and the political parties suspected of being "facades" for it. Since it could be argued that the "basic values" were involved in practically all governmental decisions, the military became the most effective channel through which various sectors could have their demands satisfied by the government. Thus, the military became a reflection of all the anti-Peronista sectors

---

military (in particular, the goals of their intervention) depends entirely on societal-level variables. As I hope to show, though these variables are very important, they do not eliminate the need to consider empirical (as contrasted with face-value attributions) variations in organization at the military level. These latter, "intervening" variables mediate the effects of societal-level variables and, according to their differences, may lead to quite different patterns of political behavior in the military. Although the author does not explicitly discuss the issue in these terms, the two-level focus I am proposing has been fruitfully applied to the Brazilian case in Stepan, The Military . . . . For a detailed study of the theoretical and empirical questions raised by the behavior of the military in the Argentine case, see G. O'Donnell, "Modernización y golpes militares: Teoría, comparaciones y el caso argentino," Desarrollo Económico, October-December, 1972. (An English version of this paper will be published in D. Apter and M. Barrera, eds., Embourgeoisement and Radicalization in Latin America, forthcoming.)

[84]La Prensa, April 7, 1959.

of Argentine society. This direct involvement in partisan and sectoral issues destroyed vertical military authority patterns, led to numerous internal putschs, and shortened the careers of many officers.

By supporting the traditional political parties while remaining verbally committed to "democracy," the gorila officers found themselves in the old predicament: the "correct" parties and candidates could not win fair elections.[85] When they ousted President Frondizi in 1962, the gorila officers made it clear that they intended to establish a long-term dictatorship, which they presumed was needed to restore "order and authentic democracy" in Argentina. But within the Army and the Air Force a strong reaction had taken place. Many officers protested against the deleterious effects on careers and military organization of the high fractionalization caused by direct political involvement. They proposed that military men should withdraw from politics and "return to their specific duties." In retrospect, it is clear that this was an argument for organizational survival.[86] The suspension of direct political involvement would necessarily mean rejecting the gorila plans of eliminating political parties and elections. The argument for organizational survival and career preservation had wide appeal within the military; in addition, its "back to the barracks" implication evoked immediate support from many civilian sectors alarmed by the prospect of a gorila dictatorship. The intra-military conflict was perceived as one between the dictatorial gorilas and the more democratic, professionalist, military officers.[87] The factions clashed twice (September 1962 and April 1963), ending with a decisive legalista victory. During the short frays, the legalistas issued influential communiques stating that they were fighting for democracy, for a professionalist, apolitical army, and for the right of the people to cast their ballots "without exclusions" (which

---

[85] For further analysis of this theme see Chapter IV below.

[86] Several authors have emphasized this factor; see M. Needler, Generals vs. Presidents: Neomilitarism in Latin America (New York: Praeger, 1964), pp. 107ff. An Argentine author, J.M. Saravia, also argues that, in this case, organizational concerns-- not democratic allegiance--were the major determinants of the actions of the legalista military officers. This interpretation is endorsed in a Prologue to Saravia's book by one of the most influential military officers during these events (and until the present)--(Hacia la salida [Emecé, 1968]; Prologue by General A. López Aufranc).

[87] The latter were given the denomination of legalistas, with obvious positive connotations.

necessarily meant a lifting of the electoral ban on Peronistas).
But after their victory the legalistas found that, even though
they agreed on the professionalism issue, they were as divided as
ever concerning the question of whether or not to allow Peronistas
to run (and very likely win) in the next elections. After some
internal debate the opinion prevailed that "totalitarian parties
could not be granted the benefits of democracy"--i.e., the electoral arena remained closed for Peronistas. The legalistas pre-
sided over the messy Presidential elections of 1963 in which
Illía, the candidate of the old Radicales, was elected with less
than one-fourth of the total vote cast.[88]

    After the legalistas won control of the Armed Forces in
1963, important organizational changes took place. The Navy,
stronghold of the gorilas, had been decisively defeated, and the
Army established its clear hegemony over the Navy and the small
Air Force. The Armed Forces, under the strong leadership of
General Onganía, the Army Chief of Staff, and aided by numerous
U.S. advisory missions, were able to reestablish vertical authority and markedly foster professionalization. This resulted in
restoration of more normal authority and career patterns, in
increased organizational capabilities, in new modes of military
training that emphasized both the study of modern technology and
of "contemporary problems," in steady transmission of U.S. and
French "anti-subversive" and "civic action" doctrines, in a marked
decline in personal contacts with political party personnel, and
in a corresponding increase in personal contacts with those I have
called "incumbents of technocratic roles."[89] The resulting feeling of achievement within the military contrasted sharply with
the general social situation described earlier in this chapter.

    The fresh memory in the military of the high organiza-
tional costs of fractionalization made it determine to avoid
situations that might risk reintroducing it. As a consequence,
planteos and, in general, the channeling of sectoral demands were
explicitly rejected by the new military leadership (and the 1963-
1966 period was by and large free of them).[90] Professionalism

---

[88]See, on this election, Chapter IV below.

[89]The results I have described here are reasonably well-supported by the literature. The one exception is the reference
to the changes in patterns of personal contacts; for this matter
I rely mainly on my own impressions as a participant-observer
during the period.

[90]For an interesting statement of the "orthodox" legalista
position (and its manifold unresolved ambiguities), see General
B. Rattenbach, El sector militar de la sociedad (Círculo Militar
Argentino, 1966).

entailed redefining the Armed Forces' role as "above politics."
As General Onganía repeatedly observed, the Armed Forces should
abstain from political intervention except "under extreme circumstances." (What "extreme circumstances" would be was of course
left to the Armed Forces to determine.) First, military disen-
gagement from direct political involvement would not only facilitate professionalism, but it would also make possible a much
more general and severe condemnation of civilian authorities:
their failures could not be attributed to military intervention
any longer. Second, a role "above politics" would mean a
refusal to take sides in purely "civilian" conflicts, but not
a loss of interest in whatever national affairs the military
deemed deserving of its attention. This was clearly indicated
in a speech in which General Onganía stated his conception of the
Armed Forces' role:

> [The Armed Forces exist] to guarantee the sovereignty and
> the territorial integrity of the state, to preserve the moral
> and spiritual values of Western civilization, to ensure public
> order and internal peace, to promote general welfare, and to
> sustain the Constitution, its essential rights and guarantees,
> and the republican institutions it has established . . . .
> [In order to achieve those goals] two fundamental premises
> must hold: the need [of the Armed Forces] to maintain apti-
> tude and capability for the custody of the highest interests
> of the nation, and the economic and social development of
> the country.[91]

The functions of the Armed Forces, according to this conception,
are even broader than those envisioned by the gorila leaders. It
was quite clear that the main practical difference between the
two factions consisted in the legalistas' refusal to engage in
planteos and direct partisan involvement.

But perhaps of greater significance were the requirements
referred to by General Onganía as "basic premises." If the Armed
Forces were to properly perform their functions, both their organizational strength and the socio-economic development of the
country were necessary conditions. Hence anything that menaced
or hindered the achievement of either condition could be construed
as impeding the fulfillment of the Armed Forces' functions. Since
the performance of these functions was so essential, anything
that threatened their necessary conditions was a threat to the
most fundamental interests of the nation. Since governments could
jeopardize, by action or by omission, these necessary conditions,
it was obvious--given this conception of the military's role--

---

[91]La Prensa, August 6, 1964; translated from Spanish by this
author.

that government personnel could not receive the allegiance of the military. In the same speech, General Onganía went on to say:

> Obedience is due, in the last analysis, to the Constitution and its laws, never to men and political parties that may eventually hold power. If this were not the case, the fundamental mission of the Armed Forces would be subverted. They would not be apolitical any more; they would become a praetorian guard at the service of some persons or groups.

The fact that the Radicales had supported the defeated gorila faction tended to increase the likelihood of systemic breakdown. In addition, the persistence of the socio-economic problems described earlier in this chapter could be interpreted as indicating that the "basic premise" of socio-economic development was not being met. The combination of this factor with the consistently high degree of social unrest contributed to fears of the spread and final victory of "subversion," which would implant "totalitarian extremism" and eliminate the Armed Forces. Government inefficiency and a low rate of socio-economic development interacted to generate "subversion." The elimination of subversion was part of the military's "specific duties" (the custody of "national security"), and according to this interpretation, it was at the socio-economic and governmental levels that the fundamental "causes" of subversion could best be attacked and its elimination achieved. Thus the military saw the whole set of social problems (all that could be included within the broad definitions of "achieving socio-economic development" and "ensuring governmental efficiency") as within the range of its "national security" duties.[92] The scope of these social problems suggests that their solution can only be achieved by direct control of government,[93] and since their existence is interpreted as a threat to "national security," it follows that the Armed Forces will not have fulfilled their duties until the problems have been "solved." Hence, direct control of the government by the military will be

---

[92]This analysis was clearly the basis of the military's perception of its role, its appraisal of the social situation, and its justification for intervention, as is evident in the informal interviews and the military publications of the period. See, e.g., Colonel M. Orsolini, Ejército argentino y crecimiento nacional (Editorial Arayú, 1965), and General O. Villegas, Guerra revolucionaria comunista (Pleamar, 1963). For a useful survey of the period, see C. Fayt, El político armado: Dinámica del proceso político argentino 1960-1971 (Ediciones Pannedille, 1971).

[93]For a comprehensive statement of this position, see General O. Villegas, Políticas y estrategias para el desarrollo y la seguridad nacional (Pleamar, 1969). Villegas was the Secretary of the National Security Council in 1966-1968.

necessary for the indefinite period required for achieving these
"solutions."[94]

These conclusions were necessarily based on the Armed
Forces being convinced of their superior capabilities for dealing
with the problems of a slow rate of socio-economic development and
government inefficiency. This conviction stemmed in part from the
poor performance of government authorities and the deteriorating
social conditions under the continued mass praetorianism, after
the legalistas won control of the Armed Forces, but it was probably mainly the result of the successful professionalist drive.
Through professionalization, the military had established clearly
defined authority patterns, and military training had greatly improved. The Armed Forces had been able to solve "their" problems
while civilian sectors continued in the midst of crisis, which
could not help but greatly enhance the military's perception of
its own superior capabilities for dealing with problems.[95] The
ultimate military conviction of the legitimacy of its rule would
derive from the anticipated historical demonstration of its superior capacity to govern (as compared with previous civilian governments).[96]

Of course, the military's concern for the state of the
society included more direct organizational considerations. The
aggravation (or the mere persistence) of social conditions prevailing under mass praetorianism might reintroduce fractionalization within the military, whatever the effects of its professionalization efforts. Since in the legalista conception, military
fractionalization would hinder the fulfillment of its essential
functions, any risk in this respect must also be interpreted as
a threat to the highest interests of the nation. Thus military
intervention to eliminate threats to its internal cohesion would
be justified to whatever extent might seem necessary to the
military itself.[97]

---

[94] For some of the many statements of this position, see the
official publications cited in footnote 3 of this chapter.

[95] The "non sequitur" in this perception should have been clearly
evident, considering that the military had means for solving its
"internal" problems (e.g., purges and open combat) rarely available to civilian sectors.

[96] The "discovery" that the military's expectations were largely
wrong, as well as of the resistance of social problems to mili-
tary-style decision-making, are part of the study of the evolution
of the political system inaugurated in 1966, which will not be
undertaken here.

[97] In this examination of military perceptions and motivations,
I have limited myself to what seem to be the more important facets,

Local elections held in 1965 showed that the <u>Peronistas</u> retained the first plurality of the electorate. Besides the formerly overthrown <u>Peronistas</u> and <u>Frondizistas</u>, the governing <u>Radicales</u> were the only party that could attract more than 10 percent of the total vote. By this time there were abundant indications that a "ceiling consensus" had been reached by most of the civilian sectors, and consequently the inducements for a new military intervention became very strong. Social unrest was high, with numerous strikes, occupations of factories, and manifold acts of less organized violence. President Illia had acquired the reputation of being a slow and ineffective decision-maker, while Parliament seemed to have been reduced to a forum for personal quarrels which produced no legislation. Meanwhile the military had greatly enhanced its own capabilities (and even more greatly enhanced its assessment of those capabilities).

In short, the conditions for a final systemic breakdown had reached a critical stage when, in 1965-1966, the organizational evolution of the military gave it the internal cohesion and sense of capability that made intervention possible without seeming to risk failure and fractionalization. The situation pointed strongly to a coup that, rather than attempting to repair the existing political system, would try to implant an entirely different system. This tendency was reinforced by the fact that all the major political parties in Argentina had already been given "a chance" and "had failed" and thus "had" to be ousted by the military.

General elections were scheduled for 1967, and it was evident that the <u>legalista</u> military (as well as many other sectors in Argentine society) were as split as ever concerning the question of <u>Peronista</u> electoral participation. Given the social conditions, the organizational evolution of the military, and the fact that all the political parties with more than a minimum share of the vote had been given a "chance," it is not an exaggeration to say that by the end of 1965 the major matter of speculation

---

as expressed in informal interviews and published sources. Using this type of information, I have not been able to determine to what extent these conceptions were sincerely held, and to what extent they were "covers" for less apparent motivations. (It is my general impression that in most cases they were sincere.) As to the origins of these perceptions and motivations, besides the historical-contextual factors analyzed here, it seems very likely that other factors frequently·suggested ("anti-subversive doctrines," U.S. training missions, secondary socialization) also exerted an important influence. But with the type of information at hand, it is not possible to assess the actual relative contribution of each of these factors.

had become the timing of the coup (not its perpetration or its goals).[98] The timing was largely determined by the risk of military fractionalization around the old Peronismo issue: the coup had to occur late enough for many of the officers to perceive clearly the risk of organizational fractionalization, but not after the electoral campaigns had started. In this way the military leadership would increase the probability of a high degree of military cohesion in support of the coup with a minimum of civilian opposition (particularly Peronista, if they were allowed to run in the 1967 elections) to their decision to intervene.[99] On June 28, 1966, the Army Chief of Staff, General Pistarini, declared:

> [The achievement] of efficiency, cohesion, and high professional capabilities [by the Armed Forces] has taken time and great sacrifice . . . . Any attempt to put the Army at the service of secondary interests, or to identify it with political, economic, or social sectors, is an attempt against the [military] institution, because it seeks to create internal division and conflict. For this very reason it is also an attempt against the nation.[100]

Soon afterward the coup took place smoothly, and a new political system was inaugurated.

Well before June 1966 numerous civilian sectors had reached a "ceiling consensus," and had been pleading for a military intervention that would drastically change the existing political system. However, for this to occur it was also necessary that the social situation pose new threats to highly valued military organizational achievements, and that the process of military professionalization be substantially advanced. The gorila officers had intervened many times, but for the purpose of pressing relatively limited demands, and with the stated intention of

---

[98]For references to the open discussion of these factors in the months prior to the coup, see Astiz.

[99]In the pre- and post-coup interviews upon which I base these impressions, the opinion was repeatedly expressed that the fate of the Radicales government had been decided long before the coup, but that it was convenient to postpone the decision until it was "evident" to most civilian sectors and military officers that a new coup was unavoidable. But at the same time, there was apparently a major concern not to get too close to the 1967 elections, for the reasons indicated in the text.

[100]La Prensa, June 29, 1966; translated from Spanish by this author.

returning power to civilians. When in 1962 these officers attempted to assume control for a long period, they were hindered
by their precarious hold over a deeply fractionalized and scarcely
professional military institution. The new professionalist military leaders--the somewhat ironically labelled legalista officers--
intervened only when they were prepared to take government in
their own hands for a long time for achieving very ambitious
goals. For this to be possible two conditions lacking in 1962
had to be present in 1966: first, the state of the social-level
variables necessary for a "ceiling consensus," and second, the
organizational-level variables (the degree of internal cohesion
and the feeling of enhanced capabilities) that resulted from the
process of professionalization and constitution of an "apolitical"
Armed Forces.

It seems ironic that those military leaders who epitomized
professionalism and an anti-interventionist stand were those who
led the coup that liquidated the existing political system.[101]
But this apparent inconsistency must be seen in the light of the
preceding circumstances. Mass praetorianism and high modernization induced the fractionalization of the military, who collaborated in the extreme political instability that characterized a
good part of the period over which praetorianism spanned. This
situation adversely affected the military, leading to a period of
withdrawal from direct political involvement and to concerted efforts at enhancing military organization. The continuation of
mass praetorianism led many civilian sectors to reach a ceiling
consensus, but the final systemic breakdown had to "wait" until
the military felt that it could intervene again.[102] This discrepancy in the timing of the civilian and military decisions

---

[101]This observation and the others that follow apply to a large
extent to the other two bureaucratic-authoritarian systems inaugurated in the 1960's in countries of high modernization:
Brazil and Greece. With reference to the evolution of the military, they also apply to another highly "professionalist" coup--
the one in Perú. But the different constellation of factors
that result from similar military professionalization but a lower
level of social modernization generated, in the Peruvian case,
important differences in the composition of the coalition which
the military officers formed, as well as in the politically incorporating and economically expanding goals of the resulting
authoritarian system.

[102]It should be recalled that for the inauguration of a bureaucratic-authoritarian system few economic and psychological payoffs
are available, and that consequently the use of coercion is indispensable for the inauguration and implementation of the socio-
economic policies characteristic of that type of political system.

made the period that immediately preceded the final breakdown essentially a political vacuum, in which everything had been determined except the exact moment of military intervention.

In the period of withdrawal from direct political involvement, the military enhanced its capabilities--and enhanced even more its self-assessment of those capabilities. In addition, military personnel increased their personal contacts with the incumbents of technocratic roles, who would participate in the coup coalition and occupy most of the high civilian government positions in the post-coup regime.

The continuation of mass praetorianism and, with it, the further deterioration of the social context contrasted with the military's feeling of its enhanced capabilities. Also, whatever precautions are taken for isolating the Armed Forces from the social situation, sooner or later they create problems that threaten the reintroduction of military fractionalization. The combination of these two factors led to goals of military intervention that were far more drastic than those that had been envisioned by the military during its interventionist period. The goals were a radical transformation of the social situation along the lines analyzed in Chapter II above.

Thus, "apoliticism" and "professionalism" of the Armed Forces during mass praetorianism at high modernization significantly raised the threshold for military intervention; the hectic pattern of coups and planteos ended. But once that threshold was reached, military intervention occurred again--with more cohesion, for much more ambitious goals, and aimed at a far more complete political domination than anything before. Contrary to what many analysts and policy-makers have expected since the 1950's, "apoliticism" and "professionalism" have not solved the endemic problem of militarism. They merely trade off a higher threshold for a far more comprehensive military intervention.

Chapter IV

AN IMPOSSIBLE "GAME": PARTY COMPETITION IN ARGENTINA,
1955-1966

For the study of party competition and coalition behavior
among Argentine political parties during the 1955-1966 period, I
shall use the model of a "game," in the tradition of "economic"
approaches to the study of political behavior. As one commentator
points out, the practitioner of this approach

> will postulate the existence of a number of individual actors,
> with certain ends (such as maximising their incomes), and will
> then try to work out deductively how they will act in a situa-
> tion of a kind which presents certain alternatives to them, on
> the assumption that they pursue their goals rationally. . . .
> The power of the "economic" method is that, in appropriate
> kinds of situations, it enables us, operating with simple
> premises concerning rational behaviour, to deduce by logic and
> mathematics interesting conclusions about what will happen.[1]

Deductions from the model are checked against actual processes.
If in several trials there is good fit between the behavior predicted by the model and actual behavior, one can assume that the
model includes the essential elements and relationships, and that
their causal patterns correspond to the real processes. This is
the logic of axiomatic-deductive economic models, of computer
simulation,[2] of game theory,[3] and of certain efforts to build a
theory of coalitions.[4]

---

[1] B. Barry, Sociologists, Economists and Democracy (London: Collier-Macmillan Ltd., 1970). Barry's discussion focuses primarily
on two studies: M. Olson, The Logic of Collective Action (Cambridge: Harvard University Press, 1965), and A. Downs, An Economic Theory of Democracy (New York: Harper, 1957). The influence of Downs' work will be clearly evident in my discussion.

[2] See G. Brewer and R. Brunner, Organized Complexity: Empirical
Theories of Political Development (New York: Free Press, 1971).

[3] For recent surveys see Anatol Rapoport, Two-Person Game Theory:
Concepts and Applications (Ann Arbor: University of Michigan
Press, 1969), and N-Person Game Theory: Concepts and Applications
(Ann Arbor: University of Michigan Press, 1970).

[4] For recent surveys see B. Collins and B. Raven, "Group Struc-

The structure of the problem to be studied here is close to the situations dealt with by game theory. It is focused on "players" (political parties) competing under certain rules to build coalitions and maximize votes, with the purpose of winning a "prize" (elections). The players are rational, in the sense that they try to maximize gains and minimize losses, and the rules are constraints that the players must observe while competing. The model proposed here specifies the assets the players have at the start of the game, as well as the criteria for determining the end of the game. Finally, it defines the information available to the players--both about the rules and about other players' moves. Unhappily, the real situation being studied in this chapter is too complicated in several important respects to allow for direct application of the formal tools of game theory;[5] hence, the conclusions will be less rigorous than would have been possible with a simpler situation.

In all the various theories belonging to the genus of what Barry calls the "economic" approach, the independent variables are the structure of the situation specified by the model and simple assumptions about the players' motivations. These, together with certain specified initial conditions (say, the distribution of assets and preferences of the players before the game starts), make possible unequivocal deductions about the behavior of the players.

In the model proposed in this chapter, two contextual variables (the initial conditions and the structure of the situation specified by the "rules" interact with one micro-level variable (the motivational assumptions). The model says nothing about how those initial conditions and "rules" came about. In a broader perspective, the independent variables of this model would be the intervening variables through which the general social conditions were reflected in the political behavior (party competition) and coalitions under consideration here.

Background

Most of the essential background information has been given in Chapter III, but a few details should be added here.

---

ture: Attraction Coalitions, Communication and Power" in G. Lindzey and E. Aronson, eds., The Handbook of Social Psychology, Vol. IV (Reading, Mass.: Addison-Wesley, 1969), and J. Chertkoff, "Sociopsychological Theories and Research on Coalition Formation" in S. Groennings et al.

[5]Game theory requires dealing with simple situations in terms of assets, payoffs, and unidimensionality of utilities if the power of its mathematical tools is to be realized.

Before Perón's government the major Argentine parties were the Radicales, the Conservadores (under various and changing denominations), Socialists and Communists (both based in Buenos Aires City), and one regional party--the Demócrata Progresista. In 1946 they all formed the anti-Perón Unión Democrática. In this coalition the Presidential candidacy was awarded to its largest member--the Radicales. The Unión Democrática was defeated by Perón in 1946 with 1,478,372 votes to 1,211,666. In 1951 another Presidential election was held; it was evident that Perón's popularity and control of governmental resources would assure an easy victory for him. Significantly, the Radicales were not interested in renewing the Unión Democrática coalition-- the first trial of a strategy that will be considered in more detail below. Instead, the Radicales conducted a vigorous independent campaign addressed to all anti-Peronista voters in which they argued that, since they were the only party with any chance to defeat Perón, a vote for any other anti-Peronista party would be "wasted." The Radicales were easily defeated by Perón with 4,745,168 votes to 2,415,795,[6] but though they lost the election, they succeeded in virtually eliminating the other anti-Peronista parties.

The cleavage between Peronistas and anti-Peronistas (basically paralleling the cleavage between (1) working class and low middle class and (2) the rest of society) became paramount in Argentine politics. Since 1946, and particularly after 1955, the distribution of political preferences in Argentina can be represented as a bimodal pattern that reflects the polarization resulting from the extreme saliency of that cleavage (see Figure 4).[7]

Several comments on Figure 4 are in order: (1) The modes do not represent "left-right" policy stands, but positions of

_____

[6] The substantial increase in number of votes compared with the 1946 election was largely due to the introduction of woman's suffrage in the 1951 election.

[7] This is the spatial analogy first used in political science by Downs, and adopted by Dahl, Political Oppositions . . . . The model being used in this chapter deals with one political arena (electoral competition) and specializes in one outcome (election of governmental personnel) in which there is abundant evidence of the overwhelming salience of this cleavage. Though some of his requirements are unduly restrictive (see Barry, pp. 99-146), this situation meets the criteria specified by D. Stokes ("Spatial Models of Party Competition," American Political Science Review, 57 [1963]) in the sense that the spatial analogy does not seem to distort seriously the voters' actual distribution and their perception of their distribution.

Figure 4

FIGURATIVE REPRESENTATION OF DISTRIBUTION OF POLITICAL
OPINIONS (PERONISTA VS. ANTI-PERONISTA) IN ARGENTINA:
1955-1966

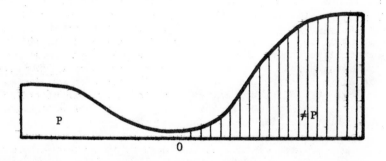

Note: Figure provides a rough approximation of the relative
voting strengths of the two political modes. Point 0
represents indifference toward both modes.

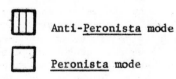

Anti-Peronista mode

Peronista mode

relative intensity with respect to the Peronismo vs. anti-Peronismo cleavage--intensity increasing as positions diverge from the center of the distribution. (2) The area covered by each mode represents the respective voting strength of each sector--in one case (Peronismo) held by a unified political leadership, in the other by a number of anti-Peronista parties. (3) The area covered by each mode is an intuitive approximation and not a precise measure of each mode's voting strength; lack of survey data, the electoral proscription of Peronismo, and the inter-party strategies to be discussed below prevent an exact (and for my purposes unnecessary) assessment of the votes for each party.[8] (4) If, instead of voting strength, the areas of the modes were intended to represent other political resources,[9] the Peronista mode would be much smaller--its only significant non-electoral resource was its control of labor unions; all other political resources were in the anti-Peronista mode.

In 1955 all the major sectors of Argentine society except labor unions were committed to preventing the return to power of Peronismo and to reversing most of the socio-economic policies that the Peronistas supported. After Perón was ousted the following governmental policies were adopted on the basis of the "need to democratize the country": (1) the Peronista party was outlawed; (2) persons who had held leadership positions during Peronismo, or who claimed allegiance to it, were forbidden to run for office or to form new political parties; (3) the formation of political parties that claimed continuity with Peronismo, or allegiance to it, or shared its "ideology," was forbidden.

One additional item of background information is needed: the Argentine electoral system provided that the party receiving the first plurality won executive office and a parliamentary

---

[8]In the only election of the period (1962) in which Peronistas were allowed to present candidates for executive office (governorships), they obtained 31.9 percent of the total vote cast. To this percentage should be added about 3 percent of the total vote received by minor provincial parties claiming allegiance to Peronismo. It seems almost certain that if Peronismo had been allowed to exist as a political party and campaign on a continued basis, had been given fair access to the mass media--and if there had not been a very high probability that elections won by Peronistas would be annulled--the Peronista share of the total vote would have been even greater. However, for the purposes of the party strategies to be analyzed here, the most important factor is the assessment by the parties of their voting strengths prior to elections (see "Players' Assets" below).

[9]Dahl, Modern Political . . . .

(II) The Rules

(1) Peronistas are not allowed to win important elections.

(2) If (for whatever reason) Peronistas win important elections, they are prohibited from taking office.

(3) Any party in power must make sure that Peronistas do not win the next important election; if it fails to do so, it is ousted.

(4) Any minor party, unless explicitly authorized by the umpire, which forms a coalition with Peronistas is construed as a "facade" of Peronismo. In this case all the prohibitions against Peronismo apply to the minor party. (Definitions: A minor party is one that has obtained less than 3 percent of the total vote cast in the last election. The umpire is the military; it may not have created the rules, but it enforces them.)

(5) Any party in power must undertake policies that, as defined by the umpire, satisfy the anti-Peronista mode and deny the Peronistas' demands; if it fails to do so, it is ousted.

(6) Peronistas are allowed to cast a blank ballot or to vote for acceptable parties.

(7) Parties are not allowed to change the rules. If they attempt to do so when in power, they are ousted; if out of government, they become unacceptable.

---

authority (without parliamentary consent) to "intervene" in the states (i.e., to oust the governor and appoint a replacement). Throughout Argentine history Presidents have made more than liberal use of this authority. Other factors contributed to make governorships a less than secure side-payment, and an incomparably less powerful position than the Presidency--particularly the intense politicization of issues at the national level (see Chapter III), and the heavy financial dependence of states on the federal government. The distinction between major and minor states makes these factors even more important. The indivisibility of payoffs hinders coalition formation because of the difficulty of establishing a "parity norm," or commonly accepted principles of "distributive" justice for allocating payoffs in some correspondence to the assets of coalition members (see W. Gamson, "Experimental Studies of Coalition Formation" in L. Berkowitz, ed., Advances in Experimental Social Psychology, Vol. I [Academic Press, 1964], and P. Homans, Social Behavior: Its Elementary Forms [New York: Harcourt, Brace and World, 1961]).

(8) A party that has been ousted from power because it violated some of the rules becomes unacceptable for the next important election.

(9) Knowledge about the rules is imperfect in the first round; players do not know if the umpire will fully enforce them. Knowledge is perfect thereafter; the rules exist as stated and are strictly enforced.

(10) Bargaining for forming coalitions may be secret, but when coalitions are formed it should become public knowledge immediately.

(III) Axioms about Motivation[12]

Parties are rational and assume that voters are also rational.

(A) Voters are rational:

(1) When, confronted with several options for voting (parties), they choose the one they most prefer;

(2) When, if there are alternatives for voting they strongly dislike and others they moderately dislike, they choose one of the latter, provided that in their assessment of the probabilities, this increases the likelihood that the alternative(s) they strongly dislike will lose;

(3) When, if they strongly dislike all the alternatives, they abstain from voting or cast a blank ballot.

(B) Parties are rational:

(4) When they try to maximize their votes and their chances to win future elections;

(5) When in power they try to implement policies that satisfy a large enough part of the electorate to win the next election;

---

[12] These axioms are derived from Downs. The only innovation is Axiom 6, but this seems to be a straightforward extension of the others. It is natural that, having in mind the U.S. and Western European polities, Downs did not feel it necessary to state or to consider this obvious implication.

(6) When in power they try to remain in office for the
full period for which they have been elected.

"Playing the Game"

It can be shown that this game cannot be won, and since
it cannot be won, it does not make sense to play it. It leads to
situations in which both "winners" and "losers" must lose. When
the players (parties), the umpire (the military), and the spec-
tators (voters) realize the game is futile, no one wants its
continuation and an entirely new "game" is inaugurated.

As William Riker has observed, the selection of coalition-
partners is fundamental for goal-attainment.[13] In the present
model, the existence of a large "forbidden mode" (i.e., the
largest individual player is forbidden to win) creates a great
probability of winning for any other player if it can obtain the
forbidden player's support (Axiom 4).[14] For _Peronistas_ the only
side-payment that can be "offered" is the promise that, when in
power, their partner will enact policies preferred by them and/or
that their partner will change the rules that forbid them to win
in a future election (Axiom 4). On that basis the _Peronista_
leaders could convince their constituency to vote in an election
for their coalition-partner (Axioms 1 and 2).

But, as the rules hold, these side-payments cannot be
delivered. The promise of policies violates Rule 5, and the

---

[13]_The Theory of Political Coalitions_ (New Haven: Yale University Press, 1962), p. 35.

[14]This contradicts predictions that coalitions will be of minimal size (Riker) or of "minimal power" (W. Gamson, "An Experimental Test of a Theory of Coalition Formation," _American Sociological Review_, 26 [1961], and "A Theory of Coalition Formation,"
American Sociological Review, 26 [1961]; see also T. Caplow, "A
Theory of Coalitions in the Triad," _American Sociological Review_,
21 [1956], and Collins and Raven). But it should be noted that
the experimental findings on which these predictions are based
stem from situations structured in a very different way from the
one studied here. Chertkoff (reported in Chertkoff, and Collins
and Raven) obtained very different results, in line with the present model, when he manipulated the experimental situation by
assigning to players not only assets (votes) but also different
probabilities of being "elected." In this case there was no
tendency toward minimal size or minimal power coalitions; on the
contrary, players tried to form coalitions with those that had
the best predetermined probability of being elected.

promise to change the rules violates Rule 7. Hence, the Peronistas' coalition-partner would be ousted from government, which violates Axiom 6. This involves a dilemma, since acting according to Axiom 6 violates Axioms 4 and 5--i.e., not delivering the side-payments will create intense hostility from the Peronistas, who will feel betrayed by their partner, and hence it will be impossible for the partner to "borrow" the votes of the single largest player again in the next election. The likelihood that the now extremely hostile Peronistas will win the next election is high (see below), while the party now in power is left with what remains of its former constituency and what it can collect in the future in the anti-Peronista mode. This is bad in terms of Axioms 4 and 5, but since the effects are not immediate (the next important election will take place years thereafter, and meanwhile "something" may happen through the party's control of the resources of government), the loss of Peronista support is preferable to the more immediate deprivation of being ousted. Hence, Axiom 6 prevails, and the side-payments to the Peronistas are not delivered.

This is the crux of the situation. If a party wants to maximize its chances of winning elections, it must make a deal with the Peronistas. The only way to achieve this is to promise to deliver intangible side-payments to the Peronistas when in power. Delivering these side-payments would mean being ousted from power; hence they are not delivered.

At this point we shall introduce a time dimension:

Period I - Game Not Yet Started: Party X of the anti-Peronista mode is fairly large, controlling 15 percent of the total vote.

Period II - Game Started, Negotiations Among Players: Party X has the following alternative: (1) "move" to the Peronista mode--i.e., express opinions and promise policies that satisfy Peronistas and, on that basis, obtain their votes--or (2) "remain" in the anti-Peronista mode. Since Party X is not the largest party in its mode, it has small hope of getting the important payoff (i.e., the Presidency), but by participating in a coalition of its mode, it can receive some governorships as side-payments.

Given the indivisibility of payoffs, only the largest party in the anti-Peronista mode has a clear interest in remaining in its mode. If the total mode is greater in size than the Peronista mode, it seems highly probable that this party will win the Presidency. The situation is different for the other, smaller parties in the anti-Peronista mode: their chances of winning the Presidency in their mode are slim, but may be very good if they can strike a bargain with the Peronistas.

As in all game situations, a rational player must take into account the probable strategies of his competitors. Since Axiom 4 holds for all parties, Party X cannot overlook the possibility that other parties will move to the Peronista mode and form a prospective winning coalition. In that case, it is likely that Party X will get no side-payments at all, and certainly not the Presidency. On the other hand, if Party X moves to the Peronista mode, it cannot be sure who else, and on what terms, may be negotiating with the Peronistas, since negotiations can be secret and it is in the obvious interest of the Peronistas to have several bidders for their votes. Party X will have to outbid any competitors.

Any competition among parties bidding for the Peronistas' votes is zero-sum. The side-payments that can create enough interest among the Peronistas to induce them to "lend" their votes can only be delivered (if at all) by the party that will occupy the Presidency after the next election. Hence if, say, Party Z makes the coalition with the Peronistas, Party X becomes unnecessary to that coalition, and the only side-payment that it could receive would be some minor governorships--and this with less probability than in its original mode, since its move will have displeased its anti-Peronista constituency, and hence its voting strength will be less than if it had remained in the anti-Peronista mode. The strongest bid for the Peronistas' votes would be mimesis--i.e., the adoption of all the policies and ideologies of Peronismo, but this would be self-defeating according to the rules. On the other hand, the zero-sum competition between X and Z will force them closer and closer to mimesis. The more this is so, the more "expensive" it will be for both X and Z in terms of their anti-Peronista constituencies. Further, the party which forms a coalition with the Peronistas on the basis of such expensive bidding will appear the more contemptible a "traitor" when it fails to honor its promises.

Period III - Negotiations Finished, Coalition Announced: Given its original size, even if Party X loses a large proportion of its own votes, it is more than compensated by the Peronistas' votes if it strikes a coalition bargain. If Party X wins in the bidding, the outbid competitors would have no significant side-payments. Hence they must "return to their mode" in order to save what they can of their constituencies (Axiom 4). For that purpose, each must campaign in a way that satisfies that constituency--i.e., take an anti-Peronista stand. However, their credibility on both sides of the cleavage will be seriously affected, and their bargaining position within the anti-Peronista mode will be weak. This high cost of "return to the mode" explains the frantic bidding for the Peronistas' votes--and the more bidding there is, the higher the costs.

Now that the Peronistas have picked a coalition-partner, we shall consider what happens in the anti-Peronista mode,

consisting of parties that never "moved" and others that are "returning." If Party X is in coalition with the Peronistas, the
anti-Peronista mode is confronted by a prospective winning coalition: it is clear that if the anti-Peronista parties run alone
they will be defeated. One possible way to avoid defeat is to
convince the umpire that the coalition violates the rules, in
which case all plays will be annulled and the game will return to
the initial stage (but now with Party X also unacceptable). Another possibility is to build a grand coalition of the anti-Peronista mode, hoping that the Peronista-based coalition cannot obtain the proportion of the total vote required to win. But among
the acceptable parties the only possible side-payments are tan-
gible (i.e., governorships), and they should bear some rough
correspondence to the assets of each of the prospective partners--
that is, to their acceptability and their varying voting strengths.
Since their acceptability is "equal" and their voting strengths
are not substantially different, the indivisibility of payoffs
creates a serious problem.

Party Y, the largest party in the anti-Peronista mode,
feels strongly that it deserves the Presidential nomination, but
it has nothing of comparable value to offer to its prospective
partners. Since there are no "fair" criteria for distributing
side-payments, negotiations soon reach a stalemate. However, Party Y still has one potentially successful strategy per Axioms 1
and 2. Appealing to the voters' rationality, it can take advantage
of the strong dislike felt toward a Peronista-based coalition.
The anti-Peronista voters can be persuaded that the only way to
prevent a Peronista victory is to vote for Party Y, even if it is
not the anti-Peronista party they otherwise would have favored.

Thus, the indivisibility of payoffs leads to a new zero-
sum situation--now within the anti-Peronista mode. Party Y, clearly the largest party in that mode, hopes to achieve electoral victory through Axiom 1 (for its own voters) and Axiom 2 (for the
voters of other anti-Peronista parties). On the basis of the
existing polarization of political preferences of the electorate,
Party Y seeks to "absorb" votes in the anti-Peronista mode. (Party Y is called an absorbing party, and its strategy an absorbing
strategy. In its mode, Party Y tries to absorb all the votes; it
is successful except for those votes that are very firmly fixed
in the other anti-Peronista parties.) The probability of success
of this strategy is a function of the bimodal distribution of
political opinion: the greater the apprehension of the anti-
Peronista voters toward the possible victory of a Peronista-based
coalition, the better are Party Y's chances to absorb anti-Peronista votes. Hence, to fulfill Axiom 4, Party Y has to attempt
to make this apprehension as great as possible. In the spatial
representation of Figure 4, Party Y has to "stretch" the distribution, pushing more voters farther away from the areas of neu-
trality or low intensity. The obvious way to do this is to depict

in the worst possible colors what would happen if a Peronista-based coalition won. Thus, acting in accordance with Axiom 4, Party Y increases the existing polarization. To the extent that the adoption of this strategy by Party Y can be predicted by parties that have moved toward the Peronista mode, it will induce even more frantic bidding for the Peronistas' votes, since absorption increases the cost of return to the anti-Peronista mode for parties that have shaken the loyalty of their constituencies by their movement toward Peronismo.

Period IV - Election Time: The winner can only be Party Y, the absorbing anti-Peronista party, or a Peronista-based coalition. If Party Y wins, given the existing polarization and the rules, the same moves will be used in the next election. However, if Party X wins with the Peronistas' support, it is in the predicament that has already been discussed: honoring its promises to the Peronistas means being ousted; not honoring them means a minimal chance of winning the next election.

Period V - Post-Election Time: If Party X has won with Peronista support and, preferring not to be ousted, has not delivered its promised side-payments, it must return to the anti-Peronista mode. The other mode "belongs" to the Peronistas, and they are intensely angered by Party X's "betrayal." In readopting an anti-Peronista stand, Party X must continue the very policies it had promised to change when in power. As a player who is perceived by all as "unreliable," Party X is bitterly resented by the Peronistas and distrusted by the anti-Peronistas.

In the election Party X has won, Party Y has absorbed votes in its mode, and its polarizing campaign has gained it credit as a "reliable" anti-Peronista party. Party X has the important advantage of controlling governmental resources, but because it is "unreliable" its voting strength is reduced to what is left of its original constituency. Party Y lacks governmental resources, but it has clearly emerged as the largest anti-Peronista party. The previously noted difficulties in building an anti-Peronista mode coalition are now compounded by a new problem. There is increased hostility between Party X and Party Y, and it is impossible to determine a priori whether control of governmental resources or being the largest anti-Peronista party in the last election is the greater advantage in terms of obtaining votes in the next election. Hence, there is no basis for deciding if Party X or Party Y should receive the Presidential nomination for the next election of an anti-Peronista coalition in which both are included. The anti-Peronista mode now has two potentially absorbing parties that cannot join in a coalition. As a consequence, since anti-Peronista voters have no way of knowing in advance which of these parties will become dominant in their mode, the individually rational decision would be to choose randomly between Party X and Party Y. But if all anti-Peronista voters followed this principle, their votes would be randomly distributed between Parties X and Y, with the result of assuring the Peronista victory they wanted to prevent.

With the possibility of an anti-Peronista mode grand coalition eliminated, the Peronistas can form a prospective winning coalition with any other party. However, playing the game has established a fundamental point: the rules exist as stated and are enforced. The Peronistas would be almost certain winners in the next election because of the two absorbing parties in the other mode, but they cannot win (i.e., take office) by themselves, and no party can deliver, when in power, the only promises (policies, changes in the rules) that can interest the Peronistas.

The other parties know that they will lose in the anti-Peronista mode, but that if they move to the Peronista mode they will be faced with the dilemma previously described--with the further difficulty of dealing with a player whose only rational goal is to blow up the game. That is to say, the Peronistas may form a new coalition, but in contrast to the first one, only if in their view the new coalition is conducive to finishing the game for good--a self-defeating course of action for their partner, who is trying to form the coalition to obtain the prize of the game. Finally, it should be noted that if the anti-Peronistas cannot vote rationally neither can the Peronistas. It would not make sense for them to vote for their own party, which is forbidden to run, or for an anti-Peronista party that has stayed in its mode, or for a party that has moved to the Peronista mode on the basis of promises which, since the rules hold, it will have to renege upon when in power. Abstention or blank votes would not be a solution because the Peronistas would be annulling one mode of the distribution and thereby assuring that the election would be won by one of the anti-Peronista absorbing parties (the one that has failed to honor its promises or the one that has aggravated the existing polarization to its advantage).

Once one round of this game has been played and knowledge of the rules is perfect, it is evident that it is a futile game which no one can win. Consequently, a rational player becomes "non-allegiant" (he rejects the game, or at least has no interest in its continuation) and "irresponsible" (since everyone will lose eventually, whatever short-term gains are possible should be pursued). Not only is the game futile, but its dynamic has increased the initial political polarization. With no players to seek its continuation, it can easily be terminated.

Collective Rationality?

It might be argued that the rationality axioms (see pp. 174-175) are exclusively individualistic and that they should include a dimension of "collective rationality,"[15] according to which all parties (or at least all anti-Peronista parties) would have a dominating interest in preserving the game and avoiding actions that would lead to its destruction. This argument merits close examination.

Once one party has moved to the Peronista mode the process previously analyzed inevitably follows. Hence, in order to be effective, "collective rationality" requires that all parties agree to remain in the anti-Peronista mode. In addition: (1) all parties must have the preservation of the game at the top of their preference schedules; (2) all parties must be perfect predictors (even before the first round of the game, they must know what consequences will follow if a party moves to the Peronista mode); and (3) all parties must have complete confidence in each other.

If we consider that knowledge of the rules of the game is imperfect in the first round, the possibilities for effective collective rationality are exceedingly remote. There is another almost insuperable difficulty. Assume that (for whatever reason--wrong prediction, disaffection with the game) Party W has decided to move to the Peronista mode. In that case, it is in its interest (in order to prevent other parties from bidding for the Peronistas' votes) to conceal its intentions from the other players. Thus, Party W will pretend to accept the "remain in the mode" agreement until the moment it can announce the formation of its coalition with the Peronistas. Given this circumstance, no rational player can be sure that all the others intend to honor the "remain in the mode" agreement. On what basis will each player determine its own behavior? Given the situation, its choice is blind, but collective rationality requires unanimous agreement, and a single "defection" will trigger the process analyzed above. Each player has to make a subjective estimate of the probability that a defection may occur. Even if all the players had sincerely agreed to remain in the mode, it is very likely that at least one of them will make a subjective estimate that the probability of a defection is high. The player that arrives at this subjective estimate will act on the assumption that the collective rationality will break down.[16] As a consequence, one prediction of high probability of violation of the agreement will lead the predictor to break it, and since it is likely that at least one

---

[15] Rapoport, N-Person Games . . ., pp. 87-89.

[16] If the prediction of the consequences of defection is correct, the move inevitably ruins the game, and it no longer makes sense to accept the constraints of collective rationality. If the prediction of the consequences of defection is incorrect, there is no basis for trying to reach the "remain in the mode" agreement.

such prediction will be made, the agreement cannot be reached or, if reached, cannot be honored, even if all players are acting in good faith.

Given the parties' imperfect knowledge of the rules and their lack of confidence in one another, the smaller the anti-Peronista party, the smaller its chances of winning in its mode, and the greater the temptation to "borrow" the Peronistas' votes. In turn, the greater the temptation for the minor parties, the greater the danger for the larger anti-Peronista parties of losing an election that they otherwise would have a good chance of winning; and the greater the danger of losing, the greater the probability that the larger parties will also change modes.

Historical Events

Their absorption of anti-Peronista votes in 1951 made the Radicales the most likely winners in the 1958 Presidential election once the Peronistas were banned. Then the "modal pulls" began to operate, with several minor and new parties trying to obtain the Peronistas' votes, thereby endangering the chances of the Radicales. The Radical party was openly supported by the 1955-1958 provisional-military government, and the prospect of victory produced an especially hard intra-party contest for the Presidential nomination. When it became apparent to one of the Radicales' leaders--Arturo Frondizi--that he would lose the Presidential nomination, a complex series of events occurred which ended with the party split into the Radicales del Pueblo, controlled by most of the old leaders, and the Radicales Intransigentes, led by Frondizi.

From the outset it was clear that the Radicales Intransigentes had decided to compete for the Peronistas' votes. In July 1957 the provisional government called an election ostensibly for reforming the Constitution, but actually to determine the strength of the various parties. It was decided that the D'Hondt system of proportional representation would be used. The Peronistas were banned. Frondizi offered them words of reconciliation and a promise to defend some Constitutional clauses presumed dear to them. There is evidence that the Radicales Intransigentes obtained some Peronista votes, but since the Radicales Intransigentes really had nothing to offer, the bulk of the Peronistas followed Perón's "orders" to cast blank ballots. (The election results are given in Table 33.)

Presidential elections were to be held seven months later, in 1958, under the first plurality electoral system. Now the Radicales Intransigentes had an attractive deal to offer to the Peronistas. Frondizi's Presidential campaign was based on the following promises: (1) when in power he would implement socio-

Table 33

ELECTION RETURNS--CONSTITUTIONAL CONVENTION: 1957

(D'Honte proportional representation system)

Blank votes	2,115,861
Radicales del Pueblo (RP)	2,106,524
Radicales Intransigentes (RI)	1,847,603
Socialists	525,721
Conservadores parties	423,920
Christian Democrats	420,606
Democratas Progresistas	263,805
Communists	228,821

Table 34

ELECTION RETURNS--PRESIDENTIAL ELECTION: 1958

Radicales Intransigentes (RI)	3,761,519
Radicales del Pueblo (RP)	2,303,180
Socialist parties	523,545
Christian Democrats	339,495
Conservadores parties	249,160
Democratas Progresistas	172,842

183

economic policies preferred by the Peronistas (and highly at odds with the policies of the 1955-1958 government), and (2) he would lift the electoral ban on the Peronistas. These offers were met with enthusiasm by the Peronista leaders and by the labor unions. Shortly before the election, it became known that Perón and Frondizi had made a "covenant" according to which Perón would deliver "his" votes to Frondizi in exchange for the future implementation of the promised policies.

Faced with a prospective winning coalition, the Radicales del Pueblo's campaign was a "crusade for democracy" against "the new demagogue," and to save the country from the nightmarish evils that would be suffered if the Peronista-supported Radical Intransigente candidate won the election. The Radicales del Pueblo insisted that all anti-Peronista voters should support them if they wanted to avoid a catastrophic Radicales Intransigentes victory. (The election results are given in Table 34.)

In spite of his record of opposition during Perón's government, Frondizi's "covenant" with Perón, the promises made to the Peronistas, and the polarizing effects of the Radicales del Pueblo campaign raised among the anti-Peronista sectors the question of whether Frondizi should be allowed to take office. Finally, in a very tense civil-military situation, Frondizi assumed the Presidency.

Am immediate, massive raise in salaries and wages, as well as the enactment of legislation favoring the labor unions, suggested that Frondizi was willing to deliver to the Peronistas at least part of the promised side-payments. But by the end of 1958 it was evident that if Frondizi did not want to be ousted, he had to meet the anti-Peronista demands. Soon Frondizi found himself doing exactly the opposite of what he had promised during the electoral campaign. The 1955-1958 policies were reenacted, resulting in unemployment and a severe recession, aggravated by drastic negative redistributions of income. This situation, added to their feeling of "betrayal," led to widespread Peronista-union unrest, which only hardened the repressive position of the anti-Peronistas.

Downs has made the important point that some minimal party reliability and responsibility is indispensable for the rationality of voting and for democracy to survive.[17] The prestige of the Argentine party system before 1958 was not high, and the Radicales Intransigentes, by so drastically changing their stand on the most salient national issues, deepened the general disaffection and cynicism toward "politics." The Peronistas saw

---

[17] Downs, pp. 105-109.

Frondizi pursuing the very policies they had hoped to change by
electing him, and the anti-Peronistas found that a party they had
many reasons to distrust was now competing for their support.
The best prediction about what Frondizi's policies would be was
that they would be exactly the opposite of his campaign promises.

The increasing Peronista disaffection made Frondizi more
dependent on the anti-Peronista sectors. In three years of government the Radicales Intransigentes "returned" to anti-Peronismo
and almost completely changed their constituency. The consequences
became evident in 1961, when an election was held for a Federal
Capital Senator. The Socialist candidate won with Peronista support, the Radicales del Pueblo were second, and the Radicales
Intransigentes ran a poor third. In 1962 an important election
for renewal of state governorships and federal and state legislatures was to be held, and the 1964 Presidential election was approaching. Minor parties were ready to repeat the 1958 move
toward the Peronistas, and the Radical del Pueblo party strongly
asserted its "rights" to hegemony in the anti-Peronista mode.
Faced with the prospect of defeat by either their old or their
determined "new" rivals, the Radicales Intransigentes lacked an
effective strategy. Only one, highly risky strategy seemed open
to them.

The dispute for hegemony in the anti-Peronista mode between the Radicales del Pueblo and the Radicales Intransigentes
all but ensured the victory of a Peronista-based coalition--even
with a minor party. However, the Peronistas had learned that no
party could honor the promises in which they [the Peronistas]
were really interested. As a consequence, their interest in a
new coalition was minimal. In this situation, having the Peronistas run on their own seemed best for both the Radicales
Intransigentes and the Peronistas. For the Peronistas, their
victory could lead to a military coup, which would perhaps create
an entirely new situation. For the Radicales Intransigentes, the
fact that Peronista candidates were running for important offices
would further intensify political polarization and increase the
apprehension of many voters toward the prospect of a Peronista
victory. Thus the Radicales Intransigentes could achieve a more
complete absorption, and with it (the anti-Peronista voters being
more numerous than the Peronistas) electoral triumph.

By allowing the Peronistas to run, Frondizi made sure
that no other party could enter into a coalition with them, while
the resulting increased polarization gave the Radicales Intransigentes some chance of winning. A fundamental obstacle to the
success of this strategy was the Radicales del Pueblo party, since
it could present the anti-Peronista voters with a strong argument
that it should be the absorbing party. Allowing the Peronistas
to run meant that the Radicales Intransigentes were assuming
responsibility vis-à-vis the anti-Peronista sectors that this was

the only way to prevent the electoral victory of the Peronista-based coalition--by impeding the very strategy that had brought the Radicales Intransigentes to power!

Although this strategy effectively increased polarization,[18] and the Radicales Intransigentes campaign reduced the number of Radicales del Pueblo votes, it did not achieve its basic aim. The Radicales del Pueblo campaign on the basis of their "pure" anti-Peronista credentials and the unreliability of the Radicales Intransigentes ensured its failure. Under the circumstances, as Table 35 shows, the Peronistas obtained the largest share of the total vote.

A military coup followed, the election was annulled, and Frondizi was ousted from the Presidency. During 1962-1963 the military ruled through appointed civilians, and (as is noted in Chapter III) the Armed Forces became split into a gorila and a legalista faction. The "back to the barracks" stand of the legalistas meant that, once they defeated the gorilas, elections had to be called again. Despite some momentary illusions, it soon became clear that the Peronistas were, once again, banned from electoral access--i.e., elections had to take place within the old rules. The Peronistas were not the only ones banned. Now the Radicales Intransigentes had become unacceptable and could not win either. Together these two parties included at least 55-60 percent of the total vote.

Compounding the problem, the Radicales del Pueblo had become convinced during Frondizi's government that, given the situation then prevailing, they would never be able to win an election. They had enthusiastically supported the gorila military faction, in whose government they would have provided the high-level civilian personnel. The legalista military officers could hardly be induced to support the party most closely related to the recently defeated gorila faction. This factor aside, the Radical del Pueblo party's less than one-third of the total vote seemed insufficient to win elections, and their sharp antagonisms with both the Peronistas and the Radicales Intransigentes made them an impractical grand coalition partner.

Nevertheless, the legalista officers "had" to call elections. This was the only way to withdraw from direct political

---

[18] In a commentary on the election, P. Snow shows how the political logic operated: "The Radicales Intransigentes candidates continually told audiences that a vote for the Radicales del Pueblo, Christian Democrats, or Conservatives was in actuality a vote for Peronistas and a vote for the return of Perón" ("Parties and Politics in Argentina: The Elections of 1962 and 1963," Midwest Journal of Political Science, IX, No. 1 [1965]).

Table 35

ELECTION RETURNS--GOVERNORS AND LEGISLATURES: 1962

Peronistas (P)	2,845,833
Radicales Intransigentes (RI)	2,423,145
Radicales del Pueblo (RP)	1,753,466
Conservadores parties	447,084
Socialist parties	405,310
Christian Democrats	205,555
Democratas Progresistas	156,114

involvement and to initiate the drive toward professionalization and organizational strengthening which they saw, after the clashes with the gorila faction, as a prerequisite for institutional survival and career preservation. Furthermore, their pro-election and anti-military dictatorship stand during the recent confrontations with the gorilas had been the primary basis of their appeal for civilian support. If shortly thereafter they had ruled out elections, their government (and their position of leadership within the Armed Forces) would have rested on shaky ground.

In the meantime split Socialist sectors and the Christian Democrats showed their willingness to move toward the Peronistas, but, as expected, they found it very difficult to persuade the Peronistas to form a coalition on the basis of promises to be honored when in power. A new party appeared, led by former provisional President General Aramburu (1955-1958), which took a strong law and order stand and based its anti-Peronista appeal on Aramburu's past performance in office.

The last clash between the gorila and the legalista military officers took place in April 1963, and Presidential elections were scheduled for July 1963. A "solution" was found along the following lines: (1) the electoral system was reformed and all elections were to be held under the D'Hondt system of proportional representation; (2) Peronistas were banned from the major elections, but they could run for parliamentary seats and for the governorships of some minor states; (3) the Radicales Intransigentes could not run for the Presidency, but were allowed to win governorships of large states; (4) with these side-payments, it

was hoped the Peronistas and Radicales Intransigentes would agree
to enter into a new coalition--the "National Front"--as the suppliers of votes, with the Presidential candidate to come from
some minor party acceptable to the recently victorious professionalist military officers.

A host of minor--many of them new, ad hoc--parties,
without any voting support, competed for the National Front's
Presidential nomination. Outside the Front, the Radicales del
Pueblo hastened to condemn it. The Christian Democrats, after
some flirtation with the Front, realized that they could not
obtain the important nominations there, and renewed their attempts
to make a direct deal with the Peronistas. At the same time,
splinter Socialist groups were trying to arrange a similar deal
with the Peronistas. Of course, the Radicales del Pueblo,
Christian Democrats, and Socialists all endeavored to point out
as loudly as they could the "trap" hidden in the Front coalition.

Negotiations within the Front proved to be particularly
difficult. The new Radical Intransigente party chairman, Oscar
Alende, had strong Presidential ambitions and argued that, in
spite of military warnings, his candidacy would not be vetoed if
he were chosen by the Front. However, one of the points stressed
by the Peronistas during their participation in the negotiations
was that, after the recent experience with Frondizi, they could
not accept another Radical Intransigente candidate. Meanwhile,
the leaders of the minor parties, with teams of "apolitical"
civilians and "independent" retired military officers, were attempting to outbid one another for the Presidential nomination
and, in the process, losing their acceptability with the anti-
Peronistas, which constituted their primary asset.

The Peronistas knew that they would not receive any of
the side-payments promised by the Front parties bidding for their
votes. Up to then Peronista voters had followed their leaders'
orders with great discipline, but after all the bitterness raised
by Frondizi's 1958-1962 government, it was evident that much more
would be required in 1963 to make them vote again for the Radical
Intransigente candidates. As for the "independent candidates"
of the minor parties, since their only asset was their acceptability with anti-Peronistas, they could not elicit much enthusiasm
either. Negotiations in the Front were stalemated when Perón
and Frondizi (neither having formal authority over his party)
announced that they had made a new "covenant" and that Solano
Lima was to be the Front's Presidential nominee. Solano Lima
was the leader of a small splinter of the Conservadores, and was
closely associated with rampant fraud that had preceded Perón's
government--fraud directed mainly against the Radicales, and of
which Perón made a major issue in his 1946 Presidential campaign.
Solano Lima was a very difficult candidate for both Peronistas
and Radicales Intransigentes to support; one can only speculate

about the reasons for the nomination. For Frondizi, the decision may have been based on the assumption that a Radical Intransigente Presidential nominee would be vetoed by the military and/or on the desire to prevent the consolidation of a strong leader who could dispute the direction of his party with him. For Perón, the desirability of not supporting a Radical Intransigente candidate was obvious, the "independent" candidates of the ad hoc parties were not appealing, and (perhaps) Solano Lima's nomination was perceived as the most effective way of destroying the Front and hastening the end of the general situation.

Immediately after the announcement of the new "covenant," and twenty days before the election, Alende convoked the Radical Intransigente party authorities, refused to withdraw his Presidential candidacy, and obtained the support of the majority of the party for his refusal to comply with the Perón-Frondizi decision. Since there was no time for a court ruling, the result was two Radical Intransigente parties--one led by Alende controlling most of the party apparatus, the other led by Frondizi participating in the Front.

Widespread Peronista uneasiness about Solano Lima's candidacy was evident, and there was little doubt that many Peronistas would refuse to vote for him. At this point the Christian Democrats made a bold move. The Front was falling apart, but in order to obtain the support of the Peronistas and to have some chance in the imminent election, the Christian Democrats had to offer the Peronistas something more than promises. Hence, they offered the most visible Peronista leader in Argentina--Raúl Mattera--the Presidential nomination on their own slate. Their Presidential candidate was given the Vice-Presidential nomination, with the governorships to be distributed between both parties. This happened a week before the election, and Mattera immediately accepted. There was no doubt that most Peronistas would be delighted to vote for him.

Thus Alende and Mattera had taken most of their parties' votes away from the Front. The Front "solution" that shortly before had seemed likely to produce a comfortable majority was now reduced to the indeterminate, but certainly small, remnants of the Peronista and Radical Intransigente vote and a handful of parties without any voting strength.

However, the new combination between Christian Democrats and Peronistas had broken the "rules," and a decree was issued vetoing Mattera's candidacy. He immediately urged his followers to cast blank votes. His decision to accept the Christian Democrat Presidential nomination had been taken without Perón's consent, and the Front's leaders circulated letters of Perón's condemning Mattera. At the same time (also during the week preceding the election) other statements of Perón's were circulated that praised Mattera and fulminated against the Front. It could not be determined which statements were authentic; one possible interpretation is that all were authentic, and that in this way "the biggest player who could not win" was following a strategy of further undermining the game.

The Front disintegrated. Two days before the election its leaders also called for blank ballots. On July 7, 1963, with the Peronistas out of the race and the Radicales Intransigentes badly split, the electoral victory--with less than one-fourth of the total vote cast--went to a party whose triumph thirty days before had seemed unimaginable: the Radicales del Pueblo (see Table 36).

When the Radicales del Pueblo made their nominations, they did not have the slightest hope of winning, and their leadership was formed by aging politicians who had been out of power since 1930. In addition, as has been noted, their relations with the military were far from good. Their government was unable to solve the manifold problems that Argentine society had accumulated. When partial elections were held in 1965, the Peronistas showed that they still retained the first plurality. In 1967 an important election was approaching, and for the government the predicament was the same as ever: ban the Peronistas and trigger the cycle of the "forbidden mode," or allow them to run, win, and be ousted. A hopeless déjà vu feeling became widespread in Argentine society. When the military ousted the Radicales del Pueblo before the scheduled 1967 election and inaugurated a bureaucratic-authoritarian system, nobody seriously opposed the move.

Table 36

ELECTION RETURNS--PRESIDENTIAL ELECTION: 1963

(D'Hondt system)

Radicales del Pueblo (RP)	2,441,064
Blank votes	1,884,435
Radicales Intransigentes (Alende)	1,593,002
Udelpas	726,861
Demócratas Progresistas	619,481
Conservadores parties	600,440
Socialists	537,643
Christian Democrats	434,823

Note: Both the Demócratas Progresistas and the Udelpas supported the Aramburu Presidential candidacy.

By the end of the 1955-1966 period all parties that could claim more than 10 percent of the total vote (Peronistas, Radicales Intransigentes, and Radicales del Pueblo) had been ousted by military coups. After the first (1958) round of the "game" its futility became clear; however, a new round took place in 1963, under the conditions and with the consequences described.[19] The exhaustion of the set of parties with significant voting strength, the final proof of the impossibility of the "game," along with the general processes analyzed in Chapters II and III, led to the inauguration of the new bureaucratic-authoritarian system.

Some Substantive Implications

The material in this chapter can now be incorporated in the general framework set forth in the preceding chapters.

At a stage of high modernization, serious social rigidities and developmental bottlenecks tend to create a barely manageable schedule of political demands. In particular, the consumption and power participation preferences of the popular sector are high and are articulated with continuity and with important organizational support. These demands, given the inherited rigidities and the developmental bottlenecks, tend to be perceived as "excessive" by the more established sectors of society.

The Argentine case is a good illustration that the political preferences of the popular sector do not become a major political concern simply because an important proportion of the voting population shares those preferences. The remarkable endurance of Peronismo over time, its successful resistance against innumerable attempts to destroy it, and its ability to mobilize strong evidence of support not only in elections but also in many non-electoral demonstrations of its active presence in the national political arena cannot be explained apart from the solid base of Peronismo in Argentine labor unions. The unions have given Peronismo the resources to finance electoral and public opinion campaigns, have provided trained workers and staff, have created a nationwide network of grass-roots organizations, and have protected a central core from the attempts to eliminate Peronismo as a political force.

---

[19] For further details on this election, see D. Rowe, "The Argentine 1963 Election" in D. Tomasek, ed., Latin American Politics: Studies of the Contemporary Scene (Garden City: Doubleday, 1966).

It is characteristic of high activation of the popular sector in situations of high modernization that differences concerning preferred policies become important issues for national policy-makers only when they are expressed as political demands by activated sectors. Where economic growth is stifled, the question of who controls the government becomes particularly important, because this determines how the national "pie" is to be allocated, and who is going to pay the costs of capital accumulation. This intense politicization of all allocational claims leads the more established sectors to conclude that, whatever the formally open channels of political access may be, they should not make it possible for "unprocessable" popular demands to dominate public policy. However, high modernization (and the resulting high political activation) has generated a large segment--or mode--of voters that cannot be overlooked in any electoral calculations.

The model proposed here can be seen as one particular instance of a more general case. Under contemporary conditions of high modernization, high popular political activation, with important organizational bases supporting continuity of political demands, is likely to follow. Given such a situation, and a history of erratic economic growth that has resulted in general zero-sum conditions, any type of political system is likely to be subject to one basic constraint--i.e., the government should not grant demands of a politically activated popular sector. In this sense, the "rules" of the model proposed here are one way (adapted to national idiosyncracies) to impose the same general constraint that apparently was imposed in pre-coup Brazil and Greece. On this more general level, the problems that democratic institutions face can be better understood. Parties can be expected to attempt to maximize their votes to win elections, as well as to gain other forms of support that will enable them to survive when in power. When most of the non-electoral political resources are found among sectors that perceive their interests as sharply at odds with the largest single aggregate of voting strength, the logic of the situation will lead most parties to adopt a sequential strategy: maximize <u>votes</u> at election time, then maximize <u>other sources of support</u> between elections.

Of course this leads to erratic, seemingly unpredictable party and governmental behavior. Lowered prestige among all sectors of parties and "politicians" follows, and political cynicism and alienation increase. Under these conditions party recruitment, as well as long-range planning and effective governmental performance, are seriously hampered. Poor governmental performance results, further undermining the public assessment of parties and "politicians."

An important effect of this "sequential" strategy, in addition to the general derogation of politicians' leadership abilities, is the question raised by the more established sectors of

"demagoguery" or "irresponsible electioneering." In the parties' competition for votes, promises are made, stands are taken, and--to some extent--policies are adopted that satisfy the activated popular sector but alienate the other sectors. However, if the governments are to survive, most of these policies will have to be reversed. Thus the sequence has increased the grievances and further activated the popular sector, with little final benefit for it, while increasing the rigidity of the more established sectors.

The performance of the system will be gauged by the persistence of the unsolved salient social problems. The adoption by the parties of sequential strategies is perceived by many established sectors as heightening the danger of further popular activation, which must be terminated even at high cost. On the other hand, these strategies undermine the commitment of the popular sector to the survival of a system that will be replaced by another system directly aimed at excluding popular demands.

The situation studied in this chapter challenges a widely prevailing assumption. It is a common practice to attribute to political parties and their leaders the decisive influence in the breakdown of South American political systems. This was the interpretation provided by the military government that emerged from the 1966 coup in Argentina, as well as of numerous works written to "explain" the coup. More generally, there is a tendency to "explain" the Argentine (and--to a considerable extent--the Latin American) political situation by attributing to party leaders and other political elites the "wrong" psychological predispositions. I cannot here provide a detailed critique of these views, but it is perhaps worth pointing out their common line of reasoning. First, political behavior is appraised as "irrational," "irresponsible," or "dysfunctional." Second, since the political behavior has been appraised in this way, it "must be" that the political actors suffer from psychological maladjustments (whether at the level of values, perception, motivation, or personality) which cause such behavior. Third, the predispositions supposedly stemming from these "maladjustments" are used to explain the macro-level dependent variables of interest (say, lack of effective decision-making, political instability, or authoritarianism). Fourth, "theories" of change and prescriptions for policy are derived, and since psychological factors are presumed to be the primum movens of the observed political situation, it is held that efforts for change should focus on the processes that, mostly by way of education, might alter these predispositions.[20] In the

---

[20]This is, of course, the approach of the presently discredited "national character" school; for an excellent criticism, see A.

meantime, it is reasonable to assume that some form of tutelary authoritarianism is the political system that is best suited to deal with these "wrong" predispositions.

However, the meaning of social action to the actor, as well as the interpretation and explanation by the observer, depends on the context in which the social action takes place.[21] If actor and observer can agree that a situation offers a choice of A, B, and C decisions but not of D, E . . . n decisions, it makes little sense to postulate that E was the "right" decision, to impute "irrationality" to the actor because he did not choose it, and to "explain" systemic patterns in terms of such "irrationality." In other words, it is impossible to ignore contextual variables and still contend that explanation and interpretation of an actor's behavior, as well as mapping of the systemic consequences of such behavior, is feasible.

Another possible method, which has a long tradition in the social sciences, consists of trying to specify the context in ways that are intellectually manageable and still adequately correspond--for the purposes of the inquiry--with the actual situation. In most cases the main focus of inquiry is description and explanation of the correspondences and differences between actors' perceptions and assessments of a certain situation and the "contextual map" of that situation drawn independently by the observer.[22] In other cases (as in this chapter) the focus is

---

Inkeles and D. Levinson, "National Character: The Study of Modal Personality and Sociocultural Systems" in G. Lindzey and E. Aronson, eds., The Handbook of Social Psychology, Vol. IV (Reading, Mass.: Addison-Wesley, 1969). But under the more fashionable rubric of "empirical research" (although they fail to do research precisely on the variables and at the levels used for "explanation"), this procedure is easily detectable in many contemporary works. See, among others, T. Fillol, Social Factors in Economic Development (Cambridge: The MIT Press, 1961); K. Johnson, Argentina's Mosaic of Discord (Institute for the Comparative Study of Political Systems, 1969); Kirkpatrick; and James Payne, Patterns of Conflict in Colombia (New Haven: Yale University Press, 1968). For an excellent critique of this latter work, which is complementary in many respects to my argument here, see A. Hirschman, "The Search for Paradigms as a Hindrance to Understanding," World Politics, XXII, No. 3 (1970).

[21] For a good recent argument in this direction, which includes a detailed critique of reductionist approaches, see Cardoso, Ideologías . . . .

[22] As may be obvious, this strategy requires obtaining data (mostly interview data) with information about perceptions and

reversed: with the contextual map previously defined and given simple motivational assumptions about the "actors" in the model, their "decisions" are deduced and checked against actual processes. Insofar as there is a close correspondence between deductions and observations, the observer-analyst can feel confident that the context and motivations assumed in the model reasonably approximate the main features of their real-world equivalents.[23]

The most important point here is that, given the context for political competition and coalitions in the situation under study in this chapter, it is the "rationality" of party leaders and voters that leads to the erosion and final destruction of the existing political system. The contrast of this outcome with the system-supportive results of the same "rational actors" in the context of Downs' model is striking. Since the motivational assumptions are the same in both cases, the different outcomes are the consequence of the different contexts in which the political actors have to operate in the two models. In the model proposed here, instead of preserving the political system, "rational actors" help to destroy it--not in spite of their "rationality" but because of it.

Apart from its theoretical-methodological interest, this insight may have important practical consequences. It is understandable that ultimate responsibility for most national evils may be attributed to party personnel, but only as a rationalization for the promotion of a coup and an unwillingness to accept the "risks" of open access to political power offered by a genuine party system. As social science such attribution of responsibility is evidence of an extreme tendency toward psychological reductionism, failure to distinguish different levels of conceptualization, and--in some cases--clearly insufficient knowledge of the socio-political phenomena that are supposedly being explained. In any event, if the argument of this chapter is correct, its

---

assessments of their social context by individuals of the population under study, which is compared with the "contextual map" drawn by the observer. At this point the theoretical-explanatory task begins. A recent, methodologically self-conscious study that uses this strategy is Cardoso, Ideologías . . . .

[23]This is the case with axiomatic-deductive models used frequently in economics; see Barry's discussion of "economic models." Of course this alternative is more parsimonious in terms of data and variables utilized, but it can be applied only to situations which are simple enough, or for which a sufficiently good theory exists, to allow precise specification of the model. Otherwise non-ambiguous deductions of "behavior" of the "actors" in the model are impossible, and the strategy becomes useless.

implications are drastically different from those of the approach I have criticized. Instead of a slow socialization process or a tutorial authoritarianism, the crux of the matter seems to be that party competition and elections become an arena where the political demands of all activated sectors are expressed without constraints. The placing of constraints such as those analyzed in this chapter may have been justified by asserting that it was the only way to save what little "democracy" was left, but given high levels of popular political activation, it has been shown that these constraints radically distort the "game" that political parties are supposed to play. It becomes plainly a "loser's game." Under these or similar constraints, party competition and coalitions suffer serious distortions, and a breakdown in an authoritarian direction becomes the most likely outcome.

Thus, given the high level of popular political activation typical of high modernization, open party competition and access to political power are necessary conditions for the survival of political democracy. The paradox is that such a level of activation, and its close interconnection with erratic socio-economic growth may lead the more established sectors to coalesce at critical junctures, feeling that they cannot afford the "risks" entailed by open political competition. Insofar as these sectors control most of the non-electoral resources, sequences of severely constrained "democracies" followed by authoritarianisms are likely to result.

In this chapter we cannot delve into the complex question of the conditions under which such a paradox might be resolved. However, it certainly will not be resolved by hoping that some cathartic experience will convert party leaders into the archetypes of rational political man.

* * * * * * *

Some Concluding Remarks. In the Preface to this work, it was described as a "preliminary" effort--for reasons which at this point should be clearly evident to the reader. The primary focus has been an analysis (with important limitations) of certain patterns and tendencies of contemporary South American politics. This is a multi-faceted theme, about which we have formulated new questions and advanced new hypotheses. After an arid, but essential, conceptual and methodological discussion, we endeavored to show that in certain countries which have achieved the social differentiation characteristic of high modernization, there is a strong tendency toward the emergence of a new type of political authoritarianism--"bureaucratic-authoritarianism." If one is willing to assume (at least as a working hypothesis) that there is a marked elective affinity between high modernization and bureaucratic-authoritarianism, a whole series of value concerns

196

and empirical questions come to the fore--none of which has a place within the "optimistic equation" or, in general, within the various conceptions that postulate linear progress toward "better" or "more mature" forms of political organization. These value concerns and empirical questions generate problems for research. Many of the problems have been noted here, but because of insufficient data, only a few have been answered. However, despite the lack of data, efforts of this kind serve a useful purpose. The perception of, and formulation of hypotheses about, what seem to be fundamental patterns and tendencies is a requisite for the analytic study of an extremely complex reality. Such efforts are preliminary steps toward research that will generate new data--data that will not be irrelevant or inadequate because they were gathered in relation to very different conceptualizations.

The concept of modernization has been broken down into several analytical and empirical components--with particular emphasis on the interrelations of these components in the most highly modernized South American countries. Within the common South American context, different patterns of modernization result in different problematic spaces, in terms of which each political system operates with the special procedures, the coalitions, and the basic public policy preferences that characterize each. One of these political systems, closely related to a high level of modernization, is bureaucratic-authoritarianism, whose emergence in South America raised the value concerns that have guided this study. It is at the level of high modernization that the flaws of the basic paradigm of social and political development literature and its "optimistic equation" are particularly evident, which is why there has been so much emphasis in this work on contemporary Argentina and Brazil--the two most highly modernized countries in the South American continent.

The main theme of the first two chapters of this study is the implantation and attempts at consolidation of bureaucratic-authoritarian political systems in both Argentina and Brazil. In the following two chapters the processes and events that preceded the military coup in Argentina in 1966 are examined in detail. We have sought to emphasize that, in contemporary South America, high modernization tends to consolidate new patterns of dependence and to lead to mass praetorianism, which introduces serious distortions in formally democratic political institutions. In addition, it increases the political activation of the popular sector, to which the more established sectors respond by becoming increasingly rigid, thereby generating new and greater obstacles to dealing effectively with the problematic space of high modernization. The combined effect of unregulated conflict, institutional distortions, and limited capability for dealing with the problematic space is the weakening of other political institutions, without which it is difficult to conceive that a political democracy can emerge and be consolidated. This induces the formation of a coalition in which various sectors that high modernization has made more powerful agree that the political exclusion of the popular sector is a requisite for overcoming a situation of stagnation and continuing conflict. From this point of view, the elimination of the electoral arena--and with it, political parties--seems essential to the achievement of such a goal. The triumph of the coalition leads to the inauguration of a new type of authoritarianism which attempts (with a significant degree of success) to extend even further the highly inequitable distribution of resources that has made its emergence possible.

One of the basic failings of the quasi-democratic systems preceding bureaucratic-authoritarianism was their inability to formulate and implement public policy. But, as we have noted at several points in the text, whatever advantages that bureaucratic-authoritarian systems might have in this respect are more than outweighed by their own inherent flaws. In the evolution of the Argentine and Brazilian cases, there have been important differences, about which we have briefly speculated. The performance of the Brazilian political system might be considered "successful" by a technocratic mentality, and in it the logical consequences of bureaucratic-authoritarianism have been largely fulfilled-- from the point of view of the author, the worst of all possibilities. The Argentine case was a failure for even a technocratic mentality, and fairly soon the country had to suffer under the very mass praetorianism that the bureaucratic-authoritarianism was intended to eliminate.

The emergence of a bureaucratic-authoritarian system is a likely response to the manifold tensions of high modernization. To hypothesize an elective affinity between such a system and high modernization leads one to ask (with some concern): Are South American countries at intermediate levels of modernization being "pushed" increasingly toward bureaucratic-authoritarian political forms? It is our impression that they are, but neither the data nor the analysis of this work enables us to advance further in exploring this question.

In the chapters focussing on Argentina--a "paradoxical" or "deviant" case in studies that utilize the basic paradigm-- the close connection between Argentina's political misfortunes and its high modernization is clear. It is evident that the deviant case is "deviant" only as a consequence of erroneous expectations derived from the paradigm.

On another level of analysis, it is evident from the text that the growing complexity of South American societies will create a need for more and more highly trained technical personnel. However, the data available concerning the political behavior

of the incumbents of technocratic roles are not very encouraging. The psychological predispositions that appear to spring
from incumbency in such roles, interacting with the interests of
the large public and private organizations they have most densely
penetrated, make these incumbents strong supporters of bureaucratic-authoritarian experiments. Given the severe tensions of
the contemporary South American social context, under what conditions is it likely that a decisive subset of these incumbents
would support an "open" political system? This is an important
question that this study can only formulate, but unhappily cannot
answer.

For a variety of reasons, some of them very personal, the
author has chosen to make his own preferences explicit. He be-
lieves that, if the goal is a more equitable society that generates more and better allocated resources, the best that could be
achieved in our present circumstances would be a political democracy open to the demands of all political actors. It is obvious
that asserting a close connection between high modernization and
bureaucratic-authoritarianism suggests that, at least for that
level of modernization, the probability of the emergence of such
democracy is not high. But this conclusion is only a point of
departure--first, for future investigation, better focused and
based on more adequate data than have been available for this
study, and second and above all, for purposive collective action
that may make the possible real and the improbable more probable.

BIBLIOGRAPHY

Adams, R. The Second Sowing. San Francisco: Chandler, 1967.

Adelman, Irma, and Morris, Cynthia Taft. Society, Politics and Economic Development. Baltimore: Johns Hopkins Press, 1967.

Aguilar, M. Alonso. Teoría y política del desarrollo latino-americano. UNAM, 1967.

Alejandro, C. Díaz. See Díaz Alejandro, C.

Alexander, Robert J. Latin American Politics and Government. New York: Harper & Row, 1965.

Alker, Hayward. "A Typology of Ecological Fallacies" in S. Rokkan and M. Doggan, eds., Quantitative Ecological Analysis in the Social Sciences. Cambridge, Mass.: The MIT Press, 1969.

Almond, Gabriel, and Verba, Sidney. The Civic Culture. Princeton: Princeton University Press, 1963.

Anderson, Charles W. Politics and Economic Change in Latin America. New York: Van Nostrand, 1967.

Apter, David A. Choice and the Politics of Allocation. New Haven: Yale University Press, 1971.

_____. Conceptual Approaches to the Study of Modernization. Englewood Cliffs: Prentice-Hall, 1969.

_____. The Politics of Modernization. Chicago: University of Chicago Press, 1965.

Arriaga, Eduardo. "A New Approach to the Measurements of Urbanization," Economic Development and Cultural Change, Vol. XVIII, No. 2 (1970). [IIS Reprint, No. 319]

Astiz, C. "The Argentine Armed Forces: Their Role and Political Involvement," The Western Political Quarterly, Vol. XXII, No. 4 (1969).

Baer, Werner. Industrialization and Economic Development in Brazil. Homewood, Ill.: Richard D. Irwin, Inc., 1965.

_____. "Inflation and Economic Efficiency: Brazil," Economic Development and Cultural Change, No. 11 (1963).

_____. "The Inflation Controversy in Latin America," Latin American Research Review, No. 2 (1967).

_____, and Kerstenetzky, Isaac, eds. Inflation and Growth in Latin America. New Haven: Yale University Press, 1970.

BIBLIOGRAPHY

Baily, Samuel L. Labor, Nationalism and Politics in Argentina. New Brunswick, N.J.: Rutgers University Press, 1967.

Banco Central de la Republica Argentina. Origen del producto y composición del gasto nacional, Suplemento del Boletín Estadistico N. 6. Buenos Aires, 1966.

Barber, Willard F., and Ronning, Neale. Internal Security and Military Power: Counterinsurgency and Civic Action in Latin America. Columbus: Ohio State University Press, 1966.

Barry, B. Sociologists, Economists and Democracy. London: Collier-Macmillan, Ltd., 1970.

Beltran, P.V., ed. El papel político y social de las fuerzas armadas en América Latina. Monte Avila Editores, 1970.

Bendix, Reinhard. Nation-Building and Citizenship. New York: John Wiley, 1964.

Bennet, D. "Ideology as Language. A Strategy for Research." Unpublished paper, Yale University, 1970.

Botana, N. La Légitimité: Probleme politique. Louvain, 1968.

_____. "La crisis de legitimidad en la Argentina y el desarrollo de los partidos políticos," Criterio, No. 1604 (1970).

Boulding, Kenneth. "Toward a General Theory of Growth," Canadian Journal of Economic and Political Science, No. 19 (1953).

Bourdieu, P., et al. Le Métier de sociologue. The Hague: Mouton and Bordas, 1969.

Bourricaud, F. "Los militares: ¿Por qué y para qué?" Aportes, No. 18 (1970).

Braun, O. El desarrollo del capital monopolista en la Argentina. Editorial Tiempo Contemporáneo, 1970.

Brewer, G., and Brunner, R. Organized Complexity: Empirical Theories of Political Development. New York: Free Press, 1971.

Brunner, R., and Liephelt, K. "Data Analysis, Process Analysis, and System Change." Paper presented at the 1970 annual meeting of the American Political Science Association.

Canitrot, A. "Nuestro desarrollo económico: Conflictos y interrogantes," Criterio, No. 1606 (1970).

Cantón, D. El parlamento argentino en epocas de cambio: 1880, 1910 y 1946. Editorial del Instituto, 1966.

_____. "Las intervenciones militares en la Argentina: 1900-1966." Instituto Torcuato di Tella, 1967.

_____. "Revolución argentina de 1966 y proyecto nacional," Revista Latinoamericana de Sociología, Vol. V, No. 3 (1969).

Caplow, T. "A Theory of Coalitions in the Triad," American Sociological Review, No. 21 (1961).

Cárdenas, G. Las luchas nacionales contra la dependencia. Editorial Galerna, 1969.

Cardoso, F. Cuestiones de sociología del desarrollo. Editorial Universitaria, 1968.

_____. Empresario industrial e desenvolvimento económico. Difusao Europeia do Livro, 1964.

_____. Ideologías de la burguesía industrial en sociedades dependientes (Argentina y Brasil). Mexico and Argentina: Siglo XXI, 1971.

_____, and Faleto, E. Dependencia y desarrollo en América Latina. Siglo XXI, 1969.

_____, and Reyna, L. "Industrialization, Occupational Structure and Social Stratification in Latin America" in C. Balsier, ed., Constructive Change in Latin America. Pittsburgh: University of Pittsburgh Press, 1968.

Casanova, P. González. La democracia en México. Mexico D.F., 1965.

Chalmers, Douglas. "Developing on the Periphery: External Factors in Latin American Politics" in J. Rosenau, ed., Linkage Politics: Essays on the Convergence of National and International Systems. New York: Free Press, 1960.

Chertkoff, J. "Sociopsychological Theories and Research on Coalition Formation" in S. Groennings, et al., eds. See Groennings.

Ciria, A. Partidos y poder en la Argentina moderna (1930-1946). Jorge Alvarez Editor, 1964.

_____. Perón y el justicialismo. Siglo XXI, 1971.

CNRS. Les Problèmes des capitales en Amérique Latine. Paris, 1965.

Coleman, James. "Conclusion: The Political Systems of Developing Areas" in G. Almond and J. Coleman, eds., The Politics of Developing Areas. Princeton: Princeton University Press, 1960.

_____. "The Mathematical Study of Change" in H. Blalock and A. Blalock, eds., Methodology in Social Research. New York: McGraw-Hill, 1968.

Collins, B., and Raven, B. "Group Structure: Attraction Coalitions, Communication and Power" in G. Lindzey and E. Aronson, eds., The Handbook of Social Psychology, Vol. IV. Reading, Mass.: Addison-Wesley, 1969.

Conde, R. Cortés. "Algunos aspectos de la expansión territorial en Argentina en la segunda mitad del siglo XIX," Desarrollo Económico, No. 29 (1968).

_____, and Gallo, E. La formación de la Argentina moderna. Paidós, 1967.

Consejo Nacional de Desarrollo. Planes de Desarrollo, various years.

Cornblit, O. "European Migrants in Argentine Industry and Politics" in C. Veliz, ed., The Politics of Ccnformity in Latin America. Oxford: Oxford University Press, 1967.

_____, Gallo, E., and O'Connell, A. "La generacion del 80 y su proyecto: Antecedentes y consecuencias" in Torcuato di Tella et al., eds., Argentina: Sociedad de masas. Eudeba, 1965.

Cornelius, W. "The Political Sociology of City-ward Migration in Latin America: Toward Empirical Theory" in F. Rabinovitz and F. Trueblood, eds., Latin American Urban Research, Vol. I. Beverly Hills: Sage Publications, 1970.

Cotler, J. "Crisis política y populismo militar en el Perú," Estudios Internacionales, Vol. IV, No. 12 (1970).

Croan, M. "Is Mexico the Future of East Europe? Institutional Adaptability and Political Change in Comparative Perspective" in Huntington and Moore, eds. See under Huntington.

Crozier, M. Le Phénomene bureaucratique. Editions du Seuil, 1963.

Cúneo, D. Comportamiento y crisis de la clase empresaria. Editorial Pleamar, 1967.

_____. El desencuentro argentino. Pleamar, 1965.

Cyert, Richard M., and March, J.G. Behavioral Theory of the Firm. Englewood Cliffs: Prentice-Hall, 1963.

Dahl, Robert A. After the Revolution. New Haven: Yale University Press, 1970.

_____. A Preface to Democratic Theory. Chicago: University of Chicago Press, 1956.

_____. Modern Political Analysis. Englewood Cliffs: Prentice-Hall, 1969.

_____. Polyarchy, Participation and Opposition. New Haven: Yale University Press, 1971.

_____. "Some Explanations" in R. Dahl, ed., Political Oppositions in Western Democracies. New Haven: Yale University Press, 1966.

Davis, Kingsley. "Problems and Solutions in International Comparisons for Social Science Purposes." Population Reprint Series, Institute of International Studies, University of California, Berkeley.

De Imaz, J.L. Los que mandan. Eudeba, 1964.

_____. Motivación electoral. IDES, 1962.

_____. "El 'tecnico' y algunos sistemas politicos latino-
americanos." Unpublished paper, 1970.

De las Casas, R. "L'Etat autoritaire: Essai sur les formes
actuelles de domination impérialiste," L'Homme et la Société,
No. 18 (1970).

Deutsch, Karl. The Nerves of Government. Glencoe, Ill.: Free
Press, 1963.

_____. "Social Mobilization and Political Development,"
American Political Science Review, No. 55 (1961).

_____. "Toward an Inventory of Basic Trends and Patterns in
Comparative and International Politics," American Political
Science Review, No. 54 (1960).

_____, and Kochen, M. "Toward a Rational Theory of Decentral-
ization," American Political Science Review, No. 63 (1969).

Diamant, A. "The Nature of Political Development" in J.
Montgomery and W. Wiffin, eds., Approaches to Development:
Politics, Administration, and Change. New York: McGraw-
Hill, 1966.

Díaz Alejandro, C. Essays on the Economic History of the Argentine Republic. New Haven: Yale University Press, 1970.

_____. Exchange Rate Devaluation in a Semi-Industrialized
Country: The Experience of Argentina 1955-1961. Cambridge:
The MIT Press, 1965.

_____. "On the Import Intensiveness of Import Substitution,"
Kyklos, Vol. III (1965).

Di Tella, Torcuato. El sistema político argentino y la clase
obrera. Eudeba, 1964.

_____. Hacia una política latinoamericana. Arca, 1969.

_____. "Populism and Reform in Latin America" in C. Véliz,
ed., Obstacles to Change in Latin America. Oxford: Oxford
University Press, 1965.

_____, and Zymmelman, M. Las etapas del desarrollo argentino.
Eudeba, 1967.

_____, et al., eds. Argentina: Sociedad de masas. Eudeba,
1965.

Dix, R. "Oppositions in Latin America" in R. Dahl et al., eds.,
Regimes and Oppositions. Forthcoming.

Donghi Halperin, T. Argentina en el callejon. Editorial Arca,
1964.

Dos Santos, T. "La Crise de la téorie de développement et les
relations de dépendence en Amérique Latine," L'Homme et la
Société, No. 12 (1969).

————. "The Structure of Dependence," The American Economic Review, Vol. LX, No. 2 (1970).

————, et al. La crisis del desarrollismo y la nueva dependencia. Moncloa Campodónico Editores, 1969.

Downs, Anthony. An Economic Theory of Democracy. New York: Harper & Row, 1957.

Dhrymes, Phoebus. Econometrics: Statistical Foundations and Applications. New York: Harper & Row, 1970.

Educacion y desarrollo económico en la Argentina (2 vols.). Argentina: Consejo Nacional de Desarrollo, 1969.

Einaudi, L. "The Peruvian Military: A Summary Political Analysis." Santa Monica: Rand Corporation, 1969.

————, and Stepan, A. "Latin American Institutional Development: Changing Military Perspectives in Peru and Brazil." Santa Monica: Rand Corporation, 1971.

Eisenstadt, S.N. Modernization: Protest and Change. Englewood Cliffs: Prentice-Hall, 1965.

Etzioni, Amitai. A Comparative Analysis of Complex Organizations. New York: Free Press, 1971.

Fayt, C. El político armado: Dinamica del proceso político argentino 1960-1971. Ediciones Pannedille, 1971.

————. La naturaleza del Peronismo. Editorial Viracocha, 1967.

Faría, V. "Dependencia e ideología empresarial," Revista Latinoamericana de Ciencia Política, Vol. II, No. 1 (April 1971).

Felix, D. "The Dilemma of Import Substitution in Argentina" in G. Papanek, ed., Development Policy: Theory and Practice. Cambridge: Harvard University Press, 1968.

Ferreira, O.S. "La geopolítica y el ejército brasileno" in P.V. Beltran, ed., El papel político y social de las fuerzas armadas en América Latina. Monte Avila Editores, 1970.

Ferrer, A. La economía argentina: Las etapas de su desarrollo y problemas actuales. Fondo de Cultura Económica, 1963.

————, et al., Los planes de estabilización en la Argentina. Paidós, 1969.

Fillol, T. Social Factors in Economic Development. Cambridge: The MIT Press, 1961.

Fisher, F.M. The Identification Problem in Econometrics. New York: McGraw-Hill, 1966.

Floria, C.A. "Una explicacion política de la Argentina," CIAS, 1967.

_____, and Belsunce, C. García. Historia de los argentinos (2 vols.). Argentina: Editorialkapelusz, 1970.

Fogel, R. "The Specification Problem in Economic History," The Journal of Economic History, Vol. XXVII, No. 3 (1967).

Freels, J.M. El sector industrial en la política nacional. Eudeba, 1970.

_____. "Industrialists and Politics in Argentina: An Opinion Survey of Trade Association Leaders," Journal of Inter-American Studies and World Affairs, Vol. XII, No. 3 (1970).

Furtado, Celso. Dialéctica del desarrollo. FCE, 1965.

_____. Subdesarrollo y estancamiento en América Latina. Eudeba, 1966.

_____. Teoría y política del desarrollo. Siglo XXI, 1968.

Gallo, E., and Sigal, S. "La formación de los partidos políticos contemporaneos: La Union Civica Radical (1880-1916)" in Torcuato di Tella et al., eds., Argentina: Sociedad de masas. Eudeba, 1965.

Gamson, William A. Power and Discontent. Homewood, Ill.: Dorsey Press, 1968.

_____. "An Experimental Test of a Theory of Coalition Formation," American Sociological Review, No. 26 (1961).

_____. "Experimental Studies of Coalition Formation" in L. Berkowitz, ed., Advances in Experimental Social Psychology, Vol. I. New York: Academic Press, 1964.

Gastaldi, A. Petreli. A economía brasileira e os problemas do desenvolvimento. Edicao Saraiva, 1968.

Germani, Gino. Política y sociedad en un epoca de transición. Paidós, 1962.

_____. Sociología de la modernización. Paidós, 1969.

_____, and Silvert, Kalman. "Politics, Social Structure and Military Intervention in Latin America," Archives Européenne de Sociologie, No. 2 (1961).

Gerschenkron, Alexander. Continuity in History and Other Essays. Cambridge: Harvard University Press, 1968. [Spanish edition: Ediciones Ariel, 1970.]

_____. Economic Backwardness in Historical Perspective. Cambridge: Harvard University Press, 1962.

Giberti, H. El desarrollo agrario argentino. Eudeba, 1964.

Graciarena, J. Poder y clases sociales en el desarrollo de América Latina. Paidós, 1967.

_____. "Estructura de poder y distribución del ingreso en

BIBLIOGRAPHY

América Latina," Revista Latinoamericana de Ciencia Política, Vol. II, No. 2 (1971).

Grondona, M. Argentina en el tiempo y en el mundo. Editorial Primera Plana, 1967.

Groennings, S., et al., eds. The Study of Coalition Behavior. New York: Holt, Rinehart and Winston, 1970.

Hagen, Everett. The Economics of Development. Homewood, Ill.: Richard D. Irwin, Inc., 1968.

Haire, M. "Biological Models and Empirical Histories of the Growth of Organizations" in Haire, ed., Modern Organization Theory. New York: John Wiley, 1959.

Hardoy, J., and Tobar, C., eds. La urbanización en América Latina. Editorial del Instituto, 1969.

Hernandez Arregui, A. La formación de la conciencia nacional. Hachón, 1964.

Hirschman, Albert O. Journeys Toward Progress: Studies of Economic Policy-Making in Latin America. New York: The Twentieth Century Fund, 1963.

_____. "Introduction" in Hirschman, ed., Latin American Issues. New York: The Twentieth Century Fund, 1960.

_____. "Introduction: Political Economics and Possibilism" in Essays in Development. New Haven: Yale University Press, forthcoming.

_____. "The Political Economy of Import-Substituting Industrialization in Latin America," The Quarterly Journal of Economics, February 1969.

_____. "The Search for Paradigms as a Hindrance to Understanding," World Politics, Vol. XXII, No. 3 (1970).

Hobsbawm, E. "Latin America as U.S. Empire Cracks," The New York Review of Books, March 25, 1971.

Holt, R., and Richardson, M. "Competing Paradigms in Comparative Politics" in R. Holt and J. Turner, eds., The Methodology of Comparative Research. New York: Free Press, 1970.

Homans, P. Social Behavior: Its Elementary Forms. New York: Harcourt, Brace and World, 1961.

Hood, William C., and Koopmans, Tjalling C., eds. Studies in Econometric Method. New York: John Wiley, 1953.

Hopkins, Raymond. "Aggregate Data and the Study of Political Development," The Journal of Politics, Vol. XXXI, No. 1 (1969).

Horowitz, Irving L. "La norma de ilegitimidad: Hacia una teoría general del desarrollo político latinoamericano," Revista Mexicana de Sociologia, Vol. XXX, No. 2 (1968).

BIBLIOGRAPHY

_____. "Politics, Urbanization and Social Development in Latin America," Urban Affairs Quarterly, No. 2 (March 1967).

_____. Three Worlds of Development. New York: Oxford University Press, 1967.

Huntington, Samuel. Political Order in Changing Societies. New Haven: Yale University Press, 1968.

_____. "The Change to Change: Modernization, Development and Politics," Comparative Politics, Vol. III (1971).

_____, and Moore, Clement H., eds. Authoritarian Politics in Modern Societies: The Dynamics of Established One-Party Systems. New York: Basic Books, 1970.

Ianni, O. Imperialismo y cultura de la violencia en América Latina. Siglo XXI, 1970.

_____. O colapso do populismo no Brasil. Editorial Civilizacao Brasileira, 1968.

Inkeles, A., and Levinson, D. "National Character: The Study of Modal Personality and Sociocultural Systems" in G. Lindzey and E. Aronson, eds., The Handbook of Social Psychology, Vol. IV. Reading, Mass.: Addison-Wesley, 1969.

Instituto Brasileiro de Estatistica. Series Estatisticas Retrospectivas. IBGE, 1970.

Instituto Torcuato di Tella. Los recursos humanos de nivel tecnico y universitario en la Argentina, 1964.

International Labour Organization. International Labour Statistics, Geneva, 1967.

_____. Yearbook of Labour Statistics, 1967.

Jaguaribe, H. Desarrollo político y desarrollo económico. Eudeba, 1964.

_____, et al., La dependencia político-económica en América Latina. Siglo XXI, 1970.

Janos, Andrew. "The One-Party State and Social Mobilization: East Europe between the Wars" in Huntington and Moore, eds. See under Huntington. [IIS Reprint, No. 357]

Johnson, John J. The Military and Society in Latin America. Stanford: Stanford University Press, 1964.

_____. Political Change in Latin America: The Emergence of the Middle Sectors. Stanford: Stanford University Press, 1958.

Johnson, K. Argentina's Mosaic of Discord. Institute for the Comparative Study of Political Systems, 1969.

Journal of the Patent Office Society, Vol. XL, No. 2 (February 1964).

BIBLIOGRAPHY

Kaplan, M. La formación del estado nacional en América Latina. Editorial Universitaria, 1969.

_____. "Aspectos políticos de la planificacion en América Latina," Aportes, No. 20 (April 1971).

Katz, J.M. "Caracteristicas estructurales del crecimiento industrial argentino," Desarrollo Económico, Vol. VII, No. 26 (1967).

Kenworthy, E. "Coalitions in the Political Development of Latin America" in S. Groennings et al., eds. See Groennings.

_____. "The Formation of the Peronist Coalition." Unpublished dissertation, Yale University, 1970.

Kirkpatrick, J. Leader and Vanguard in Mass Society: A Study of Peronism in Argentina. Cambridge: The MIT Press, forthcoming.

Klatzky, S.R. "Relationship of Organizational Size to Complexity and Coordination," Administrative Science Quarterly, Vol. XV, No. 4.

Kuhn, Thomas S. The Structure of Scientific Revolutions. Chicago: University of Chicago Press, 1962.

Lambert, D. "Repartición de los ingresos y las desigualdades en America Latina," Revista Mexicana de Sociología, Vol. XXXI, No. 2 (1969).

Lambert, J. Os dois brasís. Brazil: Companhia Editora Nacional, 1957.

Landau, Martin. "Linkage, Coding and Intermediacy: A Strategy for Institution Building," Journal of Comparative Administration, Vol. II, No. 4 (1971).

Lane, J. "Isolation and Public Opinion in Northeast Brazil," Public Opinion Quarterly, Spring 1969.

LaPalombara, Joseph. "Macrotheories and Microapplications in Comparative Politics: A Widening Gap," Comparative Politics, Vol. I, No. 1 (1968).

_____. "Penetration: A Crisis of Governmental Capability" in L. Binder et al., Crises and Sequences in Political Development. Forthcoming.

_____. "Political Science and the Engineering of National Development" in J. Powelson, ed., The Disciplines of National Development. Forthcoming.

Lasswell, Harold. World Politics and Personal Insecurity. New York: McGraw-Hill, 1935.

_____. "The Policy Sciences of Development," World Politics, Vol. XVII, No. 2 (1965).

_____, and Kaplan, Abraham. Power and Society. New Haven: Yale University Press, 1950.

Leff, Nathaniel H. The Brazilian Capital Goods Industry, 1929-1964. Cambridge: Harvard University Press, 1968.

_____. "Import Constraints and Development: Causes of the Recent Decline of Brazilian Economic Growth," Review of Economics and Statistics, November 1967.

Legg, Keith R. Politics in Modern Greece. Stanford: Stanford University Press, 1969.

Lieuwen, Edwin. Arms and Politics in Latin America. New York: Praeger, 1960.

Linz, Juan. "An Authoritarian Regime: Spain" in S. Rokkan, ed., Mass Politics. New York: Free Press, 1970.

_____. "The Breakdown of Democratic Regimes." Paper presented at the World Congress of Sociology, Varna, 1970.

Lipset, Seymour Martin. Political Man. Garden City: Doubleday, 1960.

Lopes, J.B. Sociedade industrial no Brasil. Difusao Européia do Livro, 1964.

_____. "Etude de quelques changements fondamentaux dans la politique et la société brésilienne," Sociologie du Travail, No. 3 (1965).

Macario, S. "Protectionism and Industrialization in Latin America," Economic Bulletin for Latin America, Vol. IX, No. 1 (1964).

Malinvaud, E. Statistical Methods of Econometrics. New York: American Elsevier Publications, 1970.

Mamalakis, M. "The Theory of Sectoral Clashes," Latin American Research Review, Vol. IV, No. 3 (1969).

March, James, and Simon, Herbert A. Organizations. New York: John Wiley, 1958.

Marsal, J.F. Cambio social en América Latina. Solar-Hachette, 1967.

Martins, L. Industrializacao, burguesia nacional e desenvolvimento. Editora Saga, 1968.

_____. "Aspectos políticos de la revolución brasileña," Revista Latinoamericana de Sociología, Vol. III, No. 3 (1967).

Marx, Karl. El 18 Brumario de Luis Bonaparte. Ediciones Ariel, 1968.

Maynard, G., and van Rijckeghem, W. "Stabilization Policy in an Inflationary Economy: An Analysis of the Argentine Case" in G. Papanek, ed., Development Policy: Theory and Practice. Cambridge: Harvard University Press, 1968.

Mendes, C. Nacionalismo e desenvolvimento. Instituto Brasileiro de Estudos Afro-Asiaticos, 1963.

_____. "Elite de poder, democracia e desenvolvimento," Dados, No. 5 (1969).

_____. "O governo castello branco: Paradigma e prognose," Dados, No. 3 (1967).

_____. "Sistema politico e modelos de poder no Brasil," Dados, No. 2 (1966).

Merkx, G. "Politics and Economic Change in Argentina from 1870 to 1966." Unpublished dissertation, Yale University, 1968.

_____. "Sectoral Clashes and Political Change: The Argentine Experience," Latin American Research Review, Vol. IV, No. 3 (1969).

Moore, Barrington, Jr. Social Origins of Dictatorship and Democracy. Boston: Beacon Press, 1966.

Morello, A., and Tróccoli, A. Argentina ahora y después. Editorial Platense, 1967.

Morley, Samuel. "Inflation and Stagnation in Brazil," Economic Development and Cultural Change, Vol. XIX, No. 2 (1971).

Morse, Richard. "The Heritage of Latin America" in L. Hartz, ed., The Founding of New Societies. New York: Harcourt, Brace, Jovanovich, 1966.

Murmis, M., and Portantiero, C. "Crecimiento industrial y alianza de clases en Argentina, 1930-1940." Instituto Torcuato di Tella, Centro de Investigaciones Sociales, Documento de Trabajo, 1968.

Needler, Martin. Generals vs. Presidents: Neomilitarism in Latin America. New York: Praeger, 1964.

_____. Latin American Politics in Perspective. New York: Van Nostrand, 1967.

_____. Political Development in Latin America: Instability, Violence, and Evolutionary Change. New York: Random House, 1968.

Nordlinger, E. "Soldiers in Mufti: The Impact of Military Rule upon Economic and Social Change in the Non-Western States," American Political Science Review, Vol. IXIV, No. 4 (1970).

North, Liisa. Civil-Military Relations in Argentina, Chile and Peru. Berkeley: Institute of International Studies, University of California, 1966.

Nun, José. "Marginalidad y participación social: Un planteo introductorio." Instituto Torcuato di Tella, 1969 [mimeo].

_____. "The Middle Class Military Coup" in C. Véliz, ed., The Politics of Conformity in Latin America. Oxford: Oxford University Press, 1967.

O'Donnell, Guillermo. "Modernización y golpes militares: Teoría, comparaciones y el caso argentino," Desarrollo Económico, October-December 1972. (English version to appear in D. Apter and M. Barrera, eds., Embourgeoisement and Radicalization in Latin America, forthcoming.)

OECD. Education, Human Resources and Development in Argentina, 1967.

Oficina de Estudios para la Cooperacion Económica Internacional. Argentina económica y financiera. FIAT, 1966.

Olson, Mancur, Jr. The Logic of Collective Action: Public Goods and the Theory of Groups. Cambridge: Harvard University Press, 1965.

Organski, A.F. Stages of Political Development. New York: Alfred Knopf, 1965.

Orsolini, Cl.M. Ejército argentino y crecimiento nacional. Editorial Arayú, 1965.

Ozlak, O. "Inflación y politica fiscal en la Argentina: El impuesto a los reditos en el período 1956-1965," Documento de Trabajo. Instituto Torcuato di Tella, Centro de Investigaciones en Administración Publica.

Pan American Union. America en cifras. Washington, D.C., 1967.

Panorama de la Economia Argentina, No. 3 (1967).

Papanek, G., ed. Development Policy: Theory and Practice. Cambridge: Harvard University Press, 1968.

Payne, James L. Patterns of Conflict in Colombia. New Haven: Yale University Press, 1968.

Petras, James. "Una década de democracia capitalista en Venezuela," Estudios Internacionales, Vol. IV, No. 12 (1970).

Pinto, A. Costa. Nacionalismo y militarismo. Siglo XXI, 1969.

_____. Tres ensayos sobre Chile y América Latina. Argentina: Ediciones Solar, 1971.

_____. "Naturaleza e implicaciones de la 'Heterogeneidad estructural' en América Latina," El Trimestre Económico, Vol. XXXI, No. 1 (1970).

Potash, Robert. The Army and Politics in Argentina, 1928-1945: Yrigoyen to Peron. Stanford: Stanford University Press, 1969.

Prebisch, Raul. "Change and Development: Latin America's Great Task." ILPES and IDB, 1970 [mimeo].

BIBLIOGRAPHY

Presidencia de la Nación, Argentina. "Mensaje al País del Presidente de la Nación Teniente General Juan Carlos Ongania," 1966.

_____. "Mensaje de la Junta Revolucionaria al Pueblo Argentino," 1966.

_____. "Mensaje del Presidente de la Nación en la reunión de camaradería de las Fuerzas Armadas," 1967.

_____. "Mensaje del Teniente General Juan Carlos Onganía con motivo de asumir la Presidencia de la Nación," 1966.

Price, Robert. "A Theoretical Approach to Military Rule in New States," World Politics, Vol. XXIII, No. 3 (1971).

Przeworski, A., and Teune, H. The Logic of Comparative Social Inquiry. New York: John Wiley, 1969.

Putnam, Robert. "Toward Explaining Military Interventions in Latin American Politics," World Politics, Vol. XX, No. 1 (1967).

Quijano, A. "Dependencia, cambio social y desenvolvimento social" in F. Cardoso and F. Weffort, eds., América Latina: Ensayos de interpretación sociológico-política. Chile: Editorial Universitaria, 1970.

Rabinovitz, Francine. "Data Resources for Cross-National Urban Research on Administration and Politics: A Proposal," Social Science Information, Vol. IX, No. 3 (1970).

_____. "Urban Development and Political Development in Latin America" in R. Daland, ed., Comparative Urban Research: The Administration and Politics of Cities. Beverly Hills: Sage Publications, 1969.

_____, and Trueblood, Felicity, eds. Latin American Urban Research, Vol. I. Beverly Hills: Sage Publications, 1971.

Rama, C. "El sistema político colombiano: Frente nacional y ANAPO," Centro Paraguayo de Estudios Sociologicos, 1970.

Ramos, J.A. Revolución y contrarevolución en la Argentina. La Reja, 1961.

Rapoport, Anatol. Two-Person Game Theory: The Essential Ideas. Ann Arbor: University of Michigan Press, 1966.

_____. N-Person Game Theory: Concepts and Applications. Ann Arbor: University of Michigan Press, 1969.

Rattenbach, B. El sector militar de la sociedad. Circulo Militar Argentino, 1966.

Riker, William H. The Theory of Political Coalitions. New Haven: Yale University Press, 1962.

Robinson, E.A., ed. The Economic Consequences of the Size of Nations. London: St. Martin's Press, 1960.

Rokeach, Milton. The Open and the Closed Mind. New York: Basic Books, 1960.

Rotondaro, R. Realidad y cambio en el sindicalismo argentino. Pleamar, 1971.

Rowe, D. "The Argentine 1963 Election" in D. Tomasek, ed., Latin American Politics: Studies of the Contemporary Scene. New York: Doubleday, 1966.

Russett, Bruce M. Trends in World Politics. New York: Macmillan, 1965.

_____. "The Yale Political Data Program: Experiences and Prospects" in S. Rokkan and R. Merritt, eds., Comparing Nations. New Haven: Yale University Press, 1966.

_____, et al. World Handbook of Political and Social Indicators. New Haven: Yale University Press, 1964.

Saravia, J.M. Hacia la salida. Emecé, 1968.

Sarbin, T.R., and Allen, V.L. "Role Theory" in G. Lindzey and E. Aronson, eds., The Handbook of Social Psychology, Vol. I. Reading, Mass.: Addison-Wesley, 1968.

Sartori, G. "Concept Misformation in Comparative Politics," American Political Science Review, Vol. LXIV, No. 4 (1970).

Schmitter, Philippe C. Interest Conflict and Political Change in Brazil. Stanford: Stanford University Press, 1971.

_____. "Nuevas estrategias para el análisis comparativo de la política en América Latina," Revista Latinoamericana de Sociología, Vol. V, No. 3 (1969).

Scobie, James R. Revolution on the Pampas: A Social History of Argentine Wheat. Austin: University of Texas Press, 1969.

Scott, Robert E. Mexican Government in Transition. Urbana: University of Illinois Press, 1959.

_____. "Mexico: The Established Revolution" in Lucien Pye and Sidney Verba, eds., Political Culture and Political Development. Princeton: Princeton University Press, 1965.

Silva, Couto. Geopolítica do Brasil. Livraria Jose Olimpo Editora, 1967.

Silvert, Kalman H. The Conflict Society: Reaction and Revolution in Latin America. American Universities Field Staff, 1966.

_____. Man's Power: A Biased Guide to Political Thought and Action. New York: Viking Press, 1970.

_____. "Liderazgo político y debilidad institucional en la Argentina," Desarrollo Económico, Vol. I, No. 3 (1963).

_____. "Nationalism in Latin America," The Annals of the American Academy of Political and Social Science, Vol. 334 (1961).

BIBLIOGRAPHY

Simon, H. "The Architecture of Complexity," General Systems Yearbook, No. 10 (1965).

Singer, Morris. Growth, Equality and the Mexican Experience. Austin: University of Texas Press, 1969.

Solberg, Carl. Immigration and Nationalism: Argentina and Chile, 1890-1914. Austin: University of Texas Press, 1970.

Skidmore, Thomas E. Politics in Brazil, 1930-1964: An Experiment in Democracy. New York: Oxford University Press, 1967.

Slawinski, Z. "Structural Changes in Employment in the Context of Latin America's Development," Economic Bulletin for Latin America, Vol. X, No. 2 (1965).

Smelser, Neil. The Sociology of Economic Life. Englewood Cliffs: Prentice-Hall, 1960.

Smith, Peter H. Politics and Beef in Argentina: Patterns of Conflict and Change. New York: Columbia University Press, 1969.

_____. "The Breakdown of Democracy in Argentina, 1916-1930." Paper presented to the World Congress of Sociology, Varna, 1970.

_____. "Social Mobilization, Political Participation and the Rise of Juan Perón," The Western Political Quarterly, Vol. XXXIV, No. 1 (1969).

Snow, P. "Argentine Political Parties and the 1966 Revolution." Ames: Laboratory of Political Research, University of Iowa, 1968.

_____. "Parties and Politics in Argentina: The Elections of 1962 and 1963," Midwest Journal of Political Science, Vol. IX, No. 1 (1965).

Statistical Abstract for Latin America. Los Angeles: University of California, 1966.

Statistical Abstract for Latin America---1968. Los Angeles: University of California, 1969.

Stavenhagen, R. "Seven Fallacies about Latin America" in J. Petras and M. Zeitlin, eds., Latin America: Reform or Revolution? Greenwich, Conn.: Fawcett, 1968.

Stein, Stanley J., and Stein, Barbara H. The Colonial Heritage of Latin America: Essays on Economic Dependence in Perspective. New York: Oxford University Press, 1970.

Stepan, Alfred. The Military in Politics: Changing Patterns in Brazil. Princeton: Princeton University Press, 1971.

_____. "Political Development Theory: The Latin American Experience," Journal of International Affairs, Vol. XX, No. 2.

Stokes, D. "Spatial Models of Party Competition," _American Political Science Review_, No. 57 (1963).

Sunkel, O. "La universidad latinoamericana ante el avance científico y técnico; Algunas reflexiones," _Estudios Internacionales_, Vol. III, No. 4 (1970).

_____. "Política nacional de desarrollo y dependencia externa," _Estudios Internacionales_, Vol. I, No. 1 (1968).

Tavares, M.C. "The Growth and Decline of Import Substitution in Brazil," _Economic Bulletin for Latin America_, Vol. IX, No. 1 (1964).

Thompson, D'Arcy. _On Growth and Form_. Cambridge: Cambridge University Press, 1966.

Thompson, James D. _Organizations in Action: Social Science Bases of Administrative Theory_. New York: McGraw-Hill, 1967.

Tornquist, Ernesto, and Co. _The Economic Development of the Argentine Republic in the Last Fifty Years_. Buenos Aires, 1919.

Tufte, R. "Improving Data Analysis in Political Science," _World Politics_, Vol. XXI, No. 4 (1969).

Tukey, J. _Exploratory Data Analysis_. Reading, Mass.: Addison-Wesley, 1970.

United Nations. "International Definition and Measurement of Standards of Living: An Interim Guide." E/CN.5/353.

_____. "Report on International Definition and Measurement of Standards and Levels of Living." E/CN3/3/179 and E/CN/5/299.

UN-ECLA. _Economic Bulletin for Latin America_. Vol. IX, No. 1 (April 1966).

_____. _El cambio social y la política de desarrollo social en América Latina_. New York, 1969.

_____. _El desarrollo económico de la Argentina_ (5 vols.; mimeo). New York, 1959.

_____. _El desarrollo social de América Latina en la postguerra_. Solar-Hachette, 1963.

_____. _El desarrollo económico de América Latina en la postguerra_. Solar-Hachette, 1963.

_____. _El empresario industrial en América Latina_.

_____. _Estudio económico de America Latina, 1969_. New York, 1970.

_____. "Estudios especiales: Distribucion del ingreso" in _Estudio económico de América Latina_. New York, 1970.

_____. _External Financing of Latin America_. New York, 1965.

_____. "Income Distribution in Latin America," _Economic Bulletin for Latin America_, Vol. XII, No. 2 (1968).

_____. "Industrial Development in Latin America," _Economic Bulletin for Latin America_, Vol. XIV, No. 2 (1969).

_____. _The Process of Industrial Development in Latin America_. New York, 1966.

_____. _Statistical Bulletin for Latin America_, Vol. IV, No. 2 (1964).

_____, and Consejo Nacional de Desarrollo (CONADE). _Distribución del ingreso y desarrollo económico en la Argentina_. New York, 1968.

UNESCO. _Yearbook of Educational Statistics, 1968_. Paris, 1969.

U.S. Department of Commerce. _Survey of Current Business_, August 1964.

Vekemans, R., and Segundo, L. "Essay of a Socio-Economic Typology of the Latin American Countries" in J. de Vries and J. Medina Echavarría, eds., _Social Aspects of Economic Development in Latin America_, Vol. I. 1963.

Verba, Sidney. "The Uses of Survey Research in the Study of Comparative Politics: Issues and Strategies" in S. Rokkan et al., _Comparative Survey Analysis_. The Hague: Mouton, 1969.

Verón, E. _Conducta estructura y comunicación_. Jorge Alvarez Editor, 1969.

Villanueva, J. _La inflación argentina_. Instituto Torcuato di Tella, 1964 [mimeo].

_____. "El problema del desarrollo industrial dependiente," CIAS, December 1969.

Villegas, O. _Guerra revolucionaria comunista_. Pleamar, 1963.

_____. _Políticas y estrategias para el desarrollo y la seguridad nacional_. Pleamar, 1969.

Walker, N. Aguiar. "Movilización de la clase obrera en el Brasil," _Revista Latinoamericana de Sociología_, Vol. I, No. 3 (1967).

Weffort, F. _Estado y masas en el Brasil_. ILPES, 1967.

_____. "Le Populisme," _Les Temps Modernes_, 257 (October 1967).

Whitaker, Arthur P. _Argentina_. Englewood Cliffs: Prentice-Hall, 1961.

_____. "The Argentine Paradox," _The Annals of the American Academy of Political and Social Science_, No. 334 (1961).

BIBLIOGRAPHY

Wolf, C. "The Political Effects of Economic Programs: Some Indications from Latin America," Economic Development and Cultural Change, Vol. XIV, No. 1 (1965).

Wonnacott, Ronald J., and Wonnacott, Thomas H. Econometrics. New York: John Wiley, 1970.

INSTITUTE OF INTERNATIONAL STUDIES
UNIVERSITY OF CALIFORNIA, BERKELEY

CARL G. ROSBERG,
Director

Monographs published by the Institute include:

RESEARCH SERIES

1. *The Chinese Anarchist Movement*, by Robert A. Scalapino and George T. Yu. ($1.00)
3. *Land Tenure and Taxation in Nepal*, Volume I, *The State as Landlord: Raikar Tenure*, by Mahesh C. Regmi. ($8.75; unbound photocopy)
4. *Land Tenure and Taxation in Nepal*, Volume II, *The Land Grant System: Birta Tenure*, by Mahesh C. Regmi. ($2.50)
*5. *Mexico and Latin American Economic Integration*, by Philippe C. Schmitter and Ernst B. Haas. ($1.00)
6. *Local Taxation in Tanganyika*, by Eugene C. Lee. ($1.00)
7. *Birth Rates in Latin America: New Estimates of Historical Trends*, by O. Andrew Collver. ($2.50)
8. *Land Tenure and Taxation in Nepal*, Volume III, *The Jagir, Rakam, and Kipat Tenure Systems*, by Mahesh C. Regmi. ($2.50)
9. *Ecology and Economic Development in Tropical Africa*, edited by David Brokensha. ($8.25; unbound photocopy)
10. *Urban Areas in Indonesia: Administrative and Census Concepts*, by Pauline Dublin Milone. ($10.50; unbound photocopy)
11. *Cultural Processes in the Baltic Area under Soviet Rule*, by Stephen P. Dunn. ($1.25)
12. *Land Tenure and Taxation in Nepal*, Volume IV, *Religious and Charitable Land Endowments: Guthi Tenure*, by Mahesh C. Regmi. ($2.75)
13. *The Pink Yo-Yo: Occupational Mobility in Belgrade, ca. 1915-1965*, by Eugene A. Hammel. ($2.00)
14. *Community Development in Israel and the Netherlands: A Comparative Analysis*, by Ralph M. Kramer. ($2.50)
*15. *Central American Economic Integration: The Politics of Unequal Benefits*, by Stuart I. Fagan. ($2.00)
16. *The International Imperatives of Technology: Technological Development and the International Political System*, by Eugene B. Skolnikoff. ($2.95)
*17. *Autonomy or Dependence as Regional Integration Outcomes: Central America*, by Philippe C. Schmitter. ($1.75)
18. *Framework for a General Theory of Cognition and Choice*, by Robert M. Axelrod. ($1.50)
19. *Entry of New Competitors in Yugoslav Market Socialism*, by Stephen R. Sacks. ($2.50)
*20. *Political Integration in French-Speaking Africa*, by Abdul A. Jalloh. ($3.50)
21. *The Desert and the Sown: Nomads in the Wider Society*, edited by Cynthia Nelson. ($3.50)
22. *U.S.-Japanese Competition in International Markets: A Study of the Trade-Investment Cycle in Modern Capitalism*, by John E. Roemer. ($3.95)
23. *Political Disaffection Among British University Students: Concepts, Measurement, and Causes*, by Jack Citrin and David J. Elkins. ($2.00)
24. *Urban Inequality and Housing Policy in Tanzania: The Problem of Squatting*, by Richard E. Stren. ($2.50)
*25. *The Obsolescence of Regional Integration Theory*, by Ernst B. Haas. ($2.95)

*International Integration Series

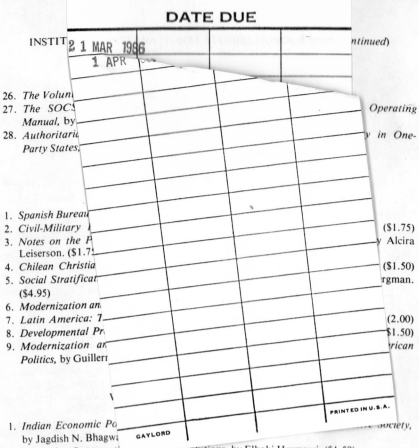

DATE DUE

2 1 MAR 1986
1 APR [...]

PRINTED IN U.S.A.

GAYLORD